AQA
GCSE science

Authors

Graham Bone

Michael Brimicombe

Simon Broadley

Philippa Gardom-Hulme

Mark Matthews

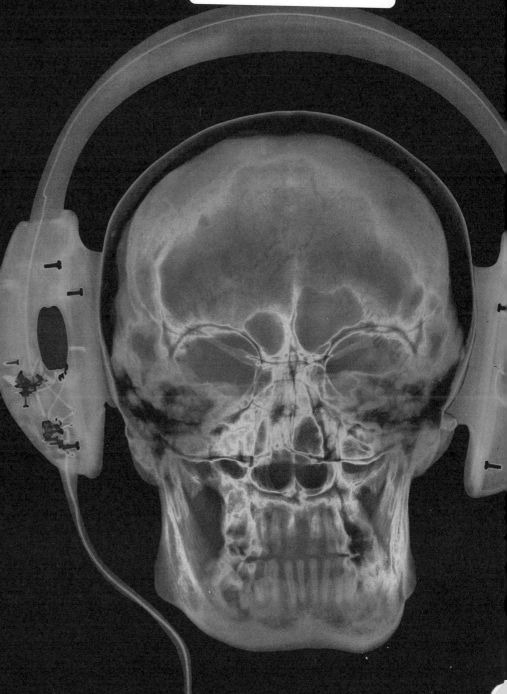

Contents

How to use this book

Welcome to your AQA GCSE Science A revision guide. This book has been specially written by experienced teachers and examiners to match the 2011 specification.

On this page you can see the types of feature you will find in this book. Everything in the book is designed to provide you with the support you need to help you prepare for your examinations and achieve your best.

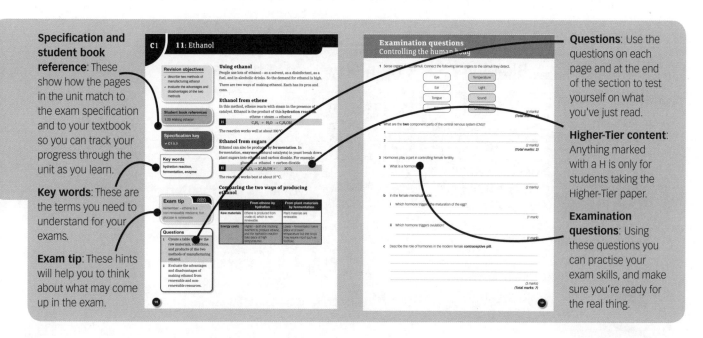

Specification and student book reference: These show how the pages in the unit match to the exam specification and to your textbook so you can track your progress through the unit as you learn.

Key words: These are the terms you need to understand for your exams.

Exam tip: These hints will help you to think about what may come up in the exam.

Questions: Use the questions on each page and at the end of the section to test yourself on what you've just read.

Higher-Tier content: Anything marked with a H is only for students taking the Higher-Tier paper.

Examination questions: Using these questions you can practise your exam skills, and make sure you're ready for the real thing.

Upgrade: Upgrade takes you through an exam question in a step-by-step way, showing you why different answers get different grades. Using the tips on the page you can make sure you achieve your best by understanding what each question needs and what an examiner is looking for in your answer.

Visual summary: Another useful revision tool is a visual summary, linking ideas together in groups so you can see how one topic relates to another. You can use this page as a start for your own summary.

Revision checklist: This is a summary of the main ideas in the unit. You can use it to check that you know and have understood the big ideas covered in the unit.

Matching your course

The units in this book have been written to match the specification, no matter what you plan to study after your GCSE Science A course.

In the diagram below you can see that the units and part units can be used to study either for **GCSE Science**, leading to **GCSE Additional Science**, or as part of **GCSE Biology**, **GCSE Chemistry** and **GCSE Physics** courses.

	GCSE Biology	GCSE Chemistry	GCSE Physics
GCSE Science	B1 (Part 1)	C1 (Part 1)	P1 (Part 1)
	B1 (Part 2)	C1 (Part 2)	P1 (Part 2)
GCSE Additional Science	B2 (Part 1)	C2 (Part 1)	P2 (Part 1)
	B2 (Part 2)	C2 (Part 2)	P2 (Part 2)
	B3 (Part 1)	C3 (Part 1)	P3 (Part 1)
	B3 (Part 2)	C3 (Part 2)	P3 (Part 2)

GCSE Science assessment

The units in this book are broken into two parts to match the different types of exam paper on offer. The diagram below shows you what is included in each exam paper. It also shows you how much of your final mark you will be working towards in each paper.

	Unit		%	Type	Time	Marks available
Route 1	Unit 1	B1 (Part 1) / B1 (Part 2)	25%	Written exam	1 hr	60
	Unit 2	C1 (Part 1) / C1 (Part 2)	25%	Written exam	1 hr	60
	Unit 3	P1 (Part 1) / P1 (Part 2)	25%	Written exam	1 hr	60
	Unit 4	Controlled Assessment	25%		1 hr 30 mins + practical	50
Route 2	Unit 5	B1 (Part 1) / C1 (Part 1) / P1 (Part 1)	35%	Written exam	1 hr 30 mins	90
	Unit 6	B1 (Part 2) / C1 (Part 2) / P1 (Part 2)	40%	Written exam	1 hr 30 mins	90
	Unit 4	Controlled Assessment	25%		1 hr 30 mins + practical	50

Understanding exam questions

When you read the questions in your exam papers you should make sure you know what kind of answer you are being asked for. The list below explains some of the common words you will see used in exam questions. Make sure you know what each word means. Always read the question thoroughly, even if you recognise the word used.

Calculate
Work out your answer by using a calculation. You can use your calculator to help you. You may need to use an equation; check whether one has been provided for you in the paper. The question will say if your working must be shown.

Describe
Write a detailed answer that covers what happens, when it happens, and where it happens. The question will let you know how much of the topic to cover. Talk about facts and characteristics. (Hint: don't confuse with 'Explain')

Explain
You will be asked how or why something happens. Write a detailed answer that covers how and why a thing happens. Talk about mechanisms and reasons. (Hint: don't confuse with 'Describe')

Evaluate
You will be given some facts, data or other information. Write about the data or facts and provide your own conclusion or opinion on them.

Outline
Give only the key facts of the topic. You may need to set out the steps of a procedure or process – make sure you write down the steps in the correct order.

Show
Write down the details, steps or calculations needed to prove an answer that you have been given.

Suggest
Think about what you've learnt in your science lessons and apply it to a new situation or a context. You may not know the answer. Use what you have learnt to suggest sensible answers to the question.

Write down
Give a short answer, without a supporting argument.

Top tips
Always read exam questions carefully, even if you recognise the word used. Look at the information in the question and the number of answer lines to see how much detail the examiner is looking for.

You can use bullet points or a diagram if it helps your answer.

If a number needs units you should include them, unless the units are already given on the answer line.

Revision objectives

- ✔ know what a healthy diet is
- ✔ know that inherited factors can affect health
- ✔ understand what the metabolic rate is, and the factors that affect it
- ✔ know the benefits of regular, frequent exercise

Student book references

1.1 Diet and exercise

1.2 Diet and health

Specification key

✔ B1.1.1

A healthy diet

We need to eat food for three reasons:
- for growth and repair
- for energy
- to keep us healthy.

Food is made out of chemicals. Biologists divide the chemicals into five main groups. All foods are a mix of these chemicals.

Food/nutrient	Why you need to eat it	Sources
Carbohydrates	for energy	bread, pasta, rice, sugary food
Fats	for energy	butter, cheese, fried food
Proteins	to build cells and repair tissue	meat, fish, cheese, nuts
Mineral ions and vitamins	needed in small amounts to keep the body healthy	fresh fruit and vegetables

A healthy diet is a **balanced** one, with the right balance of foods and energy to match the body's needs.

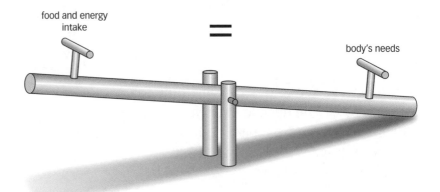

food and energy intake = body's needs

Malnourishment

A person is malnourished if their diet is not balanced. There are basically two types of malnourishment:
- Being underweight – where people do not eat enough, or they **exercise** too much. Their diet has too little food or energy. They lose body mass.
- Being overweight – where people eat too much or exercise too little. Their diet contains too much food or energy for their needs. They gain body mass.

An effect of malnourishment might be that the body lacks some food groups, such as vitamins or minerals. This can lead to **deficiency diseases**, for example, rickets, which is caused by a lack of vitamin D.

Another effect might be an excess of some food groups. Being overweight or eating too much sugar could lead to type 2 diabetes. Too much fat in the diet leads to **obesity** and a high level of cholesterol in the blood. Cholesterol can block blood vessels, leading to heart problems or strokes. Some people have inherited genes that affect their cholesterol levels, increasing their risk of heart disease.

Key words

balanced diet, deficiency disease, obesity, metabolism, metabolic rate, exercise

Metabolic rates

All the cells in your body carry out chemical reactions. This is called **metabolism**. The rate at which all of these reactions occur is called the **metabolic rate**.

Factors that affect the metabolic rate

Exercise
The more you exercise, the more reactions, like respiration, occur in the cells, so the metabolic rate is higher.

- More exercise increases the amount of energy used by the body.
- Glucose from the diet is respired to release energy for the muscles to contract.
- Using more energy in exercise than you take in through the diet causes you to lose mass.
- Exercise usually makes people healthier.

Proportion of muscle to fat
More muscle and less fat in the body will increase the metabolic rate, because reactions occur in the muscle. The more muscle, the more reactions, the higher the metabolic rate.

- Generally males have more muscle than females.

Genetic
People inherit factors that will increase their metabolic rate.

- For example, tall people have a higher metabolic rate, as they lose heat from their body surface, which is greater in area than that of a shorter person.

Questions

1 What is a balanced diet?

2 What is your metabolic rate?

3 **H** Explain why too much cholesterol is bad for your health.

Exam tip   AQA

Different people have different balanced diets. Think about the lifestyle of the person and what their needs for energy and food might be.

Revision objectives

- ✔ know what a pathogen is
- ✔ know that bacteria and viruses reproduce rapidly inside the body, and produce toxins
- ✔ know the technique for growing microorganisms
- ✔ understand the role of painkillers and antibiotics in treating diseases

Student book references

1.3 Infectious diseases

1.4 Antibiotics and painkillers

Specification key

✔ B1.1.2

Pathogens

A **pathogen** is any **microorganism** that causes an infectious disease. They include some **bacteria** and viruses.

Bacteria

Not all bacteria are pathogens. When bacteria infect our body, they reproduce rapidly, and may produce poisons, called **toxins**, which make us unwell. There are many different types of pathogenic bacteria, and they will cause different diseases. There are even millions of bacteria on our skin.

Viruses

Viruses are much smaller than bacteria. When viruses infect our body, they need to get into our cells. There they will reproduce rapidly and damage our cells, bursting out and causing the cell to release toxins, which make us ill.

Hygiene

Even before biologists had discovered that microorganisms cause disease, a Hungarian doctor, Ignaz Semmelweiss, recognised that washing hands was important. In his hospital he showed that if doctors washed their hands between patients, the numbers of deaths from infectious diseases decreased. Today washing hands is common practice in personal hygiene.

Growing microorganisms

It is important for biologists to be able to grow microorganisms like bacteria in the laboratory. This allows them to test treatments, such as **antibiotics** for disease, or to investigate how effective disinfectants might be at killing bacteria. There are now standard techniques for biologists to grow uncontaminated cultures.

move loop through flame

Sterilise the inoculating loop to kill all microorganisms, by passing through a flame.

Dip the loop into a culture of bacteria.

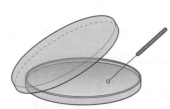

Open a **sterile** Petri dish containing culture media as a gel, and spread the microorganisms.

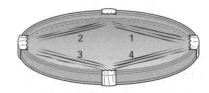

Incubate at 25 °C in school to reduce the chances of dangerous pathogens growing; in industry higher temperatures are used for more rapid growth.

Seal with tape to stop contamination with microorganisms from the air.

Medicines to treat disease

We can take medicines for two reasons when we have an infection.

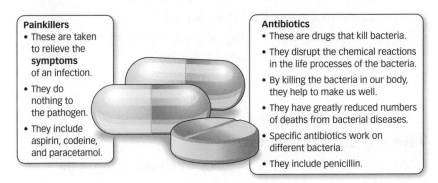

Painkillers
- These are taken to relieve the **symptoms** of an infection.
- They do nothing to the pathogen.
- They include aspirin, codeine, and paracetamol.

Antibiotics
- These are drugs that kill bacteria.
- They disrupt the chemical reactions in the life processes of the bacteria.
- By killing the bacteria in our body, they help to make us well.
- They have greatly reduced numbers of deaths from bacterial diseases.
- Specific antibiotics work on different bacteria.
- They include penicillin.

Since viruses don't carry out chemical reactions, antibiotics don't kill them. Viruses live inside our cells, so any antiviral drug often harms our own cells.

Resistance to antibiotics

By chance some bacteria can develop a mutation that gives them **resistance** to an antibiotic. They will survive by **natural selection** and form a resistant strain of the bacteria. These infect other people. Gradually the whole population of the bacteria will become resistant to the antibiotic. As antibiotic-resistant strains of bacteria have developed, scientists have had to make new antibiotics. Overuse or inappropriate use of antibiotics increases the chances of resistant bacteria developing.

There is now a problem strain of bacteria, MRSA, which is resistant to most antibiotics. It spreads rapidly as there is no effective treatment.

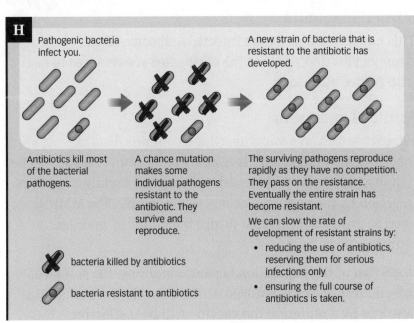

H

Pathogenic bacteria infect you.

A new strain of bacteria that is resistant to the antibiotic has developed.

Antibiotics kill most of the bacterial pathogens.

A chance mutation makes some individual pathogens resistant to the antibiotic. They survive and reproduce.

The surviving pathogens reproduce rapidly as they have no competition. They pass on the resistance. Eventually the entire strain has become resistant.

We can slow the rate of development of resistant strains by:
- reducing the use of antibiotics, reserving them for serious infections only
- ensuring the full course of antibiotics is taken.

bacteria killed by antibiotics

bacteria resistant to antibiotics

Questions

1. Name two types of pathogen.

2. What does an antibiotic do?

3. Explain why scientists need to keep producing new types of antibiotics.

Revision objectives

- ✔ know how our bodies try to prevent infection
- ✔ describe how the immune system deals with pathogens
- ✔ know how immunisation protects against some diseases

Student book references

1.5 Immunity and immunisation

Specification key

✔ B1.1.2

Key words

immune system, antibodies, antigen, immunity, white blood cell, immunisation, vaccine

Exam tip AQA

Make sure you are clear about the difference between the action of the phagocyte and the lymphocyte. Also be clear about the differences between natural and artificial immunity.

Questions

1   Name the two types of white blood cell.
2   What does immunity mean?
3   What is the difference between natural and artificial immunity?

Preventing infections

The body has a number of systems that prevent microorganisms getting in. These include:

skin – acts as a barrier

digestive system – stomach acid kills bacteria

blood clots – seal cuts

respiratory system – mucus traps bacteria.

The immune system

Once pathogens get inside the body the **immune system** comes to our rescue. It uses two types of **white blood cell**.

Phagocyte	Lymphocyte
• locates pathogen • engulfs pathogen • ingests it	• locates pathogen • reacts to **antigens** on specific pathogen • massively increases in number • produces **antibodies** • antibodies are proteins, and are specific to the antigens on the particular pathogen • antibodies destroy the specific pathogen • lymphocytes can also produce antitoxins specific to a toxin released by the pathogen

Immunisation

Immunity means the ability to resist an infection. This can be acquired in two ways.

Natural immunity

This happens when we are infected and some of the lymphocytes that produce the antibodies are retained to deal with future infections.

Artificial immunity

Here we are given a **vaccine**, which contains dead or inactivated pathogens. This triggers an immune response. The lymphocytes are retained, and will respond rapidly if a future infection by the pathogen occurs. For example, the MMR vaccine protects us against future infections of measles, mumps, and rubella.

If enough of the population becomes immune, the spread of infectious diseases is reduced. Unfortunately if a new strain develops by a mutation the vaccine will be ineffective.

Working to Grade E

1 What is the source of energy in a cell?

2 What is a balanced diet?

3 What is malnourishment?

4 What is the scientific term for being very overweight?

5 What are carbohydrates used for in the body?

6 What are fats used for in the body?

7 What are proteins used for in the body?

8 What is a pathogen?

9 What is a toxin?

10 Which are bigger, bacteria or viruses?

11 Name one harmful effect of bacteria in the body.

12 What is an antibiotic?

13 Name a painkiller.

14 Do painkillers kill pathogens?

15 Name a bacterium that is resistant to most antibiotics.

16 Name three barriers that prevent microorganisms entering the body.

17 Look at these drawings of blood cells.
   a Label the phagocyte and the lymphocyte.
   b What does a phagocyte do?

18 What is contained in a vaccine?

19 What does the MMR vaccine protect you against?

Working to Grade C

20 Suggest three things that might vary the metabolic rate.

21 Where does metabolism take place?

22 What is the relationship between the muscle-to-fat ratio in a person and their metabolic rate?

23 Name a health problem caused by being overweight.

24 Explain why it is important to wash our hands.

25 What do symptoms tell a doctor?

26 a Look at this diagram of the reproduction of viruses. Put the steps in the correct sequence.

A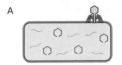
The viral genes cause the host cell to make new viruses.

B
The genetic material from the virus is injected into the host cell.

C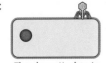
The virus attaches to a specific host cell.

D
The host cell splits open, releasing the new viruses.

b Use the diagram to describe the stages in the reproduction of a virus.

27 Explain why antibiotics have no effect on viruses.

28 What term is used for the chance changes that allow new strains of bacteria to develop resistance?

29 What does sterile mean?

30 Why is the apparatus used to grow microorganisms always sterilised before the set up of the experiment?

31 What is an inoculating loop used for?

32 Why are the lids of Petri dishes taped onto the base of the dish?

33 Why should cultures be incubated at 25 °C in a school laboratory?

34 Which organ system in your body deals with infections?

35 Describe how a lymphocyte destroys pathogens.

36 What is an antibody made of?

37 What is the difference between an antibody and an antitoxin?

38 What is immunisation?

Working to Grade A*

39 How might exercise change the muscle-to-fat ratio?

40 Explain how cholesterol might lead to a heart attack.

41 Explain how a bacterial infection makes you feel ill.

42 Explain how natural selection could lead to the development of antibiotic-resistant bacteria.

43 Explain why antibiotic resistance is of such concern to doctors.

44 What strategies do we use to reduce the development of resistant bacteria?

45 Explain why an antibody will only kill one type of bacteria.

46 Explain how a vaccination works.

Examination questions
Healthy living

1 The table below gives information about the nutrients (per 100 g of bar) in a number of chocolate snack bars and confectionery bars.

Type of bar	Energy (kJ)	Total fat (g)	Saturated fat (g)	Carbohydrates (g)	Sugars (g)	Proteins (g)
Milk chocolate bar	2200	30.0	18.6	56.8	56.6	7.5
Dark chocolate bar	2105	27.3	16.6	58.8	57.7	4.7
White chocolate bar	2315	33.3	20.6	59.7	59.7	4.5
Fruit and nut chocolate bar	2050	25.9	14.5	55.8	55.2	8.3
Raisin cereal bar	1800	15.7	8.6	65.1	42.3	5.4

a Which bar will provide the most energy?

....

(1 mark)

b Which **two** nutritional groups will provide the most energy?

.... and ....

(1 mark)

c **i** Which of the bars is the healthier bar to eat?

....

(1 mark)

ii Explain your answer.

....

....

....

(2 marks)

(Total marks: 5)

2 Look at the following graph, which shows the number of recorded cases of measles in the UK from 1940 to 2008. Measles was a common childhood disease caused by a virus.

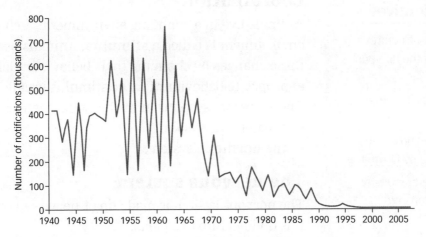

a What is the trend in the graph for numbers of cases of measles?

....

....

....

(1 mark)

b Two vaccines have been produced to combat measles. The first was a single vaccine. The second was the combined MMR vaccine.

i When do you think the first vaccine was introduced?

....

(1 mark)

ii Explain your reasoning.

....

....

(1 mark)

c This treatment of measles is an example of active immunity. Explain how active immunity works.

....

....

....

....

....

(4 marks)

(Total marks: 7)

Coordination

Animals live in a changing environment. A change in the environment is called a **stimulus**. Animals need to respond to these changes by changing their behaviour. Selecting the appropriate behaviour for the stimulus is called **coordination**. There are two systems in the body that help coordinate:

- the nervous system
- the **hormone** system.

The nervous system

The nervous system is made up of nerve cells called **neurones**. It is divided into two parts:

- the **central nervous system** (CNS) – the brain and spinal cord
- the **peripheral nervous system** – the nerves taking messages to and from the CNS.

The nervous system acts by detecting the stimulus in **receptors** called sense organs. These send an electrical message called an impulse along nerves to the CNS. The CNS coordinates an appropriate response, then sends an impulse out to an **effector**. This brings about a response, by either contracting a muscle or releasing (**secreting**) a chemical substance from a gland.

Receptors

We have different receptors for the different stimuli. Some receptors, for example, the eye, have their own special cells. Others, like those in the skin, may just be the ends of the nerve cells. All have the basic parts of all animal cells: a cell membrane, nucleus, and cytoplasm.

Sense	Receptor	Stimulus
sight	eyes	light
hearing	ears	sound
balance	ears	changes in position
smell	nose	chemicals
taste	tongue	chemicals
touch	skin	pressure, pain, and temperature

Neurones

There are three types of neurone:

- Sensory neurone – takes impulses from receptors into the CNS.
- Relay neurone – takes the impulse from the sensory neurone to the correct motor neurone inside the CNS.
- Motor neurone – takes impulses from the CNS to the effector.

The junction between two neurones is called a **synapse**. The impulse passes across a synapse as a chemical message.

Reflexes

These are rapid, protective, automatic responses in the body. The pathway taken by the impulse is called a **reflex** arc. For example, pulling the hand away from a sharp pin is a reflex arc.

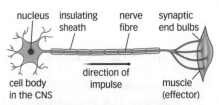

▲ Structure of a motor neurone. The nerve impulse is carried along the nerve fibre.

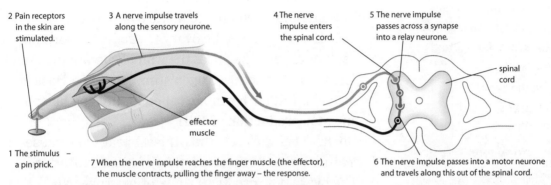

2 Pain receptors in the skin are stimulated.

3 A nerve impulse travels along the sensory neurone.

4 The nerve impulse enters the spinal cord.

5 The nerve impulse passes across a synapse into a relay neurone.

spinal cord

effector muscle

1 The stimulus – a pin prick.

7 When the nerve impulse reaches the finger muscle (the effector), the muscle contracts, pulling the finger away – the response.

6 The nerve impulse passes into a motor neurone and travels along this out of the spinal cord.

▲ A reflex arc. The impulse goes from receptor to CNS and then to effector to bring about the response. The relay neurone inside the spinal cord coordinates the response by connecting the sensory neurone to an appropriate motor neurone. The information travels from one neurone to another across a small gap called a synapse.

Hormonal control

The hormonal system plays a role in controlling the balance of our internal systems. It works by releasing hormones into the bloodstream. A hormone is a chemical messenger released in one **gland** and having its effect on a **target organ** elsewhere in the body. The effect is generally slower but longer lasting than nerve reflexes.

Internal conditions that are controlled

- Water content of the body – all cells in the body need to be bathed in water. Water enters the body in food and drink and is released during respiration. It leaves by the lungs when we breathe out, by the skin in sweat, and by the kidneys in urine.
- **Ion** content of the body – ions are needed to keep nerves and muscles healthy. Ions are taken in from the diet and lost in sweat and urine.
- Temperature – the body needs to maintain a stable temperature for its enzymes to function. The skin is particularly important in helping control temperature. For example, we sweat to cool us down.
- Blood sugar levels – sugar is needed as a source of energy for cells, but too much will lead to circulatory problems. Hormones regulate the level of blood sugar.

Key words

coordination, stimulus, central nervous system, peripheral nervous system, receptor, neurone, synapse, effector, reflex, hormone, secrete, gland, target organ, ion

Questions

1 What does coordination mean?

2 What is a receptor?

3 Explain the differences between nervous control systems and hormonal control systems.

Revision objectives

✓ understand the role of hormones in the menstrual cycle

✓ explain how oestrogen and progesterone are used in the contraceptive pill

✓ be aware that hormones are used to control fertility and in IVF treatment

✓ evaluate the benefits and difficulties of fertility treatments

Student book references

1.8 How hormones control the menstrual cycle

1.9 Using hormones to control fertility

Specification key

✓ B1.2.2

Hormonal control of the menstrual cycle

The **menstrual cycle** in females begins during puberty. The cycle is a sequence of events carefully controlled by **hormones**. It involves the exact timing of the release of an egg, and the preparation of the womb for pregnancy.

- The cycle begins with the release of a follicle stimulating hormone (**FSH**) from the pituitary gland.
- This stimulates the egg to mature in the ovary.
- FSH also stimulates the ovary to produce a hormone called **oestrogen**, which causes the wall of the womb to thicken.
- The high levels of oestrogen stimulate the release of a second pituitary hormone called luteinising hormone (**LH**), and stop production of FSH.
- On day 14 of the cycle the LH level peaks and causes a mature egg to be released; this is called **ovulation**.
- The ovary now produces a mix of oestrogen and **progesterone**.
- These hormones continue to thicken the wall of the womb, which can now receive a fertilised egg if the woman becomes pregnant.
- With high oestrogen and progesterone no FSH is produced, and no eggs mature.
- If the woman does not become pregnant, oestrogen and progesterone levels fall, and the wall of the womb is shed, together with some blood as the menstrual flow, or period.
- The cycle then starts again.

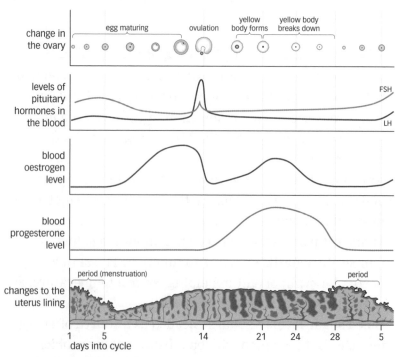

▲ Events in the menstrual cycle.

Controlling fertility

Our understanding of the hormones that control the menstrual cycle has allowed us to control **fertility** in humans.

Contraceptive treatments

Contraceptive drugs are ones that prevent pregnancy. These make use of the fact that the hormones oestrogen and progesterone will inhibit the production of FSH, and so stop eggs maturing.

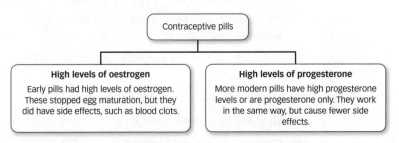

▲ Oestrogen and progesterone in the contraceptive pill.

Fertility treatments

Hormones can also be used to help women become pregnant. Some women have difficulty in maturing eggs, which may be because they have naturally low levels of FSH and LH. In such cases women can take a fertility drug, which contains both FSH and LH. This results in eggs being matured and released.

This treatment is useful in the process called **in vitro fertilisation (IVF)**.

- The woman is given a treatment of fertility drugs.
- Several eggs mature and are released; they are collected by the doctor.
- These eggs are mixed with sperm from the father.
- The fertilised eggs develop into small balls of cells, called embryos.
- One or two embryos are inserted back into the mother's womb (uterus).
- The embryos develop into a baby in the womb.

Controlling fertility in these ways has both benefits and problems.

- Some benefits include: families can control when they will start a family, and how many children they will have; IVF allows infertile couples to have children, and embryos can be screened for disorders.
- Some problems include: some people have ethical concerns about controlling fertility and disposing of unwanted embryos; IVF is expensive; there are side effects of the pill, and some women stay on the pill too long.

Exam tip

Remember that there are two pituitary hormones and two hormones made in the ovary involved in the menstrual cycle.

Questions

1 What two things does the menstrual cycle control?

2 Name two ways that doctors can use hormones to control the menstrual cycle.

3 **H** What is IVF?

Working to Grade E

1   Name three different stimuli the body can detect.

2   What stimulus is detected by the eye?

3   Which organ is sensitive to pressure?

4   Which two sense organs can detect chemicals?

5   What is an impulse?

6   Look at this drawing of a neurone.

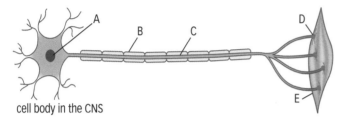

cell body in the CNS

   a   Label parts A to E.
   b   Identify the type of neurone.
   c   Label the direction the impulse takes along the neurone.

7   What is a synapse?

8   What are the two parts of the nervous system?

9   Give an example of a reflex action.

10   Give an example of a voluntary action.

11   What secrete hormones?

12   Which organ regulates the amount of water in the body?

13   What is the normal temperature of a human body?

14   What is puberty?

15   Name the female sex hormones produced in the ovaries.

16   Name the hormone that stimulates the release of eggs from the ovary.

17   Where is FSH produced?

18   What does IVF stand for?

19   What is ovulation?

Working to Grade C

20   What is the function of a sensory neurone?

21   What is the function of a motor neurone?

22   How does the impulse pass across a synapse?

23   What is a reflex action?

24   Place the following structures in the correct order to describe the pathway of a reflex action:

   motor neurone, receptor, stimulus, relay neurone, response, effector, sensory neurone

25   In which part of the nervous system do you find relay neurones?

26   How does a muscle respond to an impulse?

27   How are hormones transported?

28   Give three ways that water leaves the body.

29   Explain how the body cools down.

30   Name one process that generates heat in the body.

31   Give one way that ions pass out of the body.

32   Why is sugar needed by cells?

33   Where are hormones transported to in the body?

34   What is the function of FSH?

35   What two hormones are contained in contraceptive pills?

36   Which hormones are given to women who are having trouble conceiving?

37   Explain one medical complication caused by using hormones to control fertility.

38   What is the menstrual period?

Working to Grade A*

39   Explain why maintaining the body's temperature is important.

40   What stops the production of FSH during the menstrual cycle?

41   Which hormone combination in the contraceptive pill produces the fewest side effects?

42   Why are women who are about to undergo IVF given a course of hormone treatment?

43   List three benefits from using hormones to control fertility.

1   Sense organs detect stimuli. Connect the following sense organs to the stimuli they detect.

Eye		Temperature
Ear		Light
Tongue		Sound
Skin		Chemicals

(4 marks)
(Total marks: 4)

2   What are the **two** component parts of the central nervous system (CNS)?

1   ....

2   ....
(2 marks)
(Total marks: 2)

3   Hormones play a part in controlling female fertility.

a   What is a hormone?

....

....
(2 marks)

b   In the female menstrual cycle:

i   Which hormone triggers the maturation of the egg?

....
(1 mark)

ii   Which hormone triggers ovulation?

....
(1 mark)

c   Describe the role of hormones in the modern female **contraceptive pill**.

....

....

....

....
(3 marks)
(Total marks: 7)

4 Below is a diagram that shows the structures involved in a spinal reflex.

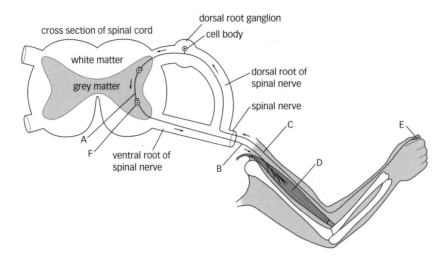

a Which of the structures labelled **A** to **F** is:

i the motor neurone? ....

ii the relay neurone? ....

iii the sensory neurone? ....

iv the sensory nerve ending?..

(4 marks)

b Describe how the labelled structures would be involved in the reflex after a drawing pin has entered the skin at **E**.

....

....

....

....

....

....

(6 marks)

c Give an example of where the brain can override the reflex action.

....

(1 mark)

(Total marks: 11)

5 A scientist carried out a test with a number of subjects to investigate human reaction times to a stimulus.
- Five subjects were selected.
- They were asked to play a computer game that had a button they could press every time they saw a red light on the screen.
- The computer showed the red light randomly a minimum of 10 times.
- The subjects' time to respond was recorded in milliseconds by the computer.
- For each game the computer calculated the average reaction time.
- The game was repeated five times for each subject.

Here are the results:

Subject	Average reaction time (ms)				
	Test 1	Test 2	Test 3	Test 4	Test 5
Nathan	120	110	109	101	98
Emily	157	122	118	101	108
James	143	133	136	126	109
Donna	128	98	103	97	90
Frankie	109	107	89	78	77

a What is the trend in the data?

....

....

(1 mark)

b Which sense organ detected the stimulus?

....

(1 mark)

c How did the scientist attempt to make the experiment:

i accurate? ....

....

ii reliable? ....

....

(2 marks)

d Emily thought her results might be wrong.

i Why does she think that? ....

....

ii Would you agree with her or not? Explain your reasoning.

....

(2 marks)

e Explain how you could adapt the experiment to show that people who regularly play computer games might react faster than people who do not play computer games.

....

....

....

....

....

....

....

(4 marks)
(Total marks: 10)

Plant hormones

Plants also need to respond to stimuli in the environment. Most plant responses are in the form of growth movements called **tropisms**. They respond to a number of stimuli.

Stimulus	Response of the shoot	Response of the root	Tropism
light	grows toward light	grows away from light	**phototropism**
gravity	grows away from gravity (up)	grows toward gravity (down)	**gravitropism (geotropism)**
moisture	grows toward moisture	grows away from moisture	hydrotropism

The growth movements in phototropism and gravitropism are brought about by a hormone called **auxin**. This is produced in the shoot and root tips, but acts behind the tip.

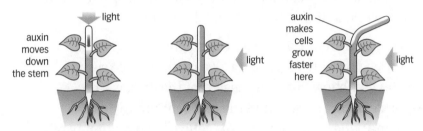

▲ Phototropism and auxin.

In the roots auxins slow plant cell elongation, and therefore the growth. In gravitropism the auxin sinks to the lower side of the plant, causing shoots to grow up away from gravity, and roots to grow down toward gravity.

Uses of plant hormones

Hormones are used commercially to affect plant growth. For example:

- weedkillers – here auxins cause the shoots of broad-leafed weeds to grow rapidly, but not the roots, so they will not be able to absorb enough water to survive.
- rooting hormones – here cuttings are dipped in rooting hormones containing auxins, which encourage the formation of new roots.

Exam tip

Be able to predict the outcome of experiments involving plant growth in response to different directional stimuli. Be able to explain why these results occur in terms of auxin distribution.

Revision objectives

- ✔ know that plants respond to environmental stimuli such as light, gravity, and moisture
- ✔ understand the role of plant hormones in the control of growth
- ✔ understand the application of plant hormones in agriculture

Student book references

1.10 Controlling plant growth

Specification key

✔ B1.2.3

Key words

tropism, auxin, phototropism, gravitropism, geotropism

Questions

1. What is a tropism?
2. What do plants use to control tropisms?
3. Explain what happens to the distribution of auxin when light is shone on the plant from one side.

Revision objectives

- ✓ know what a drug is
- ✓ know that some drugs are useful
- ✓ know that medical drugs are tested before use
- ✓ know that there are different types of recreational drugs, some legal and some illegal

Student book references

1.11 Drugs and you

1.12 Testing new drugs

Specification key

- ✓ B1.3.1

Drugs

A **drug** is a chemical that affects our body chemistry. Scientists are continually developing new drugs. Drugs are used medicinally to treat illness but they are also abused by some people.

Use of medical drugs

Many drugs are developed to treat the causes and symptoms of illness. Beneficial drugs are painkillers, antibiotics, and **statins**. Statins are drugs that have been developed to reduce blood cholesterol level. These drugs reduce the incidence of cardiovascular disease, like heart attacks.

Drug testing

New drugs are constantly being developed. They need to be tested before they can be used by doctors to make sure that the drugs work, and that they are not dangerous.

During a **clinical trial** strict rules apply.
- Large numbers of patients give more reliable results.
- Start with low doses to check that the drug is safe.
- Increase the dose to find the best (optimum) dose.
- Some patients are given a **placebo** (this is a dummy pill without the active drug) to act as a control with which to compare the experimental group.
- **Double-blind trials** are used, where neither the patients nor the doctors know who has the placebo or the real drug, to avoid bias.

Thalidomide – a mistake to learn from

Thalidomide was a drug developed in the 1950s as a sleeping pill. It also helped treat morning sickness in pregnant women. Unfortunately the testing process was not thorough enough. They did not test it on enough types of animals or pregnant women. When they used the drug commercially with pregnant women, they discovered that it had side-effects. Many of the children born to mothers who took thalidomide had severe limb abnormalities. As a result the drug was banned. Scientists made their testing procedure far more rigorous.

Interestingly thalidomide is now used again, as a treatment for conditions like leprosy.

Drug testing
Step 1 – New drug is developed by scientists to treat a disease.
Step 2 – Laboratory trials, on cells, tissues, and eventually live animals. This will check for toxicity, and whether the drug works.
Step 3 – Clinical trials. Here the drugs are tested on human volunteers.
Step 4 – If successful the drug is marketed.

Use of recreational drugs

Some people use recreational drugs.

- Some drugs are legal and some are illegal.
- Some are more harmful than others.

Drug abuse is where people take drugs for no medical reason. Drugs act by changing the chemical processes in the body, particularly the brain. Some people develop an **addiction** to, or become dependent on, drugs. This means that they need the drugs to maintain a functioning lifestyle. If these people try to give up the drug, they suffer **withdrawal symptoms**, as the body's chemical reactions fail to function fully.

Legal recreational drugs

A commonly used legal drug is alcohol. In low doses this drug relaxes people and is not normally considered drug abuse. However, high doses of alcohol can impair judgement and lead to reckless behaviour, which might affect society as a whole. Long-term use of alcohol may lead to serious damage of the liver and other organs. Other legal recreational drugs include caffeine and nicotine.

Illegal recreational drugs

There are many types of illegal drug. For example:

- **Cannabis** – the smoke contains chemicals that give a feeling of well being. It is not significantly addictive, but tends to lead the user onto more powerful drugs. In some people it may lead to mental illness. However, it can be used to treat chronic painful illnesses such as multiple sclerosis.
- **Steroids** – these are performance-enhancing drugs, leading to muscle development. They give athletes an unfair advantage, and so are banned in sport. They can cause side-effects, such as interfering with the reproductive cycle and heart problems.

Other illegal drugs include cocaine and heroin. These are very powerful and harmful drugs. They are highly addictive.

Surprisingly, it is legal drugs, not illegal drugs, that have the greater impact on health. This is because more people use the legal drugs.

Questions

1. Why do people find it difficult to stop taking some types of recreational drugs?
2. Why are large numbers of patients used in drug testing?
3. Why are laboratory trials of new drugs always carried out before clinical trials?

Exam tip

AQA

Most drugs have advantages and disadvantages. You need to look at the evidence or information in a question and balance the pros and cons of each situation.

Questions
Control in plants and drugs

Working to Grade E

1 Name three things plants are sensitive to.

2 What is a stimulus?

3 Name a plant hormone.

4 What is a drug?

5 Give some examples of beneficial drugs.

6 Why do scientists carry out tests on new drugs?

7 How might drugs be tested in a laboratory?

8 What is a clinical trial?

9 What is a placebo?

10 Thalidomide is a drug.
  a   What was thalidomide used for?
  b   Thalidomide now has a new use. What is the new use of the drug?

11 What do statins do?

12 Define the following terms:
  a   drug abuse
  b   addiction
  c   withdrawal symptoms.

13 Some athletes use steroids as an illegal drug.

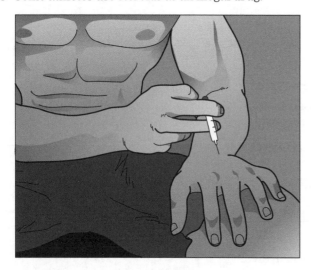

  a   Why might an athlete inject steroids?
  b   What medical problems could this cause for an athlete?

Working to Grade C

14 How do plants respond to stimuli?

15 Look at this drawing of bean seedling A.

  a   Draw the seedling as it would look after three days.
  b   Which part of the plant (the shoot or the root) responds positively to light?
  c   What is the name of this response?

16 Look at this drawing of bean seedling B.

  a   Draw the seedling as it will look after three days in an unlit box.
  b   What stimulus is the bean seedling responding to?
  c   What is the name of this type of response?

17 Name one other commercial use of plant hormones (other than weedkillers).

18 a   What is the purpose of a double-blind trial?
  b   How is a double-blind trial carried out?

19 What is a side-effect?

20 Which diseases do statins help to prevent?

21 A doctor carried out an experiment using patients on a motorbike simulator. They had to brake when the screen showed a person crossing the road. The patients then had to drink alcohol, and repeat the test. The results are shown below.

Alcohol concentration (mg/l)	Average braking time (s)
0	0.572
0.15	0.585
0.25	0.610

  a   Describe the pattern in the data.
  b   What can you conclude about the effect of alcohol on people's reaction times?

c How would a study like this improve road safety?

d How could you take the experiment further to establish the point at which alcohol might start to have an effect?

e How could you design an experiment using a placebo to support the view that alcohol is having an effect?

Working to Grade A*

22 Explain why steroids are banned in sport.

23 What is the effect of auxins on plant cells in the shoot?

24 Explain how auxins function as a weedkiller.

25 Explain how auxins cause a plant to grow toward the light.

26 Look at the diagram below of cress seedlings growing on a piece of equipment called a clinostat. The equipment rotates one full circle in an hour.

a Predict what the seedlings will look like after three days.

b Explain why this has happened.

c What would happen if the clinostat stopped working after a few hours?

27 Astronauts carried out experiments on plant growth in space. They grew bean seedlings in dark boxes for several days. Below is a drawing of the results of such an experiment.

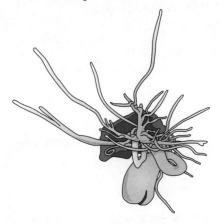

a Can you describe any clear patterns of directional growth in the seedlings?

b Explain why such results were achieved.

28 Suggest how you might modify the experiment to achieve some kind of directional growth.

29 a What problems did the drug thalidomide cause?

b What was wrong during the development process of thalidomide, which resulted in such problems?

c What precaution would a doctor take before prescribing thalidomide now?

30 Discuss the benefits of and problems with the use of cannabis.

31 A newspaper has suggested that illegal drugs such as cannabis and heroin are the most significant cause of drug-related health problems in the UK. Do you agree with this claim? What evidence can you use to support your answer?

32 Explain why someone might become dependent on a drug.

1 People use drugs for many different reasons.

   a What is a drug?

....

....

....
(1 mark)

   b Give an example of a medical drug.

....
(1 mark)

   c Give an example of a recreational drug.

....
(1 mark)

   d Scientists now think that legal recreational drugs cause more problems than illegal recreational drugs. Explain why this is the case.

....

....
(1 mark)

   e What is drug addiction?

....

....
(2 marks)
(Total marks: 6)

2 Plants show growth responses to environmental stimuli.

   a Name the response that causes roots to grow down with gravity.

....
(1 mark)

   b Explain why it is an advantage to the plants for the shoots to show phototropism.

....

....
(2 marks)

   c Explain how phototropism is caused in the shoot.

....

....

....
(2 marks)
(Total marks: 5)

Presenting and using data

Within this module there are some very good examples of the presentation and interpretation of data. You may be asked in a question to demonstrate these skills yourself.

Look at the following example; this will show you how scientists present and interpret data. There are opportunities for you to practise some of the skills, and to be guided through some of the more difficult elements that might appear in a question in the exam.

The flu pandemic of 2009

During the autumn of 2009, the world faced a new form of the flu virus (H1N1, also known as 'swine flu') that had originated in Mexico. Scientists all over the world were tracking the spread and effects of this disease. The aim was to be able to prepare countries for the arrival of the disease, and give them some indication of how it would spread.

Doctors in the UK collected data on the number of cases. This was done in every health region of the UK. The following data is for the city of Sheffield.

Week beginning	Number of swine flu cases per 100 000 of the population
14 September	8.1
21 September	28.8
28 September	35.5
5 October	50.3
12 October	50.9
19 October	46.9
26 October	52.9
2 November	70.8
9 November	33.3
16 November	22.5

1 Plot the data on a graph. Join the points.

Skill – Presenting the data

This kind of question shows how scientists try to illustrate complex data as an image (the graph). Graphs give a picture of the data and are useful for identifying patterns.

The plotting of a graph is a common exam question, but it is surprising how many students drop marks on these sorts of questions.

Here are some quick, easy tips for plotting graphs: remember the word 'SLAP':

- **S** = Scales – when spreading the scales on the axes, the values on the axes must go up in equal amounts for each square size on the graph.
- **L** = Labels – remember to label each axis with the variable and the unit.
- **A** = Axes – make sure these are plotted the correct way round: the independent variable (the one you set or change, such as 'week beginning') along the 'X' axis, and the dependent variable (the one you measure, such as 'number of cases of flu') up the 'Y' axis.
- **P** = Plotting the points – your points should be plotted with a small neat 'x' in the exact position.

Finally, remember to join the points.

Skill – Using data to draw conclusions

Once scientists have plotted the graph they can start to make sense of complex data. There are a few common types of question that scientists ask, and you could be asked these same questions in an exam.

2 What is the trend shown by the data for flu cases in Sheffield?

This type of question requires an overview of the pattern shown by the graph. Describe the overall rise/fall in the line of the graph.

Common mistakes:
- It does not require a point-by-point description.
- Do not describe the first half only and then ignore the second half, where the direction or trend might change.

3 Are there any anomalous results?

This question asks you to pick up any results that do not fit with the trend you have described. Look for any point that stands out as unusual or that distorts the shape of the curve on the graph.

4 When does the flu epidemic appear to be under control?

This is asking you for the point on the graph where the line changes direction.

5 What might have been the result for the number of cases on 23rd November?

This question asks you to continue the shape of the graph a little further, and to take a reading at that point. There is usually a little flexibility for the examiner to allow a small range in the answers, as there is no point on the graph.

Answering a question with data response

Tuberculosis (TB) is a disease caused by a bacterium.

1 How does the use of antibiotics help a patient with TB? *(1 mark)*

2 This graph shows the number of cases of TB in England and Wales since 1930. What trend is shown by the data? *(2 marks)*

3 Has the introduction of a vaccine eliminated the disease? Explain your answer using evidence. *(2 marks)*

4 By the 1970s many TB wards were closed. Suggest the reason for this. *(1 mark)*

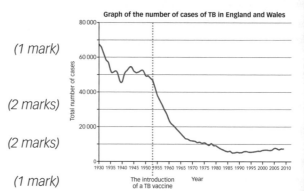

Graph of the number of cases of TB in England and Wales

G–E

1 Antibiotics fight infections.

2 In 1952 the number of cases was about 50 000.

3 No, because I can see on the graph.

4 There was a lack of money to keep them open.

Examiner: The candidate gives a vague answer, which does not describe what an antibiotic does. It is not worth a mark.

The candidate has not given a trend, but picked on one point of data. They have put effort into looking at the graph, but will not get any marks because the trend has not been given.

This candidate has got one mark for recognising that there are still cases. They have tried to use the graph, but not explained what it tells them and how. You need to quote figures or trends directly from the graph to get these marks.

No marks given because the candidate has not used the graph to suggest an explanation.

D–C

1 Antibiotics kill bacteria and viruses.

2 There has been a gradual fall in the number of cases.

3 No. People still get TB.

4 The cases have fallen.

Examiner: The answer is slightly muddled or confused. It shows some understanding of the action of antibiotics, but the use of the word virus confuses the answer, as viruses are not killed by antibiotics. No mark can be awarded, as the use of the word viruses is incorrect.

The decline has been recognised, but the significance of the introduction of the vaccine has not. This will only gain one of the two marks.

The candidate has got a mark for recognising that TB is not eliminated, but will not get the second mark because they have not referred to the data in the graph.

Whilst the candidate has recognised the decline in numbers, they have not read from the graph that the number of cases was now low. Therefore no mark can be awarded.

B–A*

1 Antibiotics kill bacteria.

2 There has been a decline in the number of cases, but there was a significant drop after 1953 when the vaccine was introduced.

3 No, because the graph still shows about 5–10 000 cases of TB even today.

4 The number of cases were so low, there was no need for them.

Examiner: Clear and accurate.

An excellent answer, not only picking out the overall trend, but also the significant drop after the vaccine.

The student has given a clear answer to both parts of the question.

Again clear answer. The candidate has recognised that the important point is that the case number being low meant that there was no need for them.

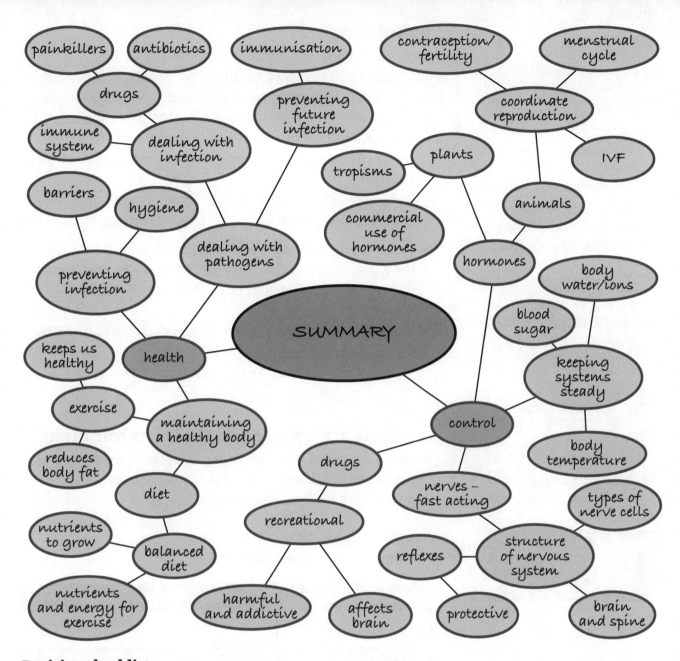

Revision checklist

- To stay healthy humans need a balanced diet. This provides enough of each nutrient and the energy for the body's needs.
- The amount of energy needed depends on your level of activity and metabolic rate.
- Pathogens are organisms, mainly bacteria and viruses, that can infect our body, multiply, and make us ill.
- Our body has a number of barriers that prevent pathogens getting into the blood.
- Our white blood cells are able to fight infections by either ingesting pathogens or making antibodies to kill them. Antitoxins are made to remove toxins.
- Vaccines can generate immunity to pathogens in our bodies.
- Drugs like antibiotics kill bacteria; painkillers can remove painful symptoms. Bacteria can develop resistance to antibiotics.
- Our bodies have a nervous system. The brain and spinal cord coordinate the correct response to any stimulus.

- Reflexes are rapid, automatic, and protective responses.
- The body is able to control its temperature, blood sugar levels, water content, and ion content at a steady level.
- Hormones are chemical messengers that coordinate the actions of cells.
- Hormones are used to control a woman's menstrual cycle. Knowledge of this can be used to control fertility and contraception.
- Plants use hormones to respond to changes in their environment. These hormones are used in agriculture to control growth.
- Drugs change the way the body or brain works. They may be medicinal or recreational. Some drugs are harmful or addictive.
- New drugs must be tested thoroughly before they can be used on patients.

Revision objectives

- ✔ know that adaptations of organisms help them to survive
- ✔ identify and explain key adaptations of plants and animals to cold or dry environments
- ✔ understand that the adaptations of an organism determine where they can live
- ✔ know that organisms live in extreme environments and show adaptations to those environments

Student book references

1.13 Animal adaptations

1.14 Plant adaptations

1.15 Extreme adaptations

Specification key

- ✔ B1.4.1

Being adapted

Successful plants and animals are well suited to their environments. They show **adaptations**. An adaptation is any feature that aids survival and reproduction. Adaptations help the organism to compete with others for limited resources:

- Adaptations may help gain materials and resources from the environment. For example, large leaves can absorb more sunlight.
- They may help gain materials from other organisms. For example, sharp teeth will help kill prey animals.

Some adaptations may be very specific to a particular feature of the environment or the organism's way of life. For example:

- Thorns on some plants, such as the acacia tree, reduce grazing by animals.
- Poisons in some plants or animals, such as the poison dart frog, reduce grazing or predation.
- Warning colours, such as the yellow and black stripes of a bee, deter predators.

Animals are adapted to their environment

Animals are successfully adapted to survive in environments from the arctic to the desert. For every adaptation you should be able to give a reason why it aids survival.

Adaptations to arctic conditions

Here are the key adaptations to remember:

Adaptation	How this aids survival
changes to **surface area**, for example, small ears	This reduced surface area reduces heat loss.
thickness of insulating coat	The thick fur coat insulates the body against the cold.
amount of body fat	The bear has a thick layer of fat, which insulates against heat loss, and can be used in respiration to generate heat.
camouflage	The white fur means that the animal blends in with the environment.

Key words

adaptation, camouflage, spines, surface area, extremophiles

Exam tip AQA

The exam question could be about any plant or animal. Practise looking at any plant or animal, identifying an adaptation, and suggesting how it might aid that plant or animal to survive.

Adaptations to desert conditions

Here are the key adaptations to remember:

Adaptation	How this aids survival
changes to surface area, for example, long legs	This lifts the body high above the hot sand.
thickness of insulating coat	The thin in fur coat traps less insulating air.
amount of body fat	The thin layer of body fat reduces heat retention. However, there is a store of fat in the hump that can be used to release energy and water.
camouflage	Sandy coloured fur blends in with the background.

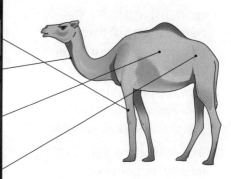

Plants are adapted to their environment

Plants are also successful in a wide range of environments. One of the most challenging environments must surely be the hot, dry environment of the desert.

Here are the key adaptations to remember:

Adaptation	How this aids survival
changes to the surface area of the leaves	Leaves are **spines**, which reduces surface area. This in turn reduces water loss.
water-storage tissues	Stems are swollen to store water.
extensive root systems	The roots of a cactus are often shallow but they cover a large area, which allows a greater absorption of water when it does rain.

Adaptations to extreme environments

Many organisms are able to withstand extreme conditions. They are called **extremophiles**. Again, they show adaptations to help them survive under such conditions.

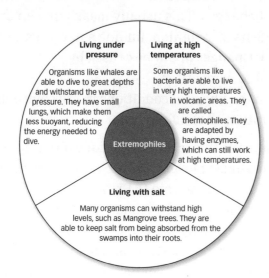

Living under pressure

Organisms like whales are able to dive to great depths and withstand the water pressure. They have small lungs, which make them less buoyant, reducing the energy needed to dive.

Living at high temperatures

Some organisms like bacteria are able to live in very high temperatures in volcanic areas. They are called thermophiles. They are adapted by having enzymes, which can still work at high temperatures.

Extremophiles

Living with salt

Many organisms can withstand high levels, such as Mangrove trees. They are able to keep salt from being absorbed from the swamps into their roots.

Questions

1. What is an adaptation?

2. Why are there so few successful plants and animals living in hot, dry deserts?

3. **H** What is the major problem for animals living in an arctic environment? Suggest one way the arctic fox is adapted to survive the conditions.

Revision objectives

✔ know that organisms compete with each other for resources and that this can affect their distribution

✔ know that the distribution of organisms is affected by changes in the environment

✔ explain how organisms are affected by pollution

✔ identify how organisms and apparatus can be used to indicate levels of pollution

Student book references

1.16 Competition for resources

1.17 Changes in distribution

1.18 Indicating pollution

Specification key

✔ B1.4.2

Distribution of an organism

A **population** is the number of individuals of a species in a named area. The **distribution** of the population is the range and extent of the area in which it lives. The distribution can be affected by:

- **competition** with other organisms
- effective adaptation to the environment
- changes in the environment
- pollution.

Competition

Organisms need **resources** to survive. In any environment the resources are limited. All organisms compete with each other for those resources.

Plants compete for: *Animals compete for:*

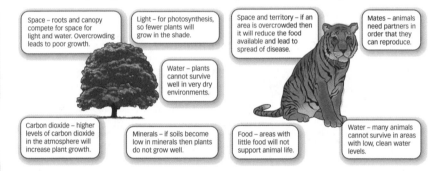

Space – roots and canopy compete for space for light and water. Overcrowding leads to poor growth.

Light – for photosynthesis, so fewer plants will grow in the shade.

Water – plants cannot survive well in very dry environments.

Carbon dioxide – higher levels of carbon dioxide in the atmosphere will increase plant growth.

Minerals – if soils become low in minerals then plants do not grow well.

Space and territory – if an area is overcrowded then it will reduce the food available and lead to spread of disease.

Mates – animals need partners in order that they can reproduce.

Food – areas with little food will not support animal life.

Water – many animals cannot survive in areas with low, clean water levels.

Adaptation

A well-adapted organism survives well in its environment. It usually means that it can obtain the resources it needs to survive.

Changes in the environment

Being well adapted to an environment causes problems if the environment changes. This usually means that an organism has to change its distribution, finding a new area to which it is better suited. Changes might be caused by:

- the arrival of competitors
- changes in the physical conditions in the environment, such as temperature or rainfall.

A good example of this is seen in various bird migration patterns. The ringed plover lives in Scandinavia during the summer, and used to migrate to Britain to overwinter in a milder climate. However, the climate has become warmer in mainland Europe during the winter. This has resulted in a change to the migration pattern, and many plovers now migrate to Europe rather than Britain during the winter.

▲ Ringed plover.

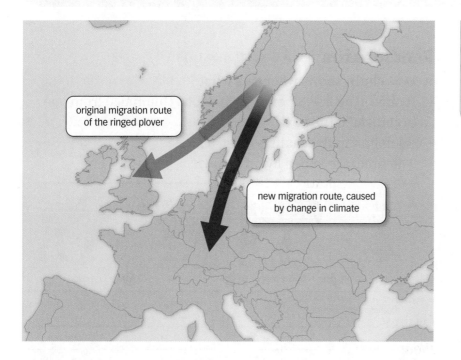

new migration route, caused by change in climate

◀ Climate change has resulted in lower numbers of ringed plover in the UK.

Pollution

Pollution is the release of harmful substances into the environment by humans. The substances are called **pollutants**. Pollutants affect the survival and distribution of organisms.

- Some species can survive well in high levels of pollution. Their presence indicates to biologists that the area is polluted.
- Other species only survive in clean areas. Their presence indicates that the area has no pollution.

Such species are known as **indicator species**.

Indicators of air pollution

Lichens are very good indicators of pollution levels in the air. Some species are particularly sensitive to sulfur dioxide. Sulfur dioxide is released as a pollutant from burning fuels. These lichens don't grow in industrial areas.

Indicators of water pollution

Polluted water contains high levels of microorganisms, which tend to massively reduce the level of oxygen in the water. Invertebrates like the rat-tailed maggot are able to survive well in polluted waters that have low oxygen levels. This is because they have a straw-like tail that can obtain oxygen from the air. The presence of these maggots indicates that the water is polluted.

Measuring pollution levels

Apart from using indicator species, scientists can also use a range of sensors that can measure physical or chemical levels in the environment. These include maximum–minimum thermometers, oxygen meters, and rainfall gauges.

Exam tip AQA

Exam questions are often based on information about a named species. Look out for information about the effects of competition, changes in the environment, and pollution on the species, and be ready to discuss how it might affect the species' distribution.

Questions

1 What is competition?

2 What might affect the distribution of an animal?

3 H How might pollution affect the distribution of organisms?

B1

10: Energy and biomass

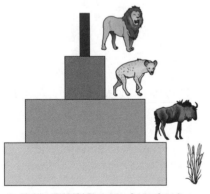

▲ Pyramid of biomass for a food chain on the African savannah.

Food chains

A **food chain** shows what eats what.

- It shows the flow of **energy** and food (**biomass**) from one organism to the next.
- Each link in the chain is given a name.
- The links are joined by an arrow.

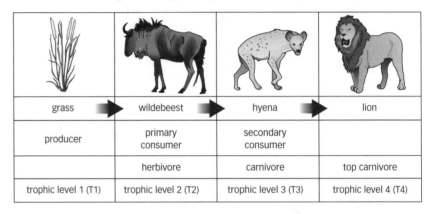

grass	wildebeest	hyena	lion
producer	primary consumer	secondary consumer	
	herbivore	carnivore	top carnivore
trophic level 1 (T1)	trophic level 2 (T2)	trophic level 3 (T3)	trophic level 4 (T4)

Biomass

Biomass is the mass of living material. The biomass of each link in the food chain can be calculated by multiplying the number of individuals in that link by the dry mass of one individual. Biologists then plot this as a **pyramid of biomass**.

Pyramids of biomass

Rules for plotting a pyramid of biomass:

- The producer is always at the base.
- Each bar represents the biomass of each trophic level.
- Each bar must be drawn to the same scale.

When plotted a typical pyramid shape is usually produced. This tells biologists that at each stage in the food chain there is less biomass than at the stage before. Biomass is lost because not all of the organism is eaten, and because some of the material eaten is lost in the waste droppings.

Energy flow through the food chain

Food chains don't only show the movement of biomass from one organism to another, but also the energy. As with biomass, some energy is lost at each link in the food chain.

Energy efficiency in farming

Many modern farmers produce meat for the human food chain. Since energy (and biomass) is lost at every link in the food chain, our scientific understanding of food chains can make the process more energy efficient.

Sun

Light radiated from the Sun is the source of energy for the food chain.

Green plants and algae absorb a small amount of the light energy (about 1%) during **photosynthesis**.

Most of the light energy (about 99%) is reflected.

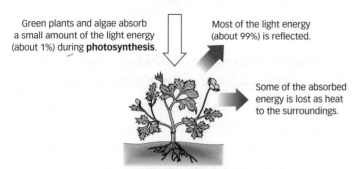

Some of the absorbed energy is lost as heat to the surroundings.

The remaining absorbed light energy is converted to chemical energy and stored in plant compounds.

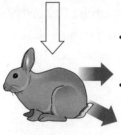

- Some plant compounds are used in respiration to supply the energy needs of the animal, including movement.
- During this transfer of energy, much is lost as heat to the surroundings.

Some energy lost in feces.

Some energy is built into animal compounds.

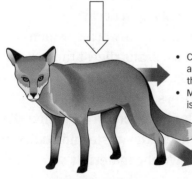

- Compounds from the rabbit are used in respiration by the fox.
- Much of the energy released is lost as heat.

Some energy lost in feces.

Some energy built into animal compounds.

▲ Energy flows through a food chain. Some energy is transferred out at each stage.

- Farming food chains are short – fewer links mean smaller losses.
- Animals kept warm – less heat energy is transferred to the surroundings.
- Animals enclosed in small pens – reduces energy loss from movement.
- Pests reduced – these compete with the organism for available energy sources.

Exam tip

This energy-loss diagram can look complicated. Focus on the loss of energy at each step, and notice that the pattern for all the animals is very similar.

Questions

1 What is the initial source of energy in all food chains?

2 What is biomass?

3 **H** How does intensive farming reduce energy loss through the food chain?

Revision objectives

- ✓ know that nature recycles by the decay of dead material
- ✓ understand the important part microorganisms play in the process of decay
- ✓ explain that elements are cycled between the living and non-living world
- ✓ understand the steps in the carbon cycle

Student book references

1.21 Recycling in nature

1.22 The carbon cycle

Specification key

✔ B1.6.1, ✔ B1.6.2

Recycling

Living things are made of energy and materials. We have seen that energy moves into and through the living world, in the

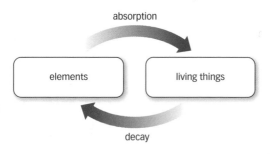

food chain. The materials are made of elements that are in a constant cycle between the living and non-living world.

When an organism dies, its body **decays** and returns the elements to the non-living world, like the soil and the air. They then become available for other organisms, such as plants, to absorb and use. This is natural **recycling**.

A stable community, like a woodland, does not require any input of materials, just a source of energy from the Sun to enable **photosynthesis**. This means that there must be a constant recycling of the elements. There must be a balance between the absorption of the elements and the return of the elements by decay.

Decay

Decay is where the waste from an organism, or the dead body of an organism, is broken down. There are two principal groups of organisms involved in decay:

- Detritivores – including earthworms, which eat bits of dead body such as dead leaves, and digest them, releasing their waste, which contains the elements and can be broken down further by decomposers.
- Decomposers – including bacteria and fungi. These **microorganisms** digest the waste and bodies by releasing enzymes to break down the materials.

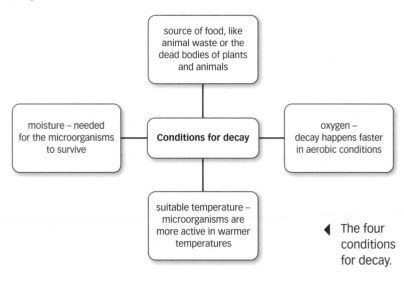

◀ The four conditions for decay.

Exam tip AQA

Learn the four conditions for decay.

The carbon cycle

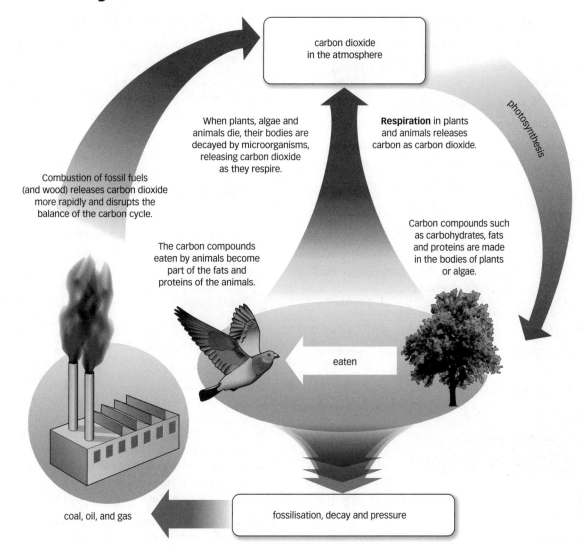

carbon dioxide
in the atmosphere

When plants, algae and
animals die, their bodies are
decayed by microorganisms,
releasing carbon dioxide
as they respire.

Respiration in plants
and animals releases
carbon as carbon dioxide.

photosynthesis

Combustion of fossil fuels
(and wood) releases carbon dioxide
more rapidly and disrupts the
balance of the carbon cycle.

Carbon compounds such
as carbohydrates, fats
and proteins are made
in the bodies of plants
or algae.

The carbon compounds
eaten by animals become
part of the fats and
proteins of the animals.

eaten

coal, oil, and gas

fossilisation, decay and pressure

▲ The major steps in the carbon cycle.

During the **carbon cycle**, the element carbon is constantly being cycled between the living and non-living world. While the elements cycle, energy goes through the cycle. When carbon dioxide is built into carbohydrates and fats in plants, they take in and store the Sun's energy in these compounds. As the compounds move through the cycle, the energy either passes from one step to the next, or is released back into the atmosphere.

Questions

1   What is decay?

2   What is the carbon cycle?

3   Explain how the action of detritivores speeds up the process of decay.

Key words

microorganism, decay, recycling, carbon cycle, photosynthesis, respiration, combustion

Working to Grade E

1   Give one way a fish is adapted to living in water.

2   Explain how a cactus is well adapted to living in dry conditions.

3   Name two extreme conditions in which microorganisms are found.

4   Sharks and dolphins have a streamlined body shape. What does this phrase mean?

5   List the five resources that plants compete for.

6   What is pollution?

7   Name one air pollutant and state where this pollutant comes from.

8   Describe one adaptation of a rat-tailed maggot that allows it to live in polluted water.

9   Where does the producer go in a pyramid of biomass?

10 Apart from energy, what is lost at every link in the food chain?

11 What is a trophic level?

12 What is a detritivore?

13 Name two decomposers.

14 Name the biological process by which living things release carbon dioxide back into the atmosphere.

15 Name three compounds that contain carbon in the body of a plant.

16 How do carbon compounds pass from plants into animals?

Working to Grade C

17 Why is a shark's streamlined body an adaptation to its way of life?

18 Whales are adapted to survive at high pressures.
    a   What does this allow the whale to do?
    b   Explain why they might need to do this.

19 Explain why the air spaces in the bones of birds are a useful adaptation for flight.

20 What is the relationship between the thickness of a mammal's fur and the habitat that it might live in?

21 Look at the drawings of the two plants below.

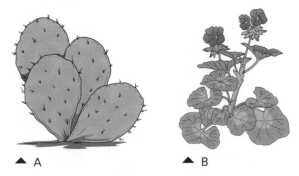

▲ A   ▲ B

    a   Which plant lives in a hot and dry environment and which lives in a wet environment?
    b   Identify two features of A that make it well adapted for its environment.
    c   Explain how the features help it to survive.

22 What is the name given to all organisms that scientists use to work out whether an area is polluted?

23 Look at this graph containing data from a river with some pollution.

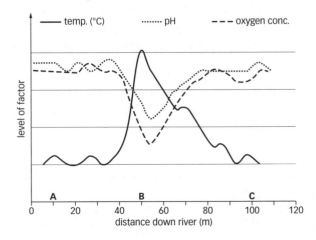

    a   At what point along the river is the greatest level of pollution?
    b   Explain the oxygen readings at this point.

24 What is light energy converted to in plants?

25 During what process does this conversion occur?

26 Explain why it is more energy efficient for a farmer to keep a herd of cows in a small barn, rather than roaming in large fields.

27 What data would you need to collect to construct a pyramid of biomass?

28 Look at the food chain below.

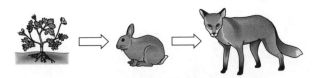

a   Sketch a pyramid of biomass for this food chain.
b   Explain the size of the bar for the fox in the pyramid.
c   Energy is lost at each link in the food chain. List three ways in which the energy is used up.
d   Explain how this loss of energy limits the length of the food chain.

29 An ideal environment, like a natural woodland, is called a stable environment. What must happen to the amount of carbon dioxide released and the amount absorbed for the environment to be stable?

30 Describe the process by which fossil fuels are formed.

31 Explain how the process of combustion upsets stable environments.

32 A biologist carried out an experiment to measure the rate of decay in bread. Below are the results.

Conditions	Time for mould to appear on bread (days)
Dry/cold	20
Dry/warm	10
Wet/cold	8
Wet/warm	3

a   Which conditions were best for decay?
b   Explain the result for the dry and warm condition.
c   How could the results be made more reliable?

Working to Grade A*

33 Look again at the plants in question 21. Predict the outcome if plant B was planted in the environment of plant A, and explain your reasoning.

34 Biologists are able to grow human gut bacteria and thermophile bacteria in the laboratory.
a   On which organisms would they choose to carry out genetic engineering experiments at 50 °C?
b   Explain your choice.

35 Look again at the graph of river pollution in question 23. In zone A on the river there are many mayfly larvae but few rat-tailed maggots. Suggest a reason for this.

36 Biologists believe that red and grey squirrels are in direct competition with each other, resulting in a change in the distribution and population size of the red squirrel. Suggest three pieces of evidence biologists would need to collect to support this theory.

37 In a recent survey, a team of biologists measured the levels of pollution in an inner city in England. They recorded the number and types of lichens, and took measurements of several air pollutants. They concluded that the pollution had been present for many years.
a   What pieces of evidence allowed the biologists to reach this conclusion?
b   Explain why you have selected this evidence.

38 Look again at the table measuring the rate of decay in bread in question 32.
a   Based on these results what advice could you give about the best conditions to store bread?
b   How could you modify this experiment to establish the ideal temperature for bread to decay?
c   In this experiment, identify two variables you would have to keep the same.

39 Some biologists believe that planting forests of trees will offset our carbon emissions. What does this mean?

40 Explain how carbon found in molecules in a dead animal might become available for a plant and end up built into the body of a plant.

1 Below is a drawing of a ring-tailed lemur. They live in the trees on the island of Madagascar.

a Use the information in the drawing to suggest **one** way in which it is adapted to life in trees.

....

....

(1 mark)

b There are several different species of lemur living in the forests of Madagascar. Below is a table of data collected by biologists studying the three lemur species.

	Ring-tailed lemur	Mouse lemur	Common brown lemur
Time of main activity	daytime	nocturnal	daytime
Type of vision	colour	black and white	colour
Diet	mainly leaves and herbs	mainly fruit and insects	mainly bark

Use the information in the table to suggest **two** reasons why the ring-tailed lemur and the mouse lemur do not compete with each other even though they live in the same environment.

....

....

....

(2 marks)

c All three species of lemur are classified into the same major group. Explain how biologists are able to group them together in this way.

....

....

....

(2 marks)

d Biologists believe that these three species are closely related. How can different species be related?

....

....

(1 mark)

(Total marks: 6)

2 Below is a diagram of the carbon cycle.

carbon dioxide in the atmosphere

When plants, algae and animals die, their bodies are decayed by microorganisms, releasing carbon dioxide as they respire.

C

B

A

Carbon compounds such as carbohydrates, fats and proteins are made in the bodies of plants or algae.

The carbon compounds eaten by animals become part of the fats and proteins of the animals.

eaten

coal, oil and gas

fossilisation, decay and pressure

a Name processes A, B, and C by writing them in the correct boxes in the diagram. *(3 marks)*

b In the carbon cycle decay is an important process that returns carbon dioxide to the air.

Which groups of organisms are involved in the decay process?

....

....

(2 marks)

c There are a number of factors that affect the rate of decay. State **two** factors that affect the rate and explain how they affect the rate.

....

....

....

....

....

....

(4 marks)
(Total marks: 9)

3 Ladybirds are common in Britain. There are 46 species in the UK. In 2004 the Harlequin ladybird arrived in Britain from northwest Europe.

- Harlequin ladybirds, like most ladybirds, tend to feed on aphids.
- The Harlequin ladybirds also feed on small insects, including other ladybirds, the eggs and larvae of butterflies, pollen, and nectar.
- They have longer periods of reproduction than most other species.
- They can fly rapidly over long distances, and therefore arrive in new territories.
- Sightings of this invading species are being logged by scientists and they produce distribution maps.

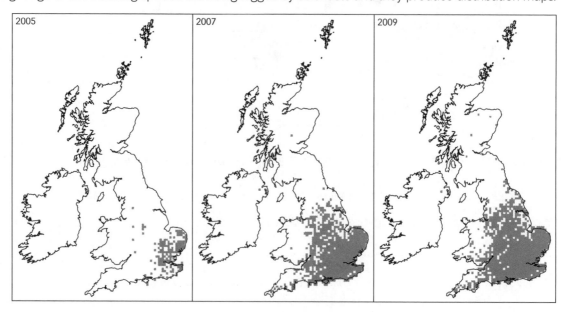

a What pattern can you see in the distribution of the Harlequin ladybird?

....

....

(1 mark)

b Use the information to suggest **two** explanations for the change in distribution of the Harlequin ladybird.

1 ....

....

2 ....

....

(2 marks)

c The arrival of the Harlequin ladybird has put many of the native species of ladybird at risk. Use the information to suggest an explanation for this.

....

....

....

....

(3 marks)

d The scientists used hundreds of members of the public throughout the UK to collect data of sightings, backed up by photographic evidence. From this data they produced their maps.

i How has this approach led to reliable results?

....

(1 mark)

ii Why did the scientists require photographic evidence?

....

(1 mark)

(Total marks: 8)

Revision objectives

- explain that differences in characteristics (variation) may be due to differences in genes, the environment, or both
- know that most body cells contain chromosomes, which carry information in the form of genes
- know that genes control the characteristics of the body
- identify the two forms of reproduction – sexual and asexual
- know that new plants can be produced from cuttings

Student book references

1.23 Variation

1.24 Reproduction

Specification key

✔ B1.7.1, ✔ B1.7.2 a – b

Variation

Variation is the differences between individuals. These differences are not only between individuals of different species but are also between individuals of the same species. For example, we all look slightly different.

Variation can be caused by:

- **Genes** – these are inherited from our parents. Examples of **characteristics** that are controlled by genes are eye colour, earlobe shape, and flower colour.
- Environment – this is where the conditions in our surroundings influence a feature. Examples of environmental characteristics are scars, and the number of flowers produced on a rose bush being dependent on the amount of sun.
- Combination – both genes and the environment interact to determine a feature. Examples of characteristics controlled by a combination are height and body mass.

Genes and variation

Genes are major contributors to variation in organisms.

What are genes?

Genes are found in the nucleus of the cell.

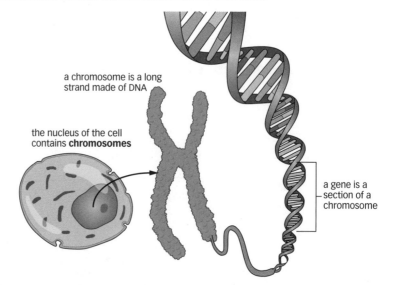

a chromosome is a long strand made of DNA

the nucleus of the cell contains **chromosomes**

a gene is a section of a chromosome

Genes are molecular codes that control the manufacture of proteins. These proteins influence the development of characteristics. For example, genes code for the pigments that colour the eyes. Different genes code for different characteristics.

Passing on genes

Genes can be passed on from generation to generation. They pass in the egg and sperm cells, which are called **gametes**. The two gametes join to form the baby.

Key words

variation, gene, chromosome, characteristic, sexual reproduction, asexual reproduction, gamete, fertilisation, cutting, clone

Reproduction

Reproduction is the production of new individuals of the same species. There are two types of reproduction.

Sexual reproduction

Sexual reproduction involves the production of sex cells or gametes by the adults. The male produces sperm cells and the female produces egg cells. During **fertilisation** the two gametes are brought together and fuse to form the offspring.

We share characteristics with our parents. This is because we have inherited half of our genes from our father in the sperm cell and half of our genes from our mother in the egg cell. This means that we are genetically different from each parent, and will be a mix of characteristics of our father and mother. Sexual reproduction leads to great variation.

Asexual reproduction

Asexual reproduction does not involve the production of gametes. This means:

- only one parent is needed
- there is no mixing of genetic information
- all offspring are genetically identical. They are called **clones**.

The advantage is that the process is quick and individuals do not need to find a mate. The disadvantage is the lack of variation. Asexual reproduction occurs in bacteria, many single-celled organisms, and plants.

Plant cuttings

Gardeners use an asexual technique to produce large numbers of plants. They take **cuttings** from a parent plant, which will grow into new plants. The advantages are that:

- the process is cheap
- the new plants are all genetically identical and so share the characteristics the gardeners want.

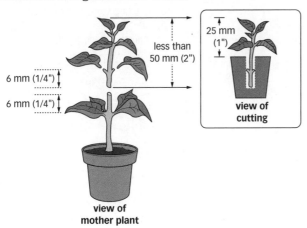

less than 50 mm (2")

25 mm (1")

6 mm (1/4")

6 mm (1/4")

view of cutting

view of mother plant

Questions

1 What do scientists call the differences in characteristics between individuals?

2 What causes these differences in characteristics between individuals?

3 **H** What is the difference between sexual and asexual reproduction?

Modern cloning techniques

A **clone** is an organism that is genetically identical to its parent. These can be produced by asexual reproduction. Modern biologists can also produce clones in the laboratory. There are three common techniques.

Tissue culture

- Small groups of plant cells are taken from the parent plant, often from the shoot tip.
- They are placed on agar jelly, containing plant hormones.
- New plants start to grow.

◀ Used to produce expensive orchids.

Embryo transplants

- Parents are selected with the desired characteristics.
- Their eggs are collected and fertilised with sperm in a dish.
- The embryos are allowed to develop into a ball of unspecialised cells.
- The ball of cells is then split up into pairs of cells.
- Each pair continues to develop, and can be transplanted into host mothers called surrogates.
- They give birth to identical offspring with the desired characteristics.

Adult cell cloning

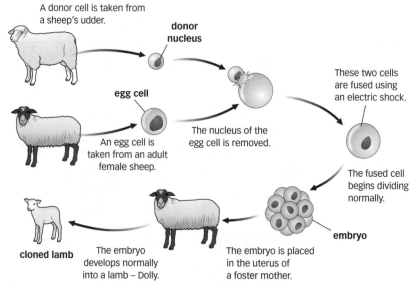

A donor cell is taken from a sheep's udder.

donor nucleus

egg cell

An egg cell is taken from an adult female sheep.

The nucleus of the egg cell is removed.

These two cells are fused using an electric shock.

The fused cell begins dividing normally.

embryo

The embryo is placed in the uterus of a foster mother.

cloned lamb

The embryo develops normally into a lamb – Dolly.

▲ Destroying embryos, lack of variation, and unknown long-term effects are ethical concerns linked to these types of animal cloning.

Genetic engineering

This is a technique where a desired gene is removed from the chromosomes of one organism (the donor) and transferred into a cell of a second organism (the host).

The host acquires the new desired characteristics, such as making new products like **insulin**. Insulin made this way is human insulin, and is better than insulin removed from pigs and cows because it is a closer match and there is no risk of disease transmission.

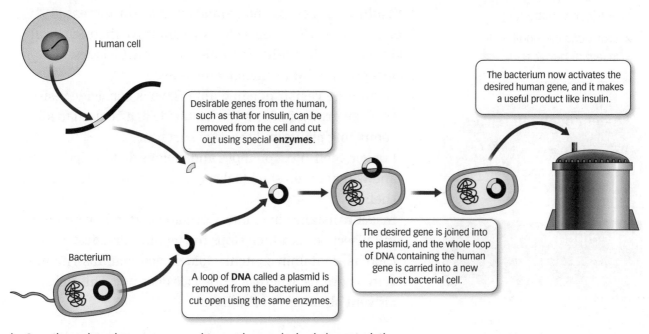

Human cell

Desirable genes from the human, such as that for insulin, can be removed from the cell and cut out using special **enzymes**.

The bacterium now activates the desired human gene, and it makes a useful product like insulin.

Bacterium

A loop of **DNA** called a plasmid is removed from the bacterium and cut open using the same enzymes.

The desired gene is joined into the plasmid, and the whole loop of DNA containing the human gene is carried into a new host bacterial cell.

▲ Genetic engineering process used to produce a desired characteristic.

Interfering with genes like this could create bacteria that could become dangerous to humans, so-called 'superbugs'. There are also ethical concerns with genetic engineering.

Questions

1 Name two methods by which scientists can produce clones.

2 Why do biologists carry out genetic engineering?

3 **H** What is genetic engineering? Suggest an ethical concern it raises.

Revision objectives

- ✔ understand that genes can be transferred to crop plants
- ✔ crops that have had their genes modified are called GM crops
- ✔ GM crops normally show increased yields or improved nutritional content
- ✔ crops can be modified to be insect or herbicide resistant

Student book references

1.27 GM crops

1.28 Concerns about GM crops

Specification key

✔ B1.7.2

Making a genetically modified organism

Biotechnologists do not only put genes into bacteria. They can also transfer genes into other organisms, including plants and animals, at an early stage in their development. These are then called **genetically modified** (GM) organisms. By adding new genes their genetic code is altered so that they develop with desired characteristics.

This technique is often used with agricultural organisms. It results in GM crops and animals that are of increased economic value. The characteristics improve their survival and therefore the **yield**. Examples of characteristics transferred by GM technology include:

- **Herbicide resistance** in plants. Soya is herbicide resistant, so when grown in fields the herbicide can be used to kill competing plants and the soya survives.
- Longer shelf life. Tomatoes and melons do not ripen as fast, and will not then start to decay and go soft on supermarket shelves.
- Insect resistance in plants. Corn and cotton have genes that kill insect pests, which stops the plants being destroyed.
- Increased vitamin content. Golden rice contains vitamin A in its grains, whereas white rice does not. This helps prevent blindness in children.

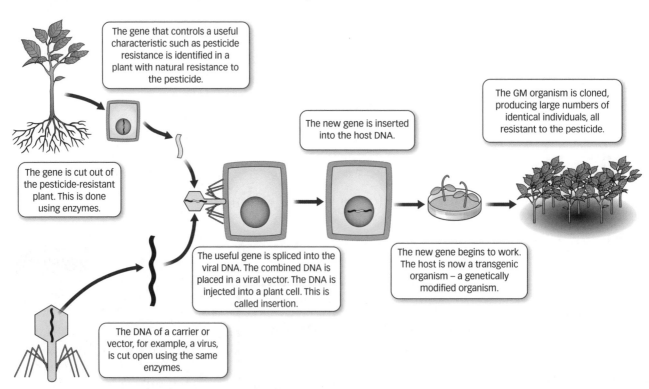

The gene that controls a useful characteristic such as pesticide resistance is identified in a plant with natural resistance to the pesticide.

The gene is cut out of the pesticide-resistant plant. This is done using enzymes.

The DNA of a carrier or vector, for example, a virus, is cut open using the same enzymes.

The useful gene is spliced into the viral DNA. The combined DNA is placed in a viral vector. The DNA is injected into a plant cell. This is called insertion.

The new gene is inserted into the host DNA.

The new gene begins to work. The host is now a transgenic organism – a genetically modified organism.

The GM organism is cloned, producing large numbers of identical individuals, all resistant to the pesticide.

▲ Creating a GM organism.

Evaluating GM crops

There are many arguments for and against the use of GM crops. Here are a few.

Arguments for GM crops	Arguments against GM crops
GM crops require fewer **pesticides** in order to grow, therefore there is less pollution in the environment.	GM crops might escape from the farms and become more successful competitors than wild flowers in the environment (superweeds).
GM crops have a higher yield and can feed larger populations. This is important in developing countries.	It disrupts the food chain if insect-resistant plants are grown, killing the insects.
GM foods have been eaten in some countries for 10 years with no ill effects noted.	There is uncertainty about the effects of eating GM crops on human health.
Some GM crops can have a higher nutritional value, for example, golden rice has a higher vitamin A content.	GM crops are expensive to develop and test. Seeds may be expensive.
The process produces crops with desired characteristics far quicker than using selective breeding.	GM crops require a lot of testing, which can take years.

Some countries are so concerned about these issues that they do not grow GM crops. There are no commercial GM crops in the UK, for example. Other countries, such as the USA and countries with greater needs for larger crops, such as India, are less concerned.

Key words

genetically modified, herbicide, resistance, yield, pesticide

Exam tip

When asked to make judgements about the pros and cons of techniques like cloning and genetic modification, use scientific arguments to back up your viewpoint.

Questions

1 What are GM crops?

2 What advantages are there to GM crops?

3 **H** Discuss an ethical concern relating to GM crops.

Revision objectives

- ✓ know that classification groups organisms based on similarities and differences
- ✓ know the causes and effects of evolution
- ✓ know that evolution can result in the formation of new species
- ✓ know that Charles Darwin produced the theory of evolution, but that other scientists have produced other explanations

Student book references

1.29 Classification

1.30 Surviving change

1.31 Evolution in action

1.32 Evolutionary theory

Specification key

✓ B1.8.1

Classification

Biologists group living organisms based on their **similarities** and differences. This is called **classification**. These studies show two types of link.

Ecological links

Here organisms may share features because they live in the same environment. For example, butterflies and birds both have wings because they fly, but the wings are very different in structure.

Evolutionary links

Here organisms with a common ancestor may share characteristics. For example, humans, chimpanzees, and lizards have limbs with digits. These limbs are similar structures, as the animals have a distant common ancestor. The more similarities in two groups of organisms, the more closely they are related. Chimpanzees and humans are more closely related than lizards and humans as their limbs are more similar.

All living things are placed first into large groups called **kingdoms**. There are three kingdoms: plant, animal, and microorganism.

Evolution

Biologists needed to be able to explain how the great variety of different **species** had developed. Did they change over time? Charles **Darwin** suggested a theory that could explain how all of these species might have developed or evolved from simple life forms that first appeared over three billion years ago. His theory was called **evolution** by **natural selection**.
Evolution is the gradual change of an organism over time. His idea suggests that gradually one type of organism, called an ancestor, might change over many generations into one or more different species. This would generate all of the different species in the world over millions of years.

The theory was only gradually accepted because:
- the theory disagreed with most religious ideas about how God created all life forms
- there was not much evidence at the time to convince other scientists
- scientists did not know about genes and how they are inherited, and cause variation, until 50 years after the theory was published, and so could not explain a mechanism for how evolution could work.

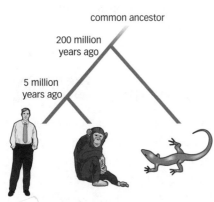

This family tree shows the relationship between three species.

Individuals in a large population of a species show variation. This is because of differences in their genes. More variation is caused by chance **mutations** in the genes.

Within any population there is always a struggle to survive because of a number of factors such as predators, shortage of food, or disease.

Some variations are more suited to the environment. They are the 'fittest', and are more likely to survive and breed.

The surviving individuals are the only ones that reproduce, passing on their genes to the next generation.

Generally evolution is quite slow but mutations cause rapid changes to an individual in the population. If this is combined with a change in the environment favouring the mutation then the evolution of change in the species as a whole is much more rapid.

Forming a new species

Where evolution continues to occur in a population of a species, there may be many changes over time. This might result in the formation of a completely new species. A good example of this is seen in the elephant population. The African and Indian elephants are separate species that have both evolved from a common ancestor over time.

Alternative theories

Charles Darwin was not the only biologist to attempt to explain the origin of all the species on Earth. Other theories have been suggested, including that of Jean Baptiste **Lamarck**. These theories often suggest that the changes occur in an individual of a species during its life, making it better suited to its environment, and that these changes would then be passed on. However, we now know that genes control our characteristics and that they do not change during an organism's lifetime.

Key words

classification, kingdom, similarities, evolution, natural selection, mutation, species, Darwin, Lamarck

Exam tip

Learn the four key steps in the process of natural selection, and be able to apply them to any organism given in a question.

Questions

1 Who was Charles Darwin?

2 What is natural selection?

3 **H** What is the key difference between Darwin's explanation of evolution and that of Lamarck?

Questions
Genetics and evolution

Working to Grade E

1. What is variation?

2. Variation is caused by several factors. Which factor is most likely to have caused:
   a. the colour of a flower?
   b. the height of a human?
   c. the colour of the fur on a dog?
   d. how much a horse weighs?

3. Which chemical is a chromosome made of?

4. Where are chromosomes found in a cell?

5. What types of cell are involved in sexual reproduction?

6. What is fertilisation?

7. Name two types of organism that carry out asexual reproduction.

8. What is a clone?

9. Name one product we get from genetic engineering.

10. What is used to cut DNA?

11. Give one way in which corn has been genetically modified.

12. Do all countries grow GM crops?

13. Give two arguments people use against GM crops.

14. What is a mutation?

15. Who proposed the theory of evolution by natural selection?

16. What are the three main kingdoms?

17. Place the following organisms into one of the three kingdoms:
    a. oak tree
    b. human
    c. fish
    d. daffodil
    e. *E. coli*
    f. crab
    g. *salmonella*

Working to Grade C

18. Look at the drawing below.

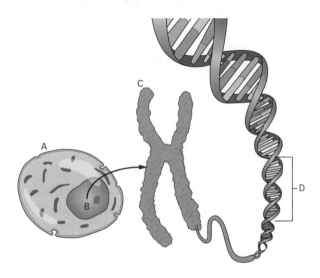

   a. Which letter labels the gene?
   b. What do genes control?

19. Describe how genes are passed on from one generation to the next.

20. Explain why we share characteristics with our parents.

21. Explain why we are not identical to our parents.

22. What is the advantage to the gardener of using cuttings of plants for reproduction?

23. During tissue culture a number of steps occur. Put the following steps into the correct order:
    a. The jelly contains special chemicals that cause roots to grow.
    b. Small groups of cells are taken from a plant.
    c. A second jelly contains chemicals that cause stems and leaves to grow.
    d. Cells are placed in a liquid or jelly.
    e. A new plant has formed, identical to the original.

24. What is a surrogate?

25. Explain why scientists carry out embryo transplants in animals.

26. Name one type of mammal that has been cloned.

27. How do biologists make an egg cell and a donor nucleus fuse?

28 Look at the diagram below, which outlines the process of genetic engineering.

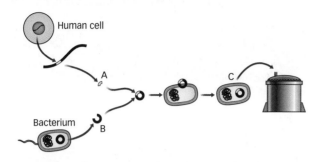

a What letter on the diagram shows the following?
   i plasmid
   ii desirable gene
   iii bacterium

b Why is insulin made by bacteria of more use to humans than insulin obtained from pigs?

29 Soya plants have been genetically modified to be resistant to weedkiller. How will this improve the yield of soya?

30 Why is genetic engineering preferred over selective breeding?

31 There are many arguments for the use of GM crops.
a Which argument would also help protect the environment?
b Which argument would suggest that our health concerns are not valid?
c Which argument shows that GM crops can help poorer countries who struggle to feed their populations?

32 How do scientists classify organisms?

33 In evolutionary terms, why are the limbs of humans and chimpanzees so similar?

34 Why will a biologist place humans and dogs as closer relatives than humans and fish?

35 Why do sharks and dolphins have similar streamlined bodies when they are not closely related?

36 Give two reasons why Darwin's theory was not initially accepted.

37 Why do biologists think that the explanation for evolution made by Lamarck is no longer acceptable?

38 How long ago do scientists think that life arose on Earth?

Working to Grade A*

39 Explain how a gene would determine the colour of your eyes.

40 Explain why humans need thousands of genes.

41 What are the major differences between sexual and asexual reproduction?

42 Outline the advantages and disadvantages of asexual reproduction.

43 Explain why taking cuttings of plants is a method of asexual reproduction.

44 Suggest one beneficial outcome that could come from cloning.

45 How would the process shown in question 28 be altered to insert a gene into a sheep?

46 A common moth in the UK is the peppered moth. It exists in two main forms, the light form and the dark form.

light moths

dark moths

light tree   dark tree

The light moth was once the only type of peppered moth. It was widespread over the whole of the UK, but now survives well in the cleaner areas of the UK, like Cornwall, whilst the darker moth developed, and survives better, in areas with heavier air pollution, like the industrial Midlands.

a Use Darwin's ideas of natural selection to explain how the darker variety became common in the industrial areas of the UK.
b Suggest why the dark moth would not survive well in the cleaner areas of the UK.
c What caused the dark moth to appear?
d How might Lamarck have explained the development of the darker moth?
e Why did the evolution of the moth happen very quickly?

1 Look at the diagram below, which shows a technique that scientists use to produce many plants from a valuable specimen.

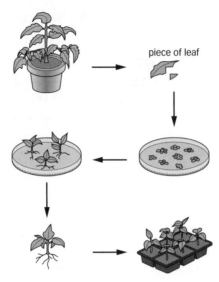

piece of leaf

a All the plants produced are identical to the parent. What is the name given to these types of organism?

....

(1 mark)

b Describe how the sections of leaf are encouraged to produce roots and shoots.

....

....

....

(2 marks)

c Explain why gardeners prefer to use this technique to produce plants, instead of allowing the plants to reproduce sexually.

....

....

....

(2 marks)

(Total marks: 5)

2 When biologists began to study the animals of South America, they discovered the anteater. Anteaters are related to the sloths. They have developed a tubelike snout with a long tongue to eat termites and ants from mounds.

Use your knowledge of the theory of evolution to explain as fully as you can how the anteater evolved the long snout.

....

....

....

....

....

....

....

....

....

....

(4 marks)
(Total marks: 4)

3 Read the following passage about the production of GM crops.

> **GM crops – growing tomorrow's food**
>
> The development of GM crops was seen by many as the solution to world hunger. Biologists are able to produce crops that are pest-resistant, pesticide-resistant, and slow to decay. In addition, crops can even be created that have increased nutritional value, such as golden rice.
>
> There are some in our society who have voiced concerns about such crops. The fear is that genes could escape from the GM crops, creating 'superweeds'. They also wonder if the GM food would cause health problems, such as allergies, to consumers.
>
> The production of such crops is expensive and some government economists think poorer countries could not afford them anyway.

Use the information and your own knowledge and understanding of biology to evaluate whether the production of GM crops is such a great benefit to the world population. Remember to give a conclusion to your evaluation.

....

....

....

....

....

....

....

....

....

(5 marks)
(Total marks: 5)

Designing investigations and using data

Within this module there are some very good examples of the design of investigations and interpretation of data. You may be asked in a question to demonstrate these skills yourself.

Look at the example below; this will show you how scientists design experiments and interpret data. There will be opportunities for you both to practise some of the skills, and to be guided through some of the more difficult elements that might appear in a question in the exam.

Pollution and indicator species

Skill – designing investigations

> Biologists were concerned about the levels of pollution being released into a river by a factory, and the impact the pollutants might have on the organisms that live in the river.
>
>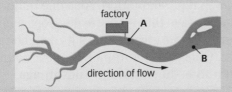
>
> Biologists set out to investigate the levels of pollution in the river. At point A on the map (where the factory was) they recorded two variables:
> - the oxygen levels in the water, using a digital oxygen probe
> - the number of rat-tailed maggots in a square metre.
>
> 1 How did the biologists ensure that the readings for the oxygen levels were:
> a accurate?
> b reliable?

These questions seem simple, but always cause trouble. Students often talk about the need to keep the experiment 'fair' here. That is the *reason* for doing these things, but not *how* these points are achieved.

You need to remember a simple rule:
For **ACCURACY** use the right **APPARATUS**.
For **RELIABILITY** do **REPEATS**.

> The biologists repeated the experiment at point B (100 metres downstream of the factory). Not only was the data for the maggots and oxygen recorded but also several other possible pollutants. The data is in the table in the next column.

Pollutant and indicator species	Point A At the factory	Point B 100 metres from factory
Oxygen	3.6 mgO$_2$/l	9.8 mgO$_2$/l
Nitrates	20.4 mgNO$_3$/l	7.8 mgNO$_3$/l
Calcium	40 ppm	39 ppm
Magnesium	24 ppm	26 ppm
Zinc	0.02 mg/l	0.02 mg/l
Lead	0.02 ppm	0.01 ppm
Total invertebrate species	14	103
Number of rat-tailed maggots	36	2

> 2 What does the distribution of the rat-tailed maggots tell us about the levels of pollution in the river?

This question is asking you to look at the data in the table.
- You must identify a specific piece of data, and then interpret that data.
- Do not get over-concerned with the other pieces of data when answering this question.
- Look at the data: it is telling us that there are more maggots in the water by the factory, which is probably polluted.
- The question then needs a link to your knowledge of the distribution of maggots.
- It is asking you to discuss the relationship between two variables: the number of maggots and the amount of pollution.

> 3 The factory is responsible for the release of the pollutants into the water.
> a How can biologists tell that the pollutants caused the growth of respiring bacteria?
> b What was the major pollutant released by the factory?

In both of these questions you are being asked to select appropriate information from the table. Remember:
- Look for pieces of data that show some significant difference or change.
- In this table only the oxygen and nitrate levels show change.
- Think about whether those pieces of data are biologically relevant to either of the questions. In this case, the oxygen levels link to the question about respiring bacteria, and the nitrates relate to the pollutants.
- Not all of the data is needed, so much of it might be ignored.

AQA Upgrade

Answering extended writing questions

Giraffes have evolved to have long necks.

1 Charles Darwin proposed a theory to explain how animals evolved.
What is the name of this theory? *(1 mark)*

2 How would Charles Darwin have explained the way the giraffe had evolved a long neck? *(4 marks)*

G–E

1 Evolution.
2 A giraffe developed a long neck to adapt to its environment. This adaption allows the animal to survive betterer in its environment. This is cause it can reach on top of the tree to get more food. Because it can get the leaves at the top of the tree it can survive better than the other giraffes which cannot get the leaves at the top of the tree. It now will survive and the short one wont. So all the giraffes now grow long necks.

Examiner: This student has either not understood the question or not learnt the correct name.

This answer is worth one mark at best. It only really gets the idea of the longer necks giving an advantage. There are a number of problems. The answer is rambling, and there is considerable repetition, so it is not logical. There are some spelling errors, and little use of technical terms. Adaption is an American term. The student appears to take the question into the wrong topic, that of adaptation. Also one major issue is that the student says that a giraffe develops a long neck, which suggests that the giraffe alters its own body to improve its survival, whereas evolution is about the random development of mutations that might give advantage.

D–C

1 Survival of the fittest.
2 Some giraffes had long necks, and they were able to eat the leaves at the tops of the trees. This gave them an advantage over the short-necked giraffes. This meant that they could have lots more food. These animals were the fittest. They grew more than the shorter ones who couldn't get food. Eventually all the giraffes had longer necks, the shorter ones died out.

Examiner: This is a shame. The candidate has clearly understood some of the ideas of evolution, but has muddled the name of the theory with the way it works.

This answer is worth two marks. Here the candidate has some understanding of evolution. However, they have not used many technical terms; for example, there is no mention of genes or mutations. Also, they have not always explained each idea clearly. For example, they have not really said what survival of the fittest is, they have just used the term. This will fail to gain them credit for these points. The answer is not a complete account of the process, as they have not mentioned reproduction and passing on characteristics at all.

B–A*

1 Natural selection.
2 In Africa there were large numbers of giraffes. They were slightly different: some had short necks, but some had grown a long neck. The long neck was caused by a mutation in one of their genes. The giraffes all competed with each other for limited food resources. The giraffes with the longer necks had an advantage in that they could reach leaves at the tops of trees, and so they survived. They could then reproduce more and pass on their genes. Gradually only the giraffes with long necks survived.

Examiner: Well answered. Candidate has learnt the correct name.

A complete and thorough answer. Full marks awarded. It makes seven clear points, far more than needed by the mark scheme. This is good practice, because if one of the statements had been poorly expressed and not worthy of the mark, there are other points that will pick up the marks. This raises a good point – in longer-answer questions there are usually more marks possible on the mark scheme than you need. This gives you room to say different things. The answer given here is also logical and well expressed. No spelling errors.

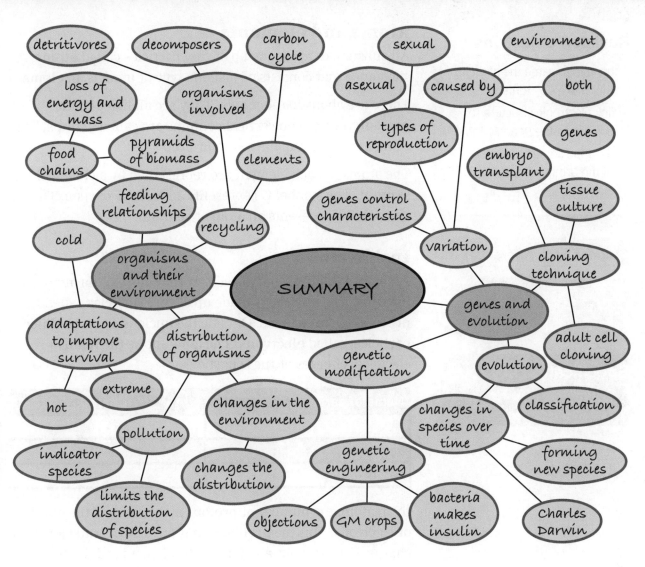

Revision checklist

- Living things show adaptations that help them to survive in their environment.
- Organisms show adaptations to hot, dry, and cold environments. Some are even adapted to survive in extreme environments.
- If the environment changes it can affect the distribution of organisms.
- Human pollution affects the environment and the organisms that live there. Indicator species are organisms that show how polluted an area is.
- Food chains show the flow of biomass and energy from one organism to the next. The mass reduces as you move along a food chain or up a pyramid of biomass.
- Energy is lost at each step of the food chain, as heat and in waste materials.
- Elements are constantly cycled between the living and non-living world.
- The carbon cycle shows how carbon moves into the living world by photosynthesis, and is released back into the non-living world by respiration and burning.
- Variation is the difference in characteristics shown between organisms of the same species. It is caused by genes, the environment, or a combination of both.

- Reproduction can be sexual, using sex cells to create variation, or asexual, with no sex cells, producing identical clones.
- Clones can be produced by tissue culture, embryo transplant, and adult cell cloning.
- Genetic engineering is the transfer of a useful gene from one organism to another. This allows us to transfer a useful characteristic. Using this method we can produce drugs like insulin.
- GM crops are crops that have been given genes that provide an advantage to them, for example, a higher yield. However, some scientists have concerns about the technique.
- Classification is the process where organisms are grouped together based on their similarities and differences.
- Evolution is the gradual change of organisms over time. Charles Darwin suggested a theory called natural selection to explain how this happened, but it took years to be accepted.

Revision objectives

- ✓ be able to name the particles that make up atoms
- ✓ link electronic structure to position in the Periodic Table
- ✓ describe some properties of the Group 1 and Group 0 elements

Student book references

1.1 Atoms and elements

1.2 Inside atoms

Specification key

✔ C1.1.1, ✔ C1.1.2

Atoms and elements

All substances are made up of tiny particles called **atoms**. A substance that consists of just one type of atom is an **element**.

There are about 100 elements. They are all listed in the **periodic table**. The vertical columns are called **groups**. The elements in a group have similar properties.

The atoms of each element are represented by a chemical **symbol**. The symbol O represents an atom of oxygen. The symbol Na represents an atom of sodium.

Inside atoms

Atoms are mainly empty space. At the centre of an atom is its **nucleus**. The nucleus is made up of tiny particles called **protons** and **neutrons**. Outside the nucleus are even tinier particles, called **electrons**. The table shows the relative electrical charges of these particles.

Name of particle	Charge
Proton	+1
Neutron	0
Electron	−1

In an atom, the number of protons is the same as the number of electrons. This means that atoms have no overall electrical charge. For example, an atom of the element sodium is made up of:

- 11 protons
- 12 neutrons
- 11 electrons.

The elements on the left of the stepped line are metals.

The elements on the right of the stepped line are non-metals.

The elements in Group 1 are silver-coloured metals. They react with water.

The elements in Group 0 are gases at room temperature. They do not usually react with other substances.

▲ The periodic table.

Atoms of the same element have the same number of protons. Atoms of different elements have different numbers of protons. For example:

- All sodium atoms have 11 protons.
- All oxygen atoms have 8 protons.

The number of protons in an atom of an element is the **atomic number** of an atom. Since sodium has 11 protons, its atomic number is 11.

The sum of the number of protons and neutrons in an atom is its **mass number**. In a sodium atom there are 11 protons and 12 neutrons. This means that the mass number of this sodium atom is 11 + 12 = 23.

Arranging electrons

Electrons are arranged in **energy levels**. Electrons fill the lowest energy levels first. Energy levels are also called **shells**.

Sodium has 11 electrons. Two electrons fill up the lowest energy level. Eight are in the next. The highest energy level contains one electron.

In all atoms, the lowest energy level holds a maximum of two electrons. The next energy level holds up to eight electrons.

Electron arrangements and the periodic table

Elements in the same group of the periodic table have the same number of electrons in their highest energy level. For example, atoms of Group 1 elements have one electron in their highest energy level. Atoms of elements in Group 0 have eight electrons in their highest energy level. Similar electron arrangements give elements similar properties. For example:

- Group 1 elements react vigorously with water to make hydroxides and hydrogen gas:

    potassium + water → potassium hydroxide + hydrogen

    Group 1 elements also react vigorously with oxygen to make oxides:

    potassium + oxygen → potassium oxide

- Group 0 elements are also called the **noble gases**. They are unreactive. They have stable electron arrangements, with eight electrons in the highest energy level, except for helium, which has two.

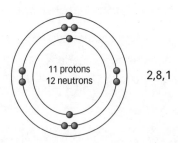

11 protons
12 neutrons

2,8,1

▲ The electronic structure of sodium.

Questions

1 List the charges on a proton, a neutron, and an electron.

2 An atom of argon has 18 electrons. Draw its electron arrangement.

3 An atom of fluorine has nine protons, nine electrons, and ten neutrons. Calculate its atomic number and its mass number.

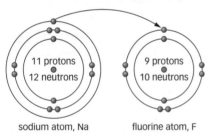

sodium atom, Na   fluorine atom, F

▲ The formation of sodium fluoride.

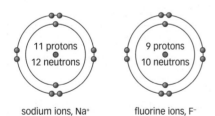

sodium ions, Na⁺   fluorine ions, F⁻

▲ The electronic structure of sodium and fluoride ions.

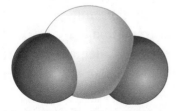

▲ A sulfur dioxide molecule.

Compounds

A **compound** is a substance made up of two or more elements. Compounds can be made from their elements, when atoms of the elements join together in chemical reactions.

Holding compounds together

Joining atoms together to form compounds involves giving and taking or sharing electrons.

Ionic bonds

Sodium fluoride is made up of a metal (sodium) joined to a non-metal (fluorine). When sodium fluoride forms from its elements, each sodium atom transfers one of its electrons to a fluorine atom.

Each atom now has eight electrons in its highest energy level. This electron arrangement is very stable.

- The sodium atom now has 10 electrons and 11 protons. It has a charge of +1.
- The fluorine atom now has 10 electrons and 9 protons. It has a charge of –1.

Charged atoms are called **ions**. Sodium fluoride contains two types of ion: positive sodium ions (Na^+) and negative fluoride ions (F^-).

Sodium fluoride is an **ionic compound**, like most compounds made up of a metal and a non-metal. In ionic compounds, the oppositely charged ions are strongly attracted to each other. The forces of attraction between the ions are called **ionic bonds**.

Covalent bonds

Compounds formed from non-metals consist of **molecules**. A molecule is a group of atoms held together by shared pairs of electrons. These shared pairs of electrons are **covalent bonds**.

Sulfur dioxide is made up of atoms of two non-metals. Its atoms are joined together in groups of three. Each group consists of one sulfur atom and two oxygen atoms. The atoms are joined together by strong covalent bonds.

Word equations

Word equations summarise chemical reactions. For example, when magnesium burns in oxygen the product is magnesium oxide:

$$\text{magnesium} + \text{oxygen} \rightarrow \text{magnesium oxide}$$

H Symbol equations

Every element and compound has its own formula.

- The formula of nitrogen gas is N_2. This means that nitrogen gas exists as molecules, each made up of two nitrogen atoms.
- The formula of sodium fluoride is NaF. This means that the compound is made up of sodium and fluorine. For every ion of sodium there is one fluoride ion.

When you write a symbol equation for a reaction, start by writing a word equation. Then write down the formula of every element or compound.

$$\text{magnesium} + \text{oxygen} \rightarrow \text{magnesium oxide}$$
$$Mg + O_2 \rightarrow MgO$$

Now balance the equation. There are two atoms of oxygen on the left of the arrow, and one on the right. Write a large '2' to the left of the formula for magnesium oxide:

$$Mg + O_2 \rightarrow 2MgO$$

The number of oxygen atoms is now the same on each side.

Balance the amounts of magnesium by writing a large '2' to the left of the symbol for magnesium. There are now two atoms of magnesium on each side. The equation is balanced.

$$2Mg + O_2 \rightarrow 2MgO$$

Conservation of mass

During a chemical reaction, atoms are not lost or made – so the mass of reactants is equal to the mass of the products. For example, reacting 48 g of magnesium with 32 g of oxygen produces (48 + 32) = 80 g of magnesium oxide.

Exam tip

Practise writing word equations. Practise balancing symbol equations.

Questions

1 Name the type of bonding in nitrogen dioxide and in iron oxide.

2 Write a word equation for the reaction of sodium with chlorine to make sodium chloride.

3 H Write a balanced symbol equation for the reaction of lithium with fluorine to form lithium fluoride. Formulae: Li, F_2, LiF.

Working to Grade E

1 Use the periodic table to give:
  a the symbol for an atom of oxygen
  b the name of the element whose atoms have the symbol Fe
  c the names and symbols of five elements whose names begin with the letter C
  d the names of four noble gases
  e the symbols of four elements in Group 1.

2 Name the two types of particle that make up the nucleus of an atom.

3 Complete the sentences below.
There are about _____ different elements. The _____ in the periodic table contain elements with similar properties.

4 Complete the table to show the electronic structures of some Group 1 elements.

Name of element	Number of electrons	Electronic structure
Lithium	3	
Sodium		2.8.1
Potassium	19	

5 Describe one chemical property that is common to the Group 1 elements.

6 Finish the diagrams below to show the electronic structures of atoms of carbon, silicon, and calcium.

  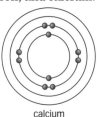

carbon (6 electrons)   silicon (14 electrons)   calcium (20 electrons)

Working to Grade C

7 Neon, argon, and krypton are noble gases.
  a Give the number of electrons in the outer energy level of an atom of each of these elements.
  b Name the noble gas that has two electrons in the outer energy level of its atoms.
  c Explain why the noble gases are unreactive.

8 An atom of an element has five protons and six neutrons.
  a What is the atomic number of the atom?
  b What is the mass number of the atom?

9 An atom of an element has an atomic number of 21 and a mass number of 45. How many neutrons are in the nucleus of the atom?

10 Use the periodic table to help you complete the table below.

Name of element	Number of protons	Number of neutrons	Number of electrons
Hydrogen			
Oxygen			
Sodium			
Aluminium			
Boron			
Calcium			

11 Annotate the diagram to represent the electron transfer when sodium reacts with chlorine to form an ionic compound.

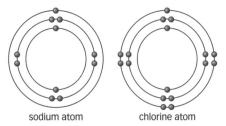

sodium atom   chlorine atom

12 Name the type of bonding in compounds formed from non-metal elements.

13 Compounds that consist of a metal and a non-metal are made of what type of particle?

14 Write word equations to represent the following reactions:
  a Carbon reacts with oxygen to make carbon dioxide.
  b Magnesium reacts with chlorine to make magnesium chloride.
  c Iron reacts with sulfur to make iron sulfide.
  d Sulfuric acid is neutralised by sodium hydroxide to make sodium sulfate and water.
  e Lead carbonate decomposes on heating to make lead oxide and carbon dioxide.

15 A chemist burns 3.2 g of sulfur in oxygen gas. She makes 6.4 g of sulfur dioxide, and no other products. What mass of oxygen reacted with the sulfur?

Working to Grade A*

16 State which of the symbol equations below are not balanced. Then balance the equations that are not balanced.
  a $Mg + O_2 \rightarrow MgO$
  b $C + O_2 \rightarrow CO_2$
  c $H_2SO_4 + NaOH \rightarrow Na_2SO_4 + H_2O$
  d $Na_2CO_3 \rightarrow Na_2O + CO_2$
  e $CuSO_4 + Zn \rightarrow Cu + ZnSO_4$
  f $CH_4 + O_2 \rightarrow CO_2 + H_2O$

Examination questions
The fundamental ideas in chemistry

1 a This diagram shows the electronic structure of an atom.

   i Explain why the element is in Group 6 of the periodic table.

   ....

   (1 mark)

   ii Give the number of protons in the nucleus of the atom above.

   ....

   (1 mark)

b An atom of another element is made up of the particles in the table.

Name of particle	Number
Proton	9
Neutron	10
Electron	9

   i What is the atomic number of the element?

   ....

   (1 mark)

   ii What is the mass number of the element?

   ....

   (1 mark)

   iii Use the periodic table to find out the name and symbol of the element in the table above.

   ....

   (2 marks)

   iv Draw the electronic structure of an atom of the element in the space below.

   (2 marks)
   (Total marks: 8)

2 This question is about the element lithium and its oxide.

a A teacher heats lithium in oxygen. It reacts to form lithium oxide.

i Complete the word equation for the reaction.

lithium + oxygen → ....

(1 mark)

H **ii** Balance the symbol equation for the reaction.

$Li + O_2 \rightarrow Li_2O$

(1 mark)

b Predict the mass of lithium oxide that would be made by reacting 28 g of lithium with 32 g of oxygen.

....

(2 marks)

c Lithium oxide consists of ions.

i Draw a ring around the correct **bold** word in the sentences below.

Lithium is a **non metal/metal**.

A lithium atom **loses/gains** an electron to form an ion with a **negative/positive** charge.

(3 marks)

ii The electronic structure of a lithium atom is 2.1.

Write down the electronic structure of a lithium ion.

....

(1 mark)

d Use the periodic table to name one element with the same number of electrons in its highest occupied energy level (outermost shell) as a lithium atom.

....

(1 mark)

e Use the periodic table to write down the number of protons and neutrons in one lithium atom.

Number of protons = ...

Number of neutrons = ...

(2 marks)

(Total marks: 11)

Using limestone

Limestone is a type of rock. It is mainly calcium carbonate, $CaCO_3$.

- Natural limestone is an attractive building material.
- Heating limestone with clay makes **cement**.
  - > Mixing cement with sand makes **mortar**. Builders use mortar to stick bricks together.
  - > Mixing cement with sand and **aggregate** (small stones) makes **concrete**. Concrete is a construction material.

Quarrying

Companies dig limestone from **quarries**. The table shows the impacts of quarrying and using limestone.

	Advantages	Disadvantages
Environmental	Old quarries can be made into lakes.	Quarries make land unavailable for other purposes, such as farming.
Social	Quarries provide jobs and limestone makes buildings and cement.	Quarries create extra traffic.
Economic	Quarry companies sell the limestone.	Tourists may stop visiting an area with a new quarry.

Thermal decomposition

On heating, calcium carbonate breaks down into simpler compounds:

calcium carbonate → calcium oxide + carbon dioxide

H $CaCO_3$ → CaO + CO_2

This is a **thermal decomposition** reaction.

The carbonates of magnesium, zinc, and copper also decompose on heating. The reactions follow a pattern, producing a metal oxide and carbon dioxide.

For example:

copper carbonate → copper oxide + carbon dioxide
     (green)   (black)

H $CuCO_3$ → CuO + CO_2

Group 1 metal carbonates do not decompose at Bunsen burner temperatures except for lithium carbonate.

Key words

cement, mortar, aggregate, concrete, quarry, limewater, thermal decomposition

Calcium oxide and calcium hydroxide

Adding water to calcium oxide makes calcium hydroxide.

calcium oxide + water → calcium hydroxide

H CaO + H_2O → $Ca(OH)_2$

Calcium hydroxide dissolves in water. The solution is alkaline. It can be used to neutralise acids.

A solution of calcium hydroxide in water is called **limewater**. Bubbling carbon dioxide gas into colourless limewater makes calcium carbonate. Tiny pieces of solid calcium carbonate make the mixture look cloudy. This is the test for carbon dioxide gas.

calcium hydroxide + carbon dioxide → calcium carbonate + water

H $Ca(OH)_2$ + CO_2 → $CaCO_3$ + H_2O

Carbonates and acids

Calcium carbonate reacts with sulfuric acid to make calcium sulfate, carbon dioxide, and water. Calcium sulfate is a salt.

calcium carbonate + sulfuric acid → calcium sulfate + carbon dioxide + water

H $CaCO_3$ + H_2SO_4 → $CaSO_4$ + CO_2 + H_2O

Sulfuric acid is one of the acids in acid rain. Since limestone is mainly calcium carbonate, it is damaged by acid rain.

Other carbonates react with acids in the same way. The products are always carbon dioxide, water, and a salt. Different acids make different salts:

- Hydrochloric acid makes chlorides.
  For example:

  copper carbonate + hydrochloric acid → copper chloride + carbon dioxide + water

  H $CuCO_3$ + $2HCl$ → $CuCl_2$ + CO_2 + H_2O

- Nitric acid makes nitrates.
  For example:

  zinc carbonate + nitric acid → zinc nitrate + carbon dioxide + water

  H $ZnCO_3$ + $2HNO_3$ → $Zn(NO_3)_2$ + CO_2 + H_2O

- Sulfuric acid makes sulphates.
  For example:

  magnesium carbonate + sulfuric acid → magnesium sulfate + carbon dioxide + water

  H $MgCO_3$ + H_2SO_4 → $MgSO_4$ + CO_2 + H_2O

Exam tip

Practise writing word equations for all the reactions in this topic.

Questions

1 Name the substances that are mixed to make mortar and concrete.

2 Identify the products of the reaction of calcium hydroxide solution with carbon dioxide gas.

3 Write word equations for the reactions of:

    a   calcium oxide with water

    b   magnesium carbonate with nitric acid.

Questions
Limestone and building materials

Working to Grade E

1 Limestone is quarried from the ground. Suggest:
- **a** a social advantage of quarrying limestone
- **b** a social disadvantage of quarrying limestone
- **c** an environmental advantage of quarrying limestone
- **d** an economic disadvantage of quarrying limestone.

2 Complete the sentences below.
Cement is made by heating together two raw materials: limestone and _____. Mixing cement with sand makes _____. Mixing cement with sand and aggregate makes _____.

3 Draw a ring around the one carbonate in the list below that cannot be decomposed at the temperatures reached by a Bunsen burner:

potassium carbonate

magnesium carbonate

copper carbonate

4 Describe how to use a solution of calcium hydroxide in water (limewater) to test for carbon dioxide gas. Describe all the changes you would expect to see.

5 Complete the flow diagram below.

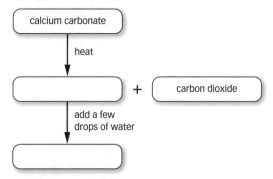

Working to Grade C

6 Calcium carbonate decomposes on heating to make calcium oxide and carbon dioxide. Write a word equation for the reaction.

7 Write word equations for the thermal decomposition reactions of:
- **a** zinc carbonate
- **b** lead carbonate.

8 Name the salts formed when the following pairs of substances react together:
- **a** copper carbonate and dilute sulfuric acid
- **b** zinc carbonate and dilute hydrochloric acid
- **c** calcium carbonate and dilute nitric acid
- **d** magnesium carbonate and dilute hydrochloric acid
- **e** sodium carbonate and dilute sulfuric acid.

9 Complete the following word equations:
- **a** sodium carbonate + nitric acid →
- **b** magnesium carbonate + nitric acid →
- **c** calcium carbonate + hydrochloric acid →
- **d** zinc carbonate + sulfuric acid →

10 A student collected secondary data about the properties of four building materials. The data is in the table below. The student also made notes about their properties. The notes are below the table.

Material	Tensile strength (MPa)	Compressive strength (MPa)	Thermal conductivity (W/m/k)
Mild steel	250	250	60.00
Oak wood	21	15	0.16
High strength concrete	Cracks if not reinforced	60	1.45
Limestone	No data	102	1.30

Notes:
- Tensile strength measures the force needed to pull something to the point where it starts breaking.
- Compressive strength measures the pushing force needed to crush a material.
- Thermal conductivity describes how well a material conducts heat. The higher the number, the better it conducts heat.

- **a** Which building material can withstand the greatest force before being crushed?
- **b** Which two materials conduct heat least well? Suggest why this might be a desirable property for a building material.
- **c** Explain why the student cannot be sure which of the four materials has the greatest tensile strength.

Working to Grade A*

11 Complete the equation below for the thermal decomposition reaction of zinc carbonate. The formulae of the products are ZnO and CO_2.
$$ZnCO_3 \rightarrow$$

12 Bubbling carbon dioxide gas through a dilute solution of calcium hydroxide produces calcium carbonate and water.
Complete the equation below to summarise the reaction.
$$Ca(OH)_2 + CO_2 \rightarrow$$

13 Check the equations below to see if they are balanced.
Balance those that are not already balanced.
- **a** $MgCO_3 + HNO_3 \rightarrow Mg(NO_3)_2 + CO_2 + H_2O$
- **b** $ZnCO_3 + HCl \rightarrow ZnCl_2 + CO_2 + H_2O$
- **c** $Na_2CO_3 + HCl \rightarrow NaCl + CO_2 + H_2O$
- **d** $CuCO_3 + H_2SO_4 \rightarrow CuSO_4 + CO_2 + H_2O$
- **e** $CaCO_3 + HNO_3 \rightarrow Ca(NO_3)_2 + CO_2 + H_2O$

1 a Every year, UK companies extract millions of tonnes of limestone from quarries.

    i Suggest an economic advantage of quarrying limestone.

    ....

    (1 mark)

    ii Suggest an environmental disadvantage of quarrying limestone.

    ....

    (1 mark)

b Limestone is mainly calcium carbonate.

When heated in lime kilns, calcium carbonate decomposes to make calcium oxide (a useful product) and carbon dioxide (a waste gas).

    i Write a word equation for the thermal decomposition reaction of calcium carbonate.

    ....

    (1 mark)

    ii Suggest why traditional lime kilns were open to the air.

    ....

    (1 mark)

    iii Calcium oxide reacts with water to make calcium hydroxide.

    Give two uses of calcium hydroxide, either as a solid or in solution.

    1 ....

    2 ....

    (2 marks)

c This statue is made of dolomite rock.

Dolomite rock is mainly calcium magnesium carbonate.

Predict the names of two salts formed when acid rain falls on the statue. Acid rain is a mixture of dilute acids, including sulfuric acid.

....

....

(2 marks)

H   **d** Balance the equation below.

It shows the reaction of calcium carbonate with hydrochloric acid.

$CaCO_3 + HCl \rightarrow CaCl_2 + CO_2 + H_2O$

(2 marks)

(Total marks: 10)

2 A student investigated the thermal decomposition reactions of some metal carbonates. He heated each metal carbonate in turn in the apparatus below.

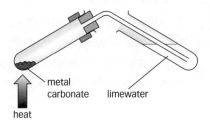

His results are in the table below.

Name of metal carbonate	Time for limewater to begin to look cloudy (seconds)
Sodium carbonate	Did not go cloudy
Calcium carbonate	275
Magnesium carbonate	153
Zinc carbonate	50
Copper carbonate	20

a **i** Identify **two** control variables for the investigation.

1 ....

2 ....

(2 marks)

ii Name the dependent variable in the investigation.

....

(1 mark)

b On heating, zinc carbonate decomposed to make zinc oxide and carbon dioxide gas. Write a word equation for this reaction.

....

(1 mark)

c Name the two products of the thermal decomposition reaction of magnesium carbonate.

.... and ....

(2 marks)

d Complete the word equation for the reaction that makes the limewater go cloudy. Limewater is a solution of calcium hydroxide in water.

calcium hydroxide + ... → .... + water

(2 marks)

(Total marks: 7)

Revision objectives

✔ outline how iron and aluminium are extracted from their ores

✔ describe new techniques of copper extraction

Student book references

1.9 Magnificent metals

1.10 Stunning steel

1.11 Copper

Specification key

✔ C1.3.1 a–h

Metal ores

An **ore** is a rock from which a metal can be extracted economically. When deciding whether to extract a metal from a particular ore, companies consider:

- the price they can get for the metal
- the costs of extracting the metal.

Economic factors change over time. If the demand for a metal increases, companies may make a profit by extracting it from an ore that contains a smaller proportion of the metal.

Processing ores

Companies dig metal ores from the ground. This is **mining**. The ore is then **concentrated** to separate its metal compounds from waste rock. Next, the metal is extracted from its compounds, and purified.

Extracting metals

How a metal is extracted depends on its position in the reactivity series.

- **Unreactive** metals, such as gold, exist in the Earth as the metals themselves, not as compounds.
- Most metals exist as compounds:
  - > Metals that are less reactive than carbon, such as iron, are extracted from their oxides by **reduction** with carbon.
  - > More reactive metals, such as aluminium, are extracted by the **electrolysis** of their molten compounds.

Extracting iron

Iron is extracted from its oxides in a **blast furnace**. Here's how:

- Put the iron ore (mainly iron(III) oxide, Fe_2O_3) into a hot blast furnace with carbon.
- Reduction reactions remove oxygen from the iron(III) oxide. The products are iron and carbon dioxide.

sodium
calcium
magnesium
aluminium
carbon
zinc
iron
tin
lead
copper
silver
gold

▲ The reactivity series.

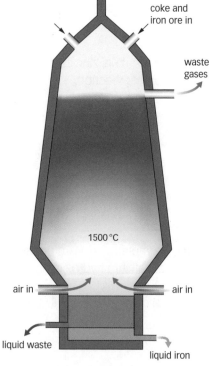

coke and iron ore in

waste gases

1500 °C

air in   air in

liquid waste

liquid iron

▲ Iron oxide is reduced in the blast furnace to make iron.

Extracting aluminium

Aluminium is extracted by electrolysis. Electricity passes through liquid aluminium oxide. The aluminium oxide breaks down and:

- positive aluminium ions move to the negative electrode; aluminium metal is produced here.
- negative oxide ions move to the positive electrode.

The process needs large amounts of energy, so aluminium is expensive.

Extracting copper from copper-rich ores

Companies heat copper-rich ores in a furnace. Chemical reactions remove other elements from the copper compounds in the ore. This is **smelting**.

The copper is then purified by **electrolysis**. The diagram on the right shows how.

Extracting copper from low-grade ores

Copper-rich ores are running out. So companies now extract copper by smelting **low-grade ores** that contain less copper. This is expensive, but the high demand for copper means companies can still make a profit. Extracting copper from low-grade ores produces huge amounts of waste. This damages the environment.

Phytomining and bioleaching

Scientists have developed new ways of extracting copper from low-grade ores. The techniques damage the environment less. They include:

- **Phytomining** – This involves planting certain plants on low-grade copper ores. The plants absorb copper compounds. Burning the plants produces an ash that is rich in copper compounds.
- **Bioleaching** – This uses bacteria to produce solutions of copper compounds. Copper metal is extracted from these solutions by chemical reactions or electrolysis.

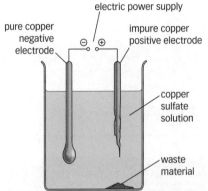

▲ The negative electrode is made of pure copper. Impure copper forms the positive electrode. During electrolysis, positive copper ions move to the negative electrode. Waste material falls to the bottom.

Questions

1 List the four main stages involved in obtaining iron from its ore.

2 Explain why aluminium is extracted from its ore by electrolysis, and not by reduction with carbon.

3 Describe two techniques of extracting copper from low-grade ores.

Exam tip

Remember:
- Metals that are less reactive than carbon are extracted from their oxides by reduction with carbon.
- Metals that are more reactive are extracted by electrolysis.

Revision objectives

- explain the benefits of recycling metals, and describe how copper is recycled
- link the properties of metals and alloys to their uses

Student book references

1.11 Copper

1.12 Titanium and aluminium

Specification key

- ✔ C1.3.1 i–j, ✔ C1.3.2, ✔ C1.3.3

Reasons for recycling

Recycling scrap metal involves melting metals and making them into new things. Governments encourage recycling because:

- some metal ores are in short supply
- extracting metals from ores creates waste and requires much energy, so is damaging to the environment.

Titanium metal cannot be extracted from its ore by reduction with carbon. The extraction of titanium is expensive because it has many stages and requires much energy. It makes economic sense to recycle titanium.

Recycling copper

One method of obtaining pure copper from scrap copper involves making solutions of copper salts. Copper metal is extracted from these solutions by:

- **Electrolysis** – positive copper ions move towards the negative electrode. Here, they gain electrons to form copper atoms.
- **Displacement** – scrap iron is added to the solution. Iron is more reactive than copper, so it displaces copper from its compounds. For example:

    copper sulfate + iron → copper + iron sulfate

Using iron

Iron from the blast furnace contains about 96% iron and 4% impurities. The impurities make it brittle – it breaks if you drop it – so it has few uses.

Some blast furnace iron is re-melted and mixed with scrap steel. This makes **cast iron**. Cast iron has a high strength in compression – you can press down on it with a great force and it will not break. Cast iron is used to make cooking pots, and has been used to make arched bridges.

Steels – vital alloys

Steel is mainly iron. The iron is mixed with carbon and other metals to change its properties and make it more useful. There are many types of steel. Each has properties that make it suitable for different uses.

Steels are examples of **alloys**. An alloy is a mixture of a metal with one or more other elements. The properties of an alloy are different to those of the elements in it.

Type of steel	Property	Uses
Low-carbon steel	Easily shaped	Food cans Car body panels
High-carbon steel	Hard	Tools
Stainless steel	Resistant to corrosion (does not rust)	Cutlery Surgical instruments

▲ A model of the structure of steel. The bigger circles represent iron atoms. The smaller ones represent atoms of another element.

Key words

recycling, displacement, alloy, cast iron, transition metal, low carbon steel, high-carbon steel, stainless steel

Other alloys

Metals like copper, gold, iron, and aluminium are too soft for many uses. So they are mixed with small amounts of similar metals to make alloys. The alloys are harder and more useful.

Properties and uses of metals

The elements in the central block of the periodic table are the **transition metals**.

																	0
1	2						H					3	4	5	6	7	He
Li	Be											B	C	N	O	F	Ne
Na	Mg											Al	Si	P	S	Cl	Ar
K	Ca	Sc	Ti	V	Cr	Mn	Fe	Co	Ni	Cu	Zn	Ga	Ge	As	Se	Br	Kr
Rb	Sr	Y	Zr	Nb	Mo	Tc	Ru	Rh	Pd	Ag	Cd	In	Sn	Sb	Te	I	Xe
Cs	Ba	La	Hf	Ta	W	Re	Os	Ir	Pt	Au	Hg	Tl	Pb	Bi	Po	At	Rn
Fr	Ra	Ac															

transition metals

Like most metals, the transition metals:

- can be bent or hammered into different shapes without cracking
- are good conductors of heat and electricity.

These properties make transition metals useful as structural materials, and for making things that must allow heat or electricity to pass through them.

For example, copper is used for:

- electrical wiring, because it is a good conductor of electricity
- plumbing, because it can be bent, but is hard enough to make pipes and tanks. Also, copper does not react with water.

Titanium and aluminium are useful metals. They have low densities and are resistant to corrosion. These properties mean that both metals are used to make aeroplanes. Aluminium makes overhead electricity cables. Titanium makes artificial hip bones.

Exam tip

Practise describing the links between the properties of metals and alloys and their uses.

Questions

1 Give three reasons for recycling metals.

2 Name three types of steel. Link their properties to their uses.

3 Explain why titanium is a suitable metal from which to make artificial hip bones and aeroplanes.

Working to Grade E

1   Name one metal that is found in the Earth as the metal itself.

2   The list below gives four stages of producing a pure metal from its ore. Put them in the correct order.
    a   Purify the metal.
    b   Mine the ore.
    c   Concentrate ore.
    d   Extract the metal from the ore.

3   Use the periodic table to identify the transition metals in the list below.

    molybdenum   sodium
    manganese   aluminium
    magnesium   titanium
    scandium

4   Give two benefits of producing aluminium drinks cans from recycled aluminium, compared to using aluminium that has recently been extracted from its ore.

5   a   Complete the table below to show the properties of three types of steel.

Type of steel	Properties
Stainless steel	
High-carbon steel	
Low-carbon steel	

    b   List one use of each type of steel in the table.

6   Highlight the correct bold word in the sentences below.
    Iron from the blast furnace is **brittle/ shatterproof**. Re-melting blast furnace iron and adding scrap steel makes **steel/cast iron**. This has high strength in **compression/tension**, so is used to make arched bridges.

7   Explain why titanium and its alloys are used to make:
    a   aeroplanes
    b   the supports for North Sea oil rigs.

8   In the blast furnace, iron oxide is reduced by heating with carbon. Explain the meaning of the word **reduced**.

Working to Grade C

9   The metals below are listed in order of their reactivity, with the most reactive at the top. One non-metal, carbon, is also included in the list.

    sodium   iron
    calcium   tin
    magnesium   lead
    aluminium   gold
    carbon

    a   Predict two metals, other than iron, that can be extracted from their oxides by reduction with carbon.
    b   Predict two metals that are extracted by the electrolysis of their molten compounds.
    c   Identify one element that is found in the Earth as the element itself.

10 Explain why it is expensive to extract titanium metal from its ore.

11 Identify two advantages of extracting copper from low-grade ores by phytomining and bioleaching, compared with extracting copper from low-grade ores by smelting.

12 The diagram below shows how copper is purified by electrolysis.

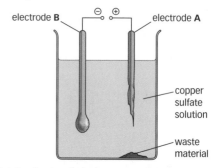

    a   Which electrode is impure copper?
    b   Towards which electrode do positively charged copper ions move?

13 Write a word equation to summarise how copper metal is extracted from copper sulfate solution by adding scrap iron.

14 The table below gives some data for aluminium and two of its alloys.

Material	Tensile strength (MPa)	Hardness (Brinell scale)*	Density (g/cm³)
Pure aluminium	90	23	2.7
Aluminium alloy 7075	572	150	2.8
Aluminium alloy 5059	160	120	2.7

*The bigger the number, the harder the material.

    a   Name the hardest material in the table.
    b   Aluminium alloy 7075 is used in making aeroplanes. Use the data in the table to suggest two reasons for this choice.
    c   Suggest one disadvantage of using aluminium alloy 7075 for making aeroplanes, compared to using pure aluminium.

1 This question is about copper.

a Describe two properties of copper that make it a suitable material for water pipes.

1 ....

2 ....

(2 marks)

b This table shows some data about three materials.

Name of material	Composition
Copper	100% copper
Nickel brass	70% copper, 24.5% zinc, 5.5% nickel
Naval brass	60% copper, 39.25% zinc, 0.75% tin

i Name the alloys in the table.

....

(1 mark)

ii Pound coins are made from nickel brass.

Suggest one advantage of making coins from nickel brass, compared to pure copper.

....

(1 mark)

c **i** Copper can be extracted by mining low-grade ores and heating the ores in a furnace.

Describe two disadvantages of obtaining copper by this method.

1 ....

2 ....

(2 marks)

ii Describe how copper can be extracted by phytomining.

....

....

(2 marks)

(Total marks: 8)

2 Read the article in the box below.

> Large deposits of a rare metal, indium, have been discovered in the UK in an old tin mine in Cornwall. The mine owners hope to dig out millions of pounds worth of indium every year.
>
> Indium tin oxide is used in touch-screen technology and to make liquid-crystal displays for flat-screen televisions, smart phones, and laptops. As more and more people have bought these products over the past 10 years, so the amount of indium needed has increased.

a Scientists analysed samples of rock from the mine. The table below shows data from six samples.

Sample number	Mass of indium per tonne of rock (g)
1	1000
2	110
3	100
4	90
5	95
6	105

i The scientists concluded that the average mass of indium per tonne of rock is 100 g.

Explain how the data in the table support this conclusion.

....

(1 mark)

ii The mine owner hopes that 400 000 tonnes of rock will be mined each year.

Estimate the mass of indium in this mass of rock.

Assume that the average mass of indium per tonne of rock is 100 g. Give your answer in tonnes.
(1 tonne = 1 000 000 g)

....

....

(2 marks)

iii Use your answer to part **ii** to estimate the mass of solid waste produced if 400 000 tonnes of rock are mined each year.

....

....

(1 mark)

iv Suggest an environmental impact of the waste rock.

....

(1 mark)

b The local council must decide whether to allow the mine to reopen to extract indium. People are discussing their ideas.

Extracting indium from the mine could create 400 jobs.

Barney – local resident

China is the biggest producer of indium. In 2009, a quarter of all indium production in the country was stopped. People were protesting about pollution linked to the process.

Lim – Chinese journalist

Our company uses copper indium gallium selenide to make solar cells. As the demand for solar cells increases, so will the demand for indium. The world needs to mine all the indium that is found.

Sarah – solar-cell manufacturer

Indium metal is harmful if swallowed or breathed in.

Meera – British scientist

Last year, 480 tonnes of indium was produced from mining, and 650 tonnes from recycling. We need to recycle more indium, so as not to put the health of humans and the environment at risk.

Catherine – environment worker

Use all the evidence given in this question to recommend whether or not the mine should be allowed to re-open to extract indium.

....

....

....

....

....

(4 marks)
(Total marks: 9)

Revision objectives

- ✔ explain the meaning of the term *hydrocarbon*
- ✔ interpret formulae of alkanes
- ✔ explain how crude oil is separated into fractions by fractional distillation

Student book references

1.13 Making crude oil useful

1.14 Looking into oil

Specification key

✔ C1.4.1, ✔ C1.4.2 a–b

Crude oil

Crude oil is a **fossil fuel**. It was formed from the decay of buried dead sea creatures over millions of years.

Crude oil contains many different compounds. Many of the compounds are **hydrocarbons**. Hydrocarbons are compounds made up of carbon and hydrogen only.

The hydrocarbons in crude oil form a **mixture**. A mixture consists of two or more elements or compounds that are not chemically combined together. In a mixture:
- the chemical properties of each substance are not affected by being in the mixture – their properties are unchanged
- the substances can be separated by physical methods, including filtering and distillation.

Fractional distillation

Crude oil is not useful as it is. But separating it into **fractions** makes valuable fuels and raw materials. A fraction is a mixture of hydrocarbons whose molecules have a similar number of carbon atoms.

Oil companies use the property of boiling point to separate crude oil into fractions by **fractional distillation**. The process is continuous – it carries on all the time.

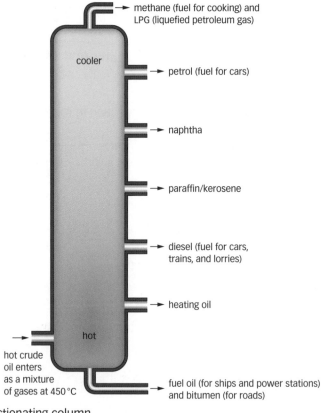

▲ Fractionating column.

Key words

hydrocarbon, mixture, fraction, fractional distillation, evaporate, fractionating column, condense, alkanes, saturated hydrocarbon, molecular formula, displayed formula, general formula

Fractional distillation involves these steps:
- Heat crude oil to about 450 °C. Its compounds **evaporate** to become a mixture of gases.
- The gases enter the bottom of a **fractionating column**. The fractionating column is hot at the bottom and cooler at the top.
- The gases move up the column. As they move up, they cool down. Different fractions **condense** to form liquids again at different levels:
  - > Compounds with the highest boiling points condense at the bottom of the column, and leave as liquids.
  - > Lower-boiling-point compounds condense higher up, where it is cooler, and leave as liquids.
  - > The lowest-boiling-point compounds leave from the top, as gases.

Alkanes

Most of the hydrocarbons in crude oil are **alkanes**. Alkanes are a family of **saturated hydrocarbons**. The carbon atoms in saturated hydrocarbons are joined together by single covalent bonds.

Alkane molecules can be represented by **molecular formulae** and by **displayed formulae**. The table below gives the names and formulae of three alkanes. There are many others.

Name	Molecular formula	Displayed formula
Methane	CH_4	H—C—H (with H above and below)
Ethane	C_2H_6	H—C—C—H (with H above and below each C)
Propane	C_3H_8	H—C—C—C—H (with H above and below each C)

In displayed formulae, each line (–) represents a covalent bond.

All alkanes have the same **general formula**, C_nH_{2n+2}. This means that the number of hydrogen atoms in an alkane molecule is twice the number of carbon atoms, plus two.

Exam tip

Make sure you can recognise alkanes from their names and formulae. Practise writing both types of formulae for methane, ethane, and propane.

Questions

1 Write definitions for these words: hydrocarbon, mixture, fraction, alkane.

2 What is a mixture? Give two characteristics of mixtures.

3 Write the molecular formulae of methane, ethane, and propane.

Revision objectives

- ✓ link the properties of hydrocarbons to the size of their molecules
- ✓ describe the impacts on the environment of burning hydrocarbon fuels

Student book references

1.14 Looking into oil

1.15 Burning dilemmas

Specification key

✓ C1.4.2 c, ✓ C1.4.3 a–d

▲ Longer-chain alkanes are more viscous because their molecules get more tangled.

Sizes and properties of hydrocarbons

Hydrocarbon properties depend on their molecule size. These properties influence how hydrocarbons are used as fuels.

- Hydrocarbons with bigger molecules are more **viscous** (thicker) than hydrocarbons with smaller molecules. Viscous liquids are more difficult to pour and do not flow as easily as runnier liquids.
- Hydrocarbons with bigger molecules have higher boiling points than those with smaller molecules.

Number of carbon atoms in hydrocarbon chain	State at room temperature
1 to 4 (smaller molecules)	gas
5 to 16	liquid
17 or more (longer molecules)	solid

Gases make good fuels for cooking because they travel easily through pipes. Liquid fuels are easy to store and transport, so are suitable for use as vehicle fuels.

- Alkanes with smaller molecules catch fire more easily than those with bigger molecules. Methane has small molecules, so it ignites easily and is useful for cooking.

Burning hydrocarbon fuels

The **combustion** (burning) of fuels releases energy. During combustion, carbon and hydrogen atoms from fuels join with oxygen from the air. The carbon and hydrogen are **oxidised**.

Burning fuels release gases to the air.

- In a good supply of air, a burning hydrocarbon produces two main products – carbon dioxide and water vapour. For example:

$$\text{methane} + \text{oxygen} \rightarrow \text{carbon dioxide} + \text{water}$$

H $\quad CH_4 \;+\; 2O_2 \;\rightarrow\; CO_2 \;+\; 2H_2O$

This is **complete combustion**.

- Burning hydrocarbons in a poor supply of air makes **carbon monoxide** gas (CO) as well as carbon dioxide and water vapour. This is **partial** or **incomplete combustion**.

Carbon monoxide and carbon dioxide cause problems:

- Carbon monoxide is poisonous.
- Carbon dioxide is a **greenhouse gas**. Its presence in the atmosphere helps to keep the Earth warm enough for life. The diagram on the next page shows how.

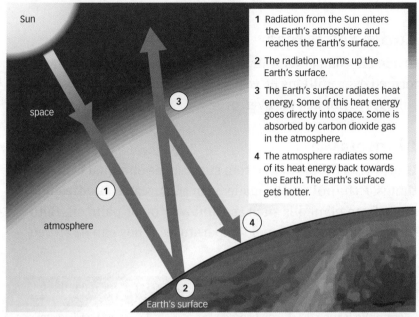

▲ Global warming.

1 Radiation from the Sun enters the Earth's atmosphere and reaches the Earth's surface.

2 The radiation warms up the Earth's surface.

3 The Earth's surface radiates heat energy. Some of this heat energy goes directly into space. Some is absorbed by carbon dioxide gas in the atmosphere.

4 The atmosphere radiates some of its heat energy back towards the Earth. The Earth's surface gets hotter.

Key words

viscous, oxidised, complete combustion, carbon monoxide, partial combustion, incomplete combustion, greenhouse gas, global warming, climate change, sulfur dioxide, oxides of nitrogen, acid rain, particulates, global dimming

- Extra carbon dioxide in the atmosphere from burning fuels causes **global warming**. The impacts of global warming include:
  > **climate change**, causing extreme weather events
  > the melting of the polar ice caps, causing sea levels to rise and coastal areas to flood.

More products of combustion

Some fuels contain atoms of sulfur, as well as carbon and hydrogen. These fuels make **sulfur dioxide** (SO_2) when they burn. At the high temperatures reached in car engines, **oxides of nitrogen**, such as nitrogen monoxide (NO) and nitrogen dioxide (NO_2), also form.

Sulfur dioxide and oxides of nitrogen cause **acid rain**. Acid rain:
- makes lakes more acidic, killing water plants and animals
- damages trees
- damages limestone buildings by reacting with calcium carbonate.

Sulfur can be removed from fuels before they are burnt. Sulfur dioxide can be removed from the waste gases of power stations.

Particulates

Burning fuels may release solid particles, or **particulates**. Particulates contain soot (a form of carbon) and unburnt fuels. Particulates cause **global dimming**. In the atmosphere, particulates reflect sunlight back into space, meaning that less sunlight reaches the Earth's surface.

Exam tip AQA

Make sure you know which environmental problems are caused by which products of combustion – it's easy to get them all confused!

Questions

1 Describe how the boiling points, viscosity, and flammability of hydrocarbons are linked to molecule size.

2 Draw a table to summarise how burning fuels produce these substances: carbon dioxide, carbon monoxide, sulfur dioxide, oxides of nitrogen, particulates.
Identify the environmental problems caused by each substance.

Revision objectives

✔ identify the benefits, drawbacks, and risks of using biofuels and hydrogen fuel

Student book references

1.16 Global warming

1.17 Biofuels

Specification key

✔ C1.4.3 e

Finite resources

Crude oil, coal, and natural gas are **non-renewable**, since they formed over millions of years. Fossil fuels are **finite** resources – they will not last for ever.

Biofuels

Biofuels are fuels made from substances obtained from living things. **Ethanol** can be made from sugar cane. **Biodiesel** is made from plant oils such as sunflower oil or palm oil. Both fuels are liquid at normal temperatures. They can be stored and transported safely.

	Advantages	Disadvantages
Economic issues	Biofuel producers sell their products.	Converting filling stations to dispense biofuels is expensive.
Social and ethical issues	Biofuels are renewable, so using them does not take supplies from future generations.	Fuel crops may be grown on land that some people think should be used to grow food.
Environmental issues	The plants from which biofuels are made remove carbon dioxide from the atmosphere as they grow.	Overall, more carbon dioxide is added to the atmosphere than is removed, since carbon dioxide is released by farm machinery and during the production of fertilisers.

Hydrogen fuel

Hydrogen can also be used as a vehicle fuel. It ignites easily, and produces just one product on burning – water vapour. Hydrogen is explosive when mixed with air, so is difficult to store and transport safely.

Hydrogen can be made from methane gas, which is renewable when produced from animal waste.

Key words

non-renewable, finite, biofuel, ethanol, biodiesel

Exam tip

Read questions on this topic carefully, and answer in detail.

Questions

1 Evaluate the environmental impacts of using biodiesel as a vehicle fuel instead of diesel.

2 List the benefits and drawbacks of using hydrogen gas as a vehicle fuel.

Questions
Crude oil and fuels

Working to Grade E

1 Highlight the statements below that are true. Then write corrected versions of the statements that are false.
  a Crude oil is a mixture of elements.
  b A mixture consists of two or more elements or compounds that are chemically combined.
  c When substances are mixed together, their chemical properties change.
  d You can separate the substances in a mixture by physical methods, such as distillation.
  e Crude oil is separated into fractions by fractional distillation.

2 In each sentence below, highlight the correct **bold** word.
  a Most compounds in crude oil are **hydrocarbons/carbohydrates**.
  b Most compounds in crude oil are made up of carbon and **hydrogen/helium** only.
  c Most compounds in crude oil are **alkenes/alkanes**.
  d Alkanes are **saturated/unsaturated** compounds.

3 The statements below describe some stages in the fractional distillation of crude oil. Write the letters of the stages in the correct order.
  a The compounds in the oil evaporate.
  b The mixture of vapours enters the fractionating column.
  c The mixture of vapours moves up the fractionating column.
  d The oil is heated.
  e Fractions of hydrocarbons with the highest boiling points condense near the bottom of the fractionating column.
  f Fractions of hydrocarbons with the lowest boiling points are removed near the top of the fractionating column.

4 Draw lines to match the name of each pollutant to show how it is formed.

Pollutant	Formed when ...
Nitrogen dioxide	hydrocarbons burn in a poor supply of air
Carbon monoxide	hydrocarbons burn in air at high temperatures
Sulfur dioxide	a sulfur-containing fuel burns

5 Name one environmental problem caused by each of these substances:
  a carbon dioxide
  b nitrogen monoxide
  c sulfur dioxide
  d particulates (solid particles)

Working to Grade C

6 Complete the table below.

Name of alkane	Molecular formula	Structural formula
Methane		
	C_2H_6	
		(structure shown: three carbons each bonded to hydrogens, H–C–C–C–H)
	C_4H_{10}	

7 Use either the word **increases** or **decreases** to complete each sentence below.
  a The boiling point of alkanes increases as their molecule size ....
  b Alkanes get less viscous as their molecule size ....
  c Alkanes get more flammable as their molecule size ....

8 Complete these word equations:
  a The complete combustion of butane.
    butane + oxygen →
  b The partial combustion of methane.
    methane + ... → carbon dioxide + ... + ...

9 The table below shows the temperature change of 100 cm³ of water when heated by burning the same mass of four different alkanes.

Alkane	Temp before heating (°C)	Temp after heating (°C)	Temp change (°C)
Methane	19	75	56
Ethane	20	72	
Propane	20	68	48
Butane	21	71	50

  a Calculate the temperature rise of the water when heated by ethane.
  b Which fuel transferred most energy to the water?
  c What happens to the atoms of carbon and hydrogen when alkanes burn?

10 Complete the table below to show the benefits and drawbacks of using ethanol as a fuel, compared to using petrol. Assume the ethanol is produced from plant material and the petrol is produced by the fractional distillation of crude oil.

	Ethanol	Petrol
Use of renewable resources	Pro: Con:	Pro: Con:
Fuel storage and use	Pro: Con:	Pro: Con:
Combustion products	Pro: Con:	Pro: Con:

1 This question is about the substances released into the atmosphere when fuels burn.

a Draw lines to link each substance to the problem it may cause. One problem is caused by more than one substance.

Substance
carbon dioxide
sulfur dioxide
solid particles
oxides of nitrogen

Problem
acid rain
global warming
global dimming

(4 marks)

b i Write a word equation for the complete combustion of methane to form carbon dioxide and water.

....
(2 marks)

ii Name the carbon compound formed as a result of the partial combustion of methane.

....
(1 mark)
(Total marks: 7)

2 The compounds in crude oil are separated by fractional distillation. This diagram shows a fractionating column.

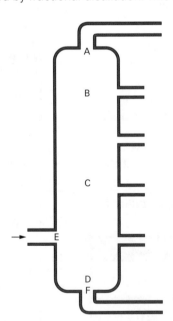

a Use words from the box to complete the following sentences. Each word may be used once, more than once, or not at all.

cool	evaporate	condense	freeze	warm

The substances in crude oil .... to become a mixture of gases. Fractions in the mixture

.... at different temperatures as they ....

(3 marks)

b Match the labels in the table below with the correct letter in the diagram of the fractionating column. Write the correct letter beside each label. You can use each letter once, more than once, or not at all.

	Letter
The place where a mixture of vapours enters the column.	
The hottest part of the column.	
The place where the fraction containing substances with the highest boiling points leaves the column.	
The place where the fraction containing the most flammable substances leaves the column.	
The place where methane gas leaves the column.	

(5 marks)

(Total marks: 8)

3 This table gives data for six alkanes.

Name of alkane	Molecular formula	Melting point (ºC)	Boiling point (ºC)
Methane	CH_4	−182	−162
Ethane	C_2H_6	−183	−89
Propane	C_3H_8	−188	−42
Butane	C_4H_{10}	−138	−0.5
Pentane	C_5H_{12}	−130	36
Hexane	C_6H_{14}	−95	69

a Draw the displayed formula for propane in the space below.

(2 marks)

b i Describe the trend in boiling points shown in the table.

....

(1 mark)

ii Name an alkane in the table that is a liquid at room temperature (20 °C).

....

(1 mark)

(Total marks: 4)

4 *In this question you will be assessed on using good English, organising information clearly, and using specialist terms where appropriate.*

Describe the benefits, drawbacks, and risks of using hydrogen as a vehicle fuel, compared with using hydrocarbon fuels such as petrol or diesel.

....

....

....

....

....

....

....

....

....

(6 marks)

(Total marks: 6)

How Science Works
Atoms, rocks, metals, and fuels

Designing an investigation and making measurements

As well as demonstrating your investigative skills practically, you are likely to be asked to comment on investigations done by others. The example below offers guidance in this skill area. It also gives you the chance to practise using your skills to answer the types of question that may come up in exams.

Comparing the energy of different fuels

Skill – Understanding the experiment

Josh tested the hypothesis that the bigger a fuel molecule, the more energy is released when it burns.

He burnt 1 g of a fuel, methanol, and used it to heat 100 cm³ of water.

Josh repeated the procedure with four other fuels. He used the apparatus below. Josh's results are in the table.

Fuel	Number of carbon atoms in one molecule	Temp before heating (°C)	Temp after heating (°C)	Temp change (°C)
Methanol	1	19	49	30
Ethanol	2	19	54	35
Propanol	3	20	61	41
Butanol	4	20	63	43
Pentanol	5	21	66	45

1 Identify the independent and dependent variables.

In an investigation:
- The independent variable is the one that is changed by the scientist or student.
- The dependent variable is the one that is measured for each change in the independent variable.

Try remembering it like this – the dependent variable *depends* on what you do to the independent one.

2 Identify three control variables.

In a fair test, only the independent variable should affect the dependent variable. The other variables must be kept the same. These are the control variables.

In Josh's investigation, one of the control variables is the volume of water. Can you identify the others?

Skill – Analysing the experiment

3 The smallest temperature change that Josh's thermometer can detect is 1 °C. Describe an advantage of using a thermometer that can detect a temperature change of 0.5 °C.

This question is asking about the resolution of the thermometer. In general, using a measuring instrument with a high resolution gives more accurate values (ones that are closer to the true value) than instruments with a lower resolution.

Skill – Evaluating the experiment

4 Do Josh's results support his hypothesis? Give a reason for your answer.

A hypothesis is an idea to explain observations. Josh uses the idea of increasing molecule size to explain why different fuels release different amounts of energy on burning. Do you think Josh's idea is correct? Why?

Skill – Using data to draw conclusions

5 Predict the temperature change of 100 cm³ of water if Josh burns 1 g of hexanol. Hexanol has six carbon atoms in one molecule.

A prediction is a statement about the way something will happen in the future. It is not the same as a hypothesis.

To answer this question properly, you would need to draw a graph or bar chart. But you can use the data in the table to make a rough prediction.

6 Rebecca does a similar investigation to Josh but she repeats the test for each fuel three times. The table below summarises her results.
Suggest two advantages of repeating the test for each fuel.

Fuel	Temperature change (°C)			
	Run 1	Run 2	Run 3	Mean
Methanol	28	32	30	30
Ethanol	39	35	37	37
Propanol	43	61	43	43
Butanol	45	45	45	45
Pentanol	48	46	47	47

This question is asking about repeatability – how similar are the measurements when repeated under the same conditions by the same person?

If repeated values are close to each other, then the results are likely to be close to the true value.

You could also mention the anomalous result. Which result is anomalous? How does repeating tests help to identify anomalous data? Why might Rebecca have chosen to ignore the anomalous result?

AQA Upgrade

Answering an extended writing question

1 *In this question you will be assessed on using good English, organising information clearly, and using specialist terms where appropriate.*

Describe three ways by which copper metal can be obtained. Include descriptions of methods for extracting copper from its ores, and by recycling. Give an advantage or disadvantage of each method.

(6 marks)

QUESTION

---

you can heat copper ores this use emergie and you can use plants this is good and recycling is good two

G–E

Examiner: This answer is typical of a grade G candidate. It is worth just one mark.

The candidate has mentioned only two methods for obtaining copper metal, and has implied only one disadvantage of one method.

The candidate has not used specialist terms. There is no punctuation, and there are errors of grammar and spelling.

You can heat copper ores in a furnness. This is bad because it uses lots of energy. You can use bioleaching. This needs bacterea. It is good because it gets copper from ores with just a teeny bit of copper in them.

D–C

Examiner: This answer is worth three marks out of six. It is typical of a grade C or D candidate. The candidate has described two methods of extracting copper from ores, and has correctly given an advantage or disadvantage for each. No mention has been made of copper recycling.

The answer is well organised, with correct grammar and punctuation. There are a few spelling mistakes.

---

1 Copper can be obtained from copper-rich ores by heating them in a furnace. This is smelting. Then the copper is made pure by electrolysis. One disadvantage of this method is that it needs electricity. If the electricity is generated by burning fossil fuels, then the process puts carbon dioxide into the air, causing global warming.

Copper can be obtained from low-grade ores by phytomining. This uses plants to take in metal compounds. Then they burn the plants and get the copper compounds out of the ash. The advantage is that its energy costs are low, and it makes little solid waste.

You can also get copper by using waste copper to make solutions of salts. Then you add scrap steel, which is mainly iron. There is a displacement reaction, which gives copper.

$$copper\ sulfate + iron \rightarrow iron\ sulfate + copper$$

This is recycling. Its advantage is that it doesn't use up copper ores, and the process does not make greenhouse gases.

B–A*

Examiner: This is a high-quality answer, typical of an A* candidate. It is worth six marks out of six.

All parts of the question have been answered accurately and in detail.

The answer is well organised, and the spelling, punctuation, and grammar are faultless. The candidate has used several specialist terms.

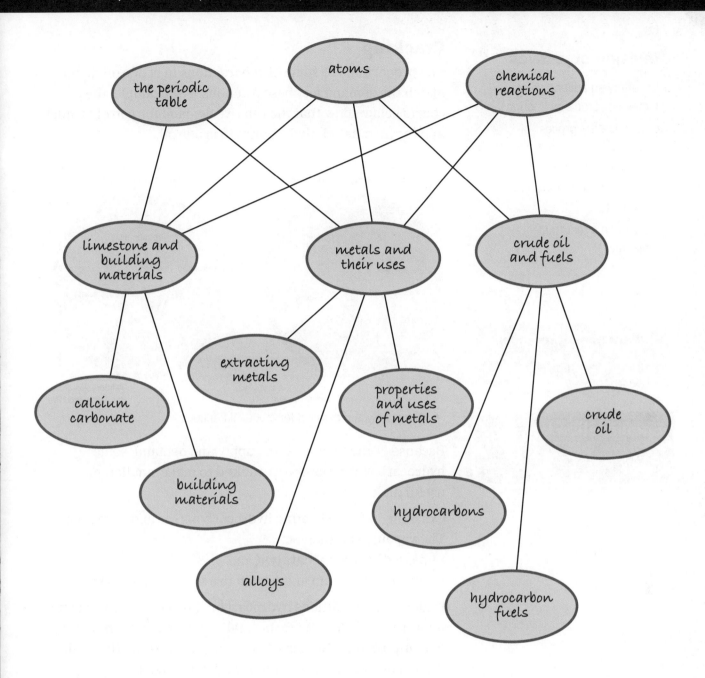

Revision checklist

- All substances are made up of atoms. Atoms are made up of protons, neutrons, and electrons.
- Elements are substances made up of one type of atom.
- There are about 100 elements listed in the periodic table.
- In the periodic table, elements in the same group have the same number of electrons in their highest energy level, and so have similar properties.
- In chemical reactions, atoms are rearranged to make new products. The mass of products equals the mass of the reactants.
- Limestone is a raw material for the manufacture of cement and concrete.
- Limestone is mainly calcium carbonate.
- Some metal carbonates decompose on heating to give carbon dioxide and a metal oxide.
- Carbonates react with acids to produce carbon dioxide, a salt, and water.

- Most metals are found combined with other elements in ores.
- Metals that are less reactive than carbon can be extracted from their ores by reduction with carbon.
- Metals that are more reactive than carbon are extracted by electrolysis of their molten compounds.
- An alloy is a mixture of a metal with small amounts of other elements. Many alloys are harder than the metals from which they are made.
- The uses of metals and alloys depend on their properties.
- Crude oil is a mixture of many hydrocarbons. Most of these are saturated hydrocarbons called alkanes.
- Fractional distillation separates the hydrocarbons in crude oil into fractions, each of which contains molecules with a similar number of carbon atoms.
- Hydrocarbon fuels burn to release energy. Some of their combustion products are pollutants.

Revision objectives

- ✔ identify an advantage of cracking crude oil fractions
- ✔ describe the process of cracking, and identify the conditions needed
- ✔ interpret the formulae of alkenes
- ✔ describe a test to identify alkenes

Student book references

1.18 Cracking crude oil

Specification key

✔ C1.5.1

Cracking

The proportions of some of the fractions in crude oil do not match the demand for these fractions. For example, the pie charts below show that the relative demand for petrol is much greater than its relative amount in crude oil.

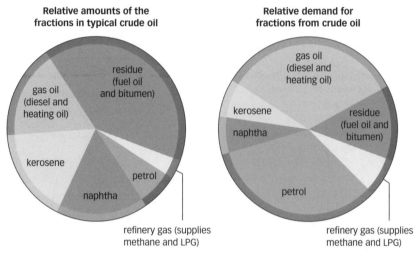

▲ The supply and demand for crude oil fractions.

Because of the mismatch in supply and demand, some hydrocarbon fractions are **cracked** to make smaller, more useful molecules.

Cracking involves heating hydrocarbons to vapourise them. The vapours can then be:

- passed over a hot **catalyst**, or
- mixed with steam and heated to a very high temperature.

Under these conditions hydrocarbon molecules in the vapour mixture break down to form smaller molecules in **thermal decomposition** reactions. The catalyst speeds up thermal decomposition reactions but is not itself used up.

Exam tip

When describing chemical tests, don't forget to describe the expected appearance of the test solution both before and after adding the substance being tested.

For example, on cracking the naphtha fraction, octane molecules may break down to make two smaller molecules – hexane and ethane.

$$\text{octane} \rightarrow \text{hexane} + \text{ethene}$$

H $\quad C_8H_{18} \rightarrow C_6H_{14} + C_2H_4$

Hexane is a useful fuel. It is added to the petrol fraction. Other products of cracking are also useful fuels.

Alkenes

Ethene, one product of cracking, has a double bond between its two carbon atoms. This means it is an **unsaturated hydrocarbon**. It is a member of a group of hydrocarbons called the **alkenes**.

The table shows two alkenes.

Name	Molecular formula	Structural formula
Ethene	C_2H_4	
Propene	C_3H_6	

The alkenes have the general formula C_nH_{2n}. This shows that the number of hydrogen atoms in an alkene molecule is double the number of carbon atoms.

Detecting alkenes

You can detect unsaturated compounds by testing with **bromine water**. Orange bromine water becomes colourless when it reacts with alkenes.

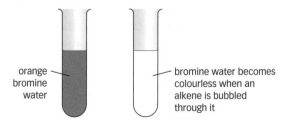

orange bromine water

bromine water becomes colourless when an alkene is bubbled through it

Key words

cracking, catalyst, thermal decomposition, unsaturated hydrocarbon, alkene, ethene, propene, bromine water

Exam tip

Make sure you can explain both *why* and *how* hydrocarbon fractions are cracked. Practise writing both types of formulae for ethene and propene.

Questions

1 Give one advantage of cracking the naphtha fraction of crude oil.

2 Give the conditions needed for cracking. Identify the two types of product of a typical cracking reaction.

3 Write the molecular formulae of ethene and propene.

4 Describe the test for identifying alkenes.

Revision objectives

- describe how polymers are made
- write equations to represent polymerisation reactions
- evaluate the impacts of the uses, disposal, and recycling of polymers

Student book references

1.19 Polymers

1.20 Designer polymers

1.21 More designer polymers

1.22 Polymer problems

Specification key

- C1.5.2

Making polymers

Alkenes are important raw materials. They are used to make **polymers**. Polymers are materials that have very big molecules. They are made by joining together many small molecules, called **monomers**. For example:

part of a poly(ethene) molecule

▲ Ethene molecules join together in long chains to make poly(ethene).

Using polymers

There are thousands of different polymers. Each has unique properties. The uses of a polymer depend on its properties. Scientists continue to develop new polymers with new applications.

Type of polymer	Properties	Uses
'Breathable' polymers	Allow water vapour to pass through their tiny pores, but not liquid water.	Making waterproof clothes.
Dental polymers	White, hard, and tough. Poor conductors of heat.	Fillings for teeth.
Hydrogels	Absorb huge volumes of liquid.	Making wound dressings and disposable nappies.
Smart materials, for example, shape-memory polymers	Change in response to their environment.	Making shrink-wrap packaging and glasses frames.

The properties of some polymers make them better for particular purposes than the material they replace. For example, metal fillings conduct heat well, making it uncomfortable to eat very hot or very cold food. New dental polymers are poor conductors of heat.

Polymer disposal

Many polymers are **non-biodegradable** – they cannot be broken down by microbes. This creates disposal problems because when put into **landfill sites** they remain unchanged for many years. When thrown away as litter, they persist in the environment for a long time, and may injure animals.

Chemists are developing ways of solving these problems, including:

* Recycling plastics – mixed plastic waste is collected and sorted into separate types of polymer, often by hand. This process is time consuming and expensive. The separate polymers are then melted and made into new products.

PET	high-density poly(ethene)	PVC	low-density poly(ethene)	poly(propene)	polystyrene

| PET | HDPE | PVC | LDPE | PP | PS |

▲ Recycling symbols found on plastic items.

* Adding starch to poly(ethene) – bacteria break down the starch once the polymer gets wet. This makes the plastic item break down into very small pieces. It has not rotted away, but it is no longer litter.
* Making bags from cornstarch – cornstarch is made from maize. It is biodegradable. There are advantages and disadvantages of making bags from cornstarch.

	Advantages	Disadvantages
Environmental	Biodegradable.	Fertiliser used to help maize grow may pollute rivers and lakes.
Economic	Growers and manufacturers have products to sell.	Cornstarch bags can be more expensive than poly(ethene) ones.
Social and ethical	Cornstarch is renewable, so using it to make bags does not take supplies from future generations.	Grown on land that could be used for food crops.

Key words

polymer, monomer, non-biodegradable, landfill site

Questions

1 Describe the properties of dental polymers, and explain why these properties make them suitable for their purpose.

2 Use ideas about properties to explain why hydrogels are used in disposable nappies.

3 Identify the environmental, economic, and social advantages of making bags from cornstarch instead of from poly(ethene).

11: Ethanol

Revision objectives

- ✔ describe two methods of manufacturing ethanol
- ✔ evaluate the advantages and disadvantages of the two methods

Student book references

1.23 Making ethanol

Specification key

✔ C1.5.3

Key words

hydration reaction, fermentation, enzyme

Exam tip

AQA

Remember – ethene is a non-renewable resource, but glucose is renewable.

Questions

1 Create a table to show the raw materials, conditions, and products of the two methods of manufacturing ethanol.

2 Evaluate the advantages and disadvantages of making ethanol from renewable and non-renewable resources.

Using ethanol

People use lots of ethanol – as a solvent, as a disinfectant, as a fuel, and in alcoholic drinks. So the demand for ethanol is high.

There are two ways of making ethanol. Each has its pros and cons.

Ethanol from ethene

In this method, ethene reacts with steam in the presence of a catalyst. Ethanol is the product of this **hydration reaction**.

ethene + steam → ethanol

$$\text{H} \qquad C_2H_4 + H_2O \rightarrow C_2H_5OH$$

The reaction works well at about 300 °C

Ethanol from sugars

Ethanol can also be produced by **fermentation**. In fermentation, **enzymes** (natural catalysts) in yeast break down plant sugars into ethanol and carbon dioxide. For example:

glucose → ethanol + carbon dioxide

$$\text{H} \qquad C_6H_{12}O_6 \rightarrow 2C_2H_5OH + 2CO_2$$

The reaction works best at about 37 °C.

Comparing the two ways of producing ethanol

	From ethene by hydration	From plant materials by fermentation
Raw materials	Ethene is produced from crude oil, which is non-renewable.	Plant materials are renewable.
Energy costs	Higher – both the cracking reaction to produce ethene, and the hydration reaction take place at high temperatures.	Lower – fermentation takes place at a lower temperature but the crops may require input such as fertiliser.

Working to Grade E

1 Tick the boxes to show which of the substances listed below are produced from crude oil:

poly(ethene) ☐   diesel ☐

petrol ☐   wool ☐

paper ☐

2 Draw lines to match each polymer use to the properties that make it suitable for this use.

Polymer use	Property
Dental fillings.	Allows water vapour to pass through its tiny pores, but not liquid water.
To make disposable nappies.	Hard and tough and a poor conductor of heat.
To make 'breathable' waterproof fabrics.	Changes shape in response to warming or pressure.
To make mattresses that mould to the body.	Absorbs large volumes of liquid.

3 Highlight the statements below that are true. Then write corrected versions of the statements that are false.

  a Monomers are small molecules that join together to form polymers.

  b A molecule of poly(ethene) is made by joining together thousands of ethane molecules.

  c Polymers have very big molecules.

  d The monomer propene makes poly(propane).

4 Choose words from the box below to fill in the gaps in the sentences that follow. The words in the box may be used once, more than once, or not at all.

> decomposition bigger smaller catalyst
> condense steam vapourise vapours
> liquids combustion

Hydrocarbons are cracked to make substances with _____ molecules. The process involves heating the hydrocarbons to _____ them. Next the _____ are passed over a hot _____, or mixed with _____ and heated to a very high temperature. Thermal _____ reactions then occur.

Working to Grade C

5 Draw lines to match each name below to a molecular formula and a structural formula.

Molecular formula	Name	Structural formula
C_2H_4	Ethene	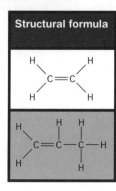
C_3H_6	Propene	

6 Alkenes have the general formula C_nH_{2n}. Tick the boxes to show which of the hydrocarbons below are alkenes.

C_4H_8 ☐ C_5H_{12} ☐

$C_{12}H_{26}$ ☐ C_7H_{14} ☐

7 A student bubbles four hydrocarbons through bromine water. Complete this table to show his expected observations.

Name of hydrocarbon	Results
Ethane	
Propene	
Ethene	
Butane	

8 Complete the equations below to show how poly(ethene) and poly(propene) are made from their monomers.

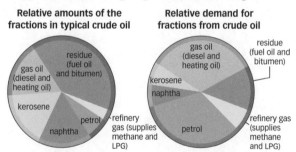

9 Oil companies often crack the naphtha fraction in crude oil. The process produces hydrocarbons in the petrol fraction. Use data from these pie charts to suggest how cracking might benefit oil companies.

Relative amounts of the fractions in typical crude oil

Relative demand for fractions from crude oil

10 Complete this table to summarise the two ways of manufacturing ethanol.

Starting materials	Type of reaction	Conditions
Glucose		
		needs catalyst

11 Complete this table to show the environmental advantages and disadvantages of making ethanol from ethene and from glucose.

	Advantages	Disadvantages
From **ethene**		
From **glucose**		

12 A city council is deciding whether or not to provide a plastic recycling collection to all homes in the city. Describe the benefits and problems of recycling polymer waste.

1   This diagram shows the apparatus that can be used to crack a hydrocarbon in the laboratory.

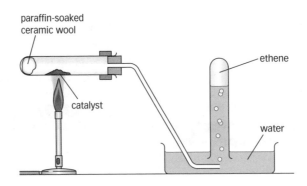

a   What type of reaction occurs in the boiling tube?

Tick the **one** correct box.

Type of reaction	Tick
Reduction	
Oxidation	
Combustion	
Thermal decomposition	

(1 mark)

b   The aluminium oxide shown in the apparatus above is not used up in the reaction. What is its purpose?

....

(1 mark)

c   One product of the cracking reaction is ethene.

The displayed formula of ethene is

$$\underset{H}{\overset{H}{>}}C=C\underset{H}{\overset{H}{<}}$$

i   Give the molecular formula of ethene.

....

(1 mark)

ii   Describe a chemical test to show that ethene has a double bond. Include the name of the chemical you need, brief instructions for doing the test, and the changes you would expect to see.

....

....

....

(3 marks)
(Total marks: 6)

2 In 2002, Bangladesh became one of the first countries to ban the use of all polythene bags in its capital city. The bags were found to have blocked the city's drainage system, which helped to cause severe flooding in 1988 and 1998.

a Give a scientific reason to explain why some polythene bags remained in drainage ditches for many years.

....
(1 mark)

b Today, many bags in Bangladesh are made from a plant material, jute. Suggest two advantages of making bags from jute compared to making them from polythene.

1 ....

2 ....
(2 marks)
(Total marks: 3)

3 Read the information in the box below, then answer the questions that follow.

Poly(butene) is a polymer. It is flexible and withstands large forces without being damaged. It is slightly elastic (stretchy). It does not react with detergents, oils, fats, acids, bases, alcohols, or hot water. Over time, it may react with chlorine and its compounds.

Poly(butene) has been used to make water pipes since the early 1970s. In Vienna, Austria, hot water from underground travels through poly(butene) pipes to heat homes. In the UK, many water pipes are made from poly(butene).

a Complete the equation below to show how poly(butene) is made from its monomer. Include the structural formula of poly(butene).

(3 marks)

b **i** Explain why poly(butene) is a suitable material from which to make water pipes.

....

....
(2 marks)

ii In Canada, poly(butene) pipes are no longer used to transport drinking water to which chlorine and its compounds have been added. Suggest why.

....

....
(2 marks)
(Total marks: 7)

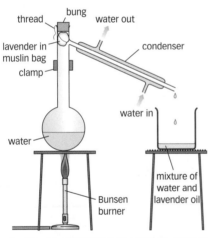

▲ Steam distillation is used to extract lavender oil. Note: in this diagram, the apparatus has been simplified.

Vegetable oils

The fruit, seeds, and nuts of some plants are rich in natural oils. These oils are called **vegetable oils**.

Extracting vegetable oils

Oils are extracted from different plants in different ways:

- Olive oil is extracted by crushing and **pressing** olives. The oil is then separated from water and other impurities.
- The flow diagram below shows how sunflower oil is extracted from sunflower seeds.

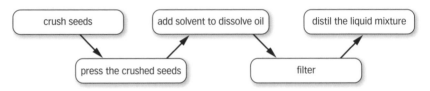

▲ Extracting sunflower oil from sunflower seeds.

- Lavender oil is extracted by **steam distillation**. The process produces a mixture of water and lavender oil. Water is removed from the mixture, and pure lavender oil remains.

Vegetable oils as food

Vegetable oils are important foods. They provide **nutrients**, such as vitamin E. They also release a lot of energy when digested, so eating large amounts of oil-rich foods can make people gain weight.

Vegetable oils boil at higher temperatures than water. So oils can cook foods at higher temperatures than boiling water. This means that:

- food cooks more quickly in oil
- a food cooked in oil tastes different to the same food cooked in water.

Vegetable oils as fuels

Since vegetable oils release large amounts of energy on burning, they are useful as vehicle fuels.

Questions

1	Name three plant parts from which oils may be extracted.
2	Describe how olive oil is extracted from olives.
3	Explain why vegetable oils can be used as vehicle fuels.

Emulsions

You cannot mix vegetable oils with water. This is because their particles are too different. Vegetable oil molecules include long hydrocarbon chains. These chains cannot interact with small water molecules.

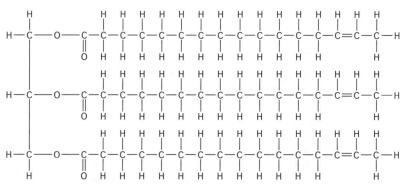

▲ A typical vegetable oil molecule.

But if you add an **emulsifier** to oil and water and shake well, the oil and water no longer separate out. The emulsifier stabilises the mixture. An **emulsion** forms.

Emulsions are thicker than oil or water. Their uses depend on their properties. Emulsions include:
- salad dressing – its thickness means it coats salad well
- icecream – its texture helps make it enjoyable to eat
- paints – their thickness means they coat walls well
- cosmetics such as hand creams, shaving cream, and sun screens

H Emulsifiers

Emulsifiers include egg – this prevents the oil and vinegar in mayonnaise separating. Emulsifier molecules have two ends:
- One end interacts with water molecules. This is the **hydrophilic end**.
- One end interacts well with oil molecules, and does not interact with water molecules. This is the **hydrophobic end**.

This diagram shows how emulsifier molecules stop an oil droplet separating from water.

Emulsifier safety

Egg is a natural emulsifier. Some foods contain artificial emulsifiers. These are identified by **E-numbers**. Additives with E-numbers have been safety tested and licensed by the European Union.

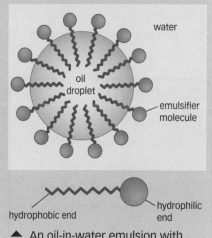

▲ An oil-in-water emulsion with emulsifier molecules.

Unsaturated oils

Sunflower oil is **unsaturated**. It contains double bonds between some of the carbon atoms in its molecules. You can represent a carbon–carbon double bond like this:

$$C=C$$

You can use bromine water to detect carbon–carbon double bonds.

orange bromine water

bromine water becomes colourless when an unsaturated oil is mixed with it.

▲ Orange bromine water becomes colourless when shaken with an unsaturated vegetable oil.

Coconut oil is **saturated**. Its molecules do not have double bonds between their carbon atoms. Saturated fats raise blood cholesterol and increase the risk of heart disease. Unsaturated fats are better for health.

Exam tip AQA

Remember the difference between saturated and unsaturated fats, and how to test for unsaturation.

Questions

1 Explain what an emulsion is.

2 Describe how to test a vegetable oil to find out whether or not it is unsaturated.

3 H Describe how unsaturated vegetable oils can be hardened.

H Hardening vegetable oils

Most vegetable oils are liquid at room temperature. Food companies harden unsaturated vegetable oils by adding hydrogen gas to them. The conditions for the reaction are:

- a temperature of 60 °C
- a nickel catalyst.

In these **hydrogenation** reactions, hydrogen atoms add to the carbon atoms on both sides of a double bond:

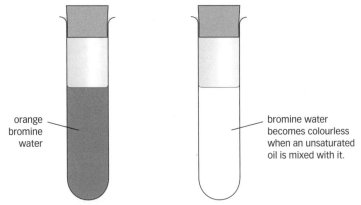

▲ This diagram shows just part of a plant oil molecule.

Hydrogenation reactions convert unsaturated oils into **saturated** ones. Saturated fats have higher melting points that unsaturated ones. So they are useful as spreads and for making cakes and pastries.

Working to Grade E

1 Tick the boxes to show the plant parts from which oils may be extracted.

seeds ☐   roots ☐
stem ☐   fruit ☐
nuts ☐

2 The statements below describe the steps in extracting sunflower oil from sunflower seeds. Write the letters of the steps in the best order.
   a Add a solvent.   c Distil the mixture.
   b Crush the seeds.   d Press the crushed seeds.

3 Highlight the statements below that are true. Then write corrected versions of the statements that are false.
   a Oils dissolve well in water.
   b A vegetable oil and water can be used to make an emulsion.
   c Emulsifiers make emulsions less stable.
   d A student shakes a mixture of oil, vinegar, and sugar. Afterwards, he sees two layers of liquid. This shows that sugar is an emulsifier.

4 This diagram shows the laboratory apparatus used to extract lavender oil from lavender plants.

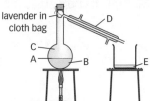

Answer each question below with the letter A, B, C, D or E. You may use each letter once, more than once, or not at all.
   a Where in the apparatus is a gas condensing?
   b Where is a liquid evaporating?
   c Which piece of apparatus contains water and lavender oil?
   d Which piece of apparatus contains tap water?

Working to Grade C

5 A student adds four plant oils to separate samples of bromine water. Her results are in the table below.

Name of oil	Observations on adding the oil to bromine water
Sunflower oil	Colour change from orange to colourless.
Coconut oil	Orange colour of bromine water is unchanged.
Palm oil	Orange colour of bromine water is unchanged.
Olive oil	Colour change from orange to colourless.

   a Name the oils that are saturated.
   b Name the oils that contain no double bonds between carbon atoms (C = C bonds).

6 Catherine and Sarah cook potatoes. Each uses a different cooking method. The table shows the energy released when they eat the potatoes.

Cook	Energy released per 100 g (kJ)
Catherine	1012
Sarah	288

   a Who cooked the potatoes in oil? Give a reason for your decision.
   b Give two advantages of cooking potatoes in oil, compared to boiling in water.
   c Give one disadvantage of cooking potatoes in oil, compared to boiling in water.

7 a A doctor tells Alan to reduce the total amount of fat that he eats. Suggest why.
   b A doctor tells Jim to avoid saturated fats, and to eat unsaturated oils instead. Suggest why.

8 A student does an investigation to compare the energy released by three plant oils. He uses the apparatus below.
   a Identify the dependent and independent variables for the investigation.
   b Identify two control variables.
   c Explain how the student can use results from the investigation to work out which oil releases the most energy on burning.

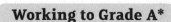

Working to Grade A*

9 The diagram opposite shows a droplet of water surrounded by oil in an emulsion, and some emulsifier molecules. Which end of the emulsifier molecule is hydrophilic? Give a reason for your choice.

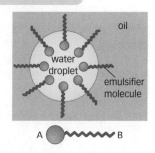

10 A company produces hardened oils from unsaturated vegetable oils.
   a Name the chemical that is added to unsaturated oils in order to harden them.
   b Give the conditions for the hardening process.
   c Describe one difference in the properties of an unsaturated oil and the hardened oil that is made from it.
   d Give two uses of hardened vegetable oils. Explain how their properties make them suitable for this use.

1 A student does an experiment to identify substances that act as emulsifiers.

- He places 3 cm³ of corn oil and 3 cm³ of water in a boiling tube.
- He adds a small amount of detergent.
- He puts a bung in the top of the boiling tube, and shakes.
- He repeats the experiment, using different substances instead of the detergent.

His results are given in the table below.

Name of substance	Observations
Detergent	Thick cream liquid. Can't see through it.
Salt	Two separate layers.
Mustard powder	Thick yellow liquid. Can't see through it.
Egg yolk	Thick yellow liquid. Can't see through it.
Flour	Two separate layers.

a Name the substances in the table that are emulsifiers.

....

(1 mark)

b i Salad dressing is an emulsion made from oil and vinegar. Explain why its properties make it suitable for use as a salad dressing.

....

(1 mark)

ii Name **two** other uses of emulsions.

....

(2 marks)

H

c This diagram shows a droplet of oil surrounded by water in an emulsion, and some emulsifier molecules.

Which end of an emulsifier molecule is hydrophobic?
Give a reason for your choice.

....

....

....

....

....

....

(2 marks)

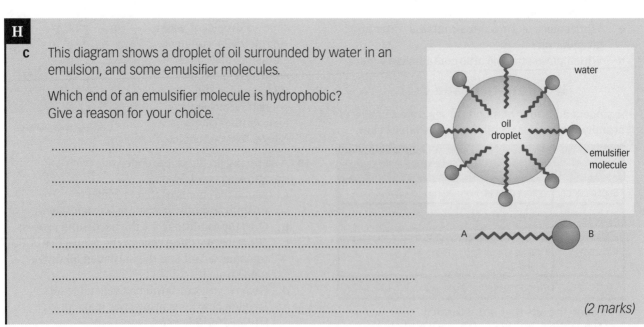

(Total marks: 6)

2 Describe **three** advantages and/or disadvantages of cooking potatoes in oil compared to cooking them in water.

....

....

....

(3 marks)

(Total marks: 3)

3 A teacher added bromine water to samples of four vegetable oils, then shook the mixtures. Her results are in the table below.

Vegetable oil sample	Observations
A	Orange bromine water became colourless.
B	Orange bromine water became colourless.
C	Orange colour did not change.
D	Orange colour did not change.

a **i** Give the letters of the **two** saturated vegetable oils in the table.

.... and ....

(1 mark)

ii Draw a ring around the one correct **bold** word or phrase in the sentence below.

Saturated vegetable oils have **zero/one/more than one** double bonds between carbon atoms.

(1 mark)

H

b **i** Describe and explain how unsaturated vegetable oils can be hardened to make hydrogenated vegetable oils.

....

....

....

(3 marks)

ii Give **two** uses of hydrogenated vegetable oils, and explain what makes them suitable for these uses.

1 ....

2 ....

(2 marks)

(Total marks: 7)

Revision objectives

- ✓ describe the structure of the Earth
- ✓ give evidence for Wegener's theory of crustal movement
- ✓ explain what tectonic plates are and how they move
- ✓ explain why it is not possible to predict exactly when earthquakes and volcanic eruptions will occur

Student book references

1.28 Inside the Earth

1.29 Moving continents

Specification key

✓ C1.7.1

Inside the Earth

The Earth consists of a **core**, **mantle**, and **crust**.

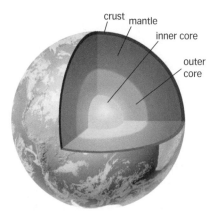

▲ The structure of the Earth.

Surrounding the Earth is a mixture of gases. This is the **atmosphere**. All the minerals and other resources that humans need come from the Earth's crust, the oceans, or the atmosphere.

Tectonic plates

The Earth's crust and upper part of the mantle are cracked into approximately 12 huge pieces, called **tectonic plates**.

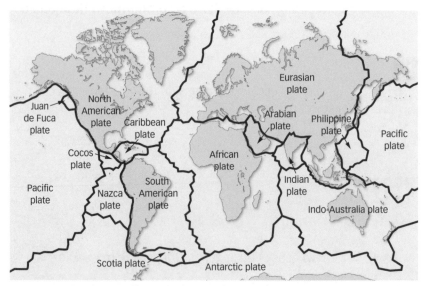

▲ Tectonic plates.

Tectonic plates are less dense than the part of the mantle that is below them, so they rest on top of it. The mantle is mostly solid but can move slowly.

Deep inside the Earth, natural radioactive processes heat the mantle. The heat drives convection currents within the mantle. These convection currents make tectonic plates move. They move slowly, at relative speeds of a few centimetres a year.

Earthquakes and volcanoes

Earthquakes and volcanic eruptions occur where tectonic plates meet.

- **Earthquakes** happen when tectonic plates move against each other suddenly. Scientists cannot predict when these movements will happen, so people living on plate boundaries can expect an earthquake at any time.
- Many **volcanoes** are at tectonic plate boundaries. Volcanoes often show signs of eruption in advance but the timing of an eruption depends on many factors. It is difficult to predict eruptions exactly.

Wegener's theory

For many years, some scientists thought that mountains and valleys were formed by the shrinking of the crust as the Earth cooled following its formation.

In 1912, Wegener put forward a new theory to explain the features of the Earth. He suggested that the continents were once joined together, and had gradually moved apart. Wegener supported his theory with evidence:

- The shapes of Africa and South America look as if they might once have fitted together.
- There are fossils of the same plants on both continents.
- There are rocks of the same type at the edges of the two continents where they might once have been joined.

At the time, most scientists did not accept Wegener's theory of **crustal movement**, or **continental drift**. This was because:

- Wegener was not a geologist
- they could not see *how* the continents might have moved.

Since the 1950s, scientists have discovered more evidence supporting Wegener's theory. Now his ideas are generally accepted.

Exam tip

Practise interpreting diagrams about Wegener's theory, and about the locations of earthquakes and volcanoes.

Questions

1. List the three sources of all the minerals and other resources that humans need.

2. At what speeds do tectonic plates move?

3. Explain what makes the Earth's mantle move.

4. Give three pieces of evidence to support Wegener's theory of crustal movement.

Revision objectives

- state the proportions of gases in the modern atmosphere
- describe one theory that explains how the early atmosphere was formed, and why the proportion of carbon dioxide decreased
- describe a scientific theory that explains how life began

Student book references

1.30 Gases in the air

1.31 Forming the atmosphere

Specification key

✔ C1.7.2 a–g

The modern atmosphere

For 200 million years, the proportions of gases in the atmosphere have been much the same as they are today.

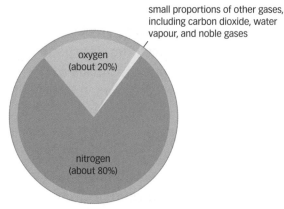

small proportions of other gases, including carbon dioxide, water vapour, and noble gases

oxygen (about 20%)

nitrogen (about 80%)

▲ This pie chart shows the proportions of the main gases in the air

Forming the atmosphere

During the first billion years of the Earth's existence, many volcanoes erupted. The gases from these eruptions formed the early atmosphere. Water vapour from the eruptions condensed to form the oceans.

There are several theories about how the atmosphere was formed. One theory suggests that the early atmosphere was mainly carbon dioxide gas. There were small amounts of water vapour, methane, and ammonia. There was little or no oxygen gas, like the modern atmospheres of Mars and Venus.

H Life begins

In this early atmosphere, life began. No one can be sure exactly how, or when, because no one was around to make observations at the time. There are several scientific theories to explain the origin of life.

One of these theories, the **primordial soup theory**, involves the interaction between:
- hydrocarbon compounds
- ammonia
- lightning.

According to the theory, gases in the early atmosphere reacted with each other in the presence of lightning, or sunlight, to make the complex molecules that are the basis of life.

In 1953, two scientists did an experiment to test the theory. The **Miller–Urey experiment** simulated a lightning spark in a mixture of the gases of the early atmosphere. A week later, more than 2% of the carbon in the system had formed compounds from which the proteins in living cells are made.

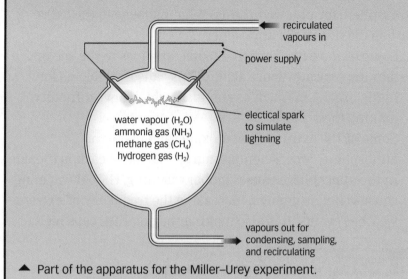

▲ Part of the apparatus for the Miller–Urey experiment.

Where did the oxygen come from?

Plants make their food by **photosynthesis**. They take carbon dioxide from the atmosphere and release oxygen gas.

carbon dioxide + water → glucose + oxygen

The photosynthesis of early plants and algae removed carbon dioxide from the atmosphere, and added oxygen gas to it.

What happened to the carbon dioxide?

Some of the carbon dioxide from the early atmosphere was removed by plants. But not all of it. What happened to the rest?

Locking up carbon in rocks

Much carbon dioxide dissolved in the oceans. Shellfish and other sea creatures used some of this dissolved carbon dioxide in making their shells and skeletons. The animals died and fell to the bottom of the sea. After many years, limestone, a **sedimentary rock**, formed from their shells and skeletons. The carbon atoms were locked away in the calcium carbonate of the limestone.

Locking up carbon in fossil fuels

Millions of years ago, dead animals and plants decayed under swamps. The dead organisms formed **fossil fuels**. The carbon atoms of the plants and animals were locked up in underground stores of coal, oil, and gas.

Questions

1 List the main gases in the modern atmosphere, and give their proportions.

2 Explain why the proportion of carbon dioxide in the atmosphere is less now than it was millions of years ago.

3 Explain why no one knows how life began.

Revision objectives

- ✓ describe some impacts of the recent increase in the proportion of carbon dioxide in the atmosphere
- ✓ name some products that we obtain from the air, and state how they are extracted

Student book references

1.32 The carbon cycle

Specification key

✓ C1.7.2 h–j

Exam tip   AQA

Remember the problems caused by adding extra carbon dioxide to the oceans and to the atmosphere.

Carbon dioxide – on the up

Today, humans burn fossil fuels. This puts extra carbon dioxide into the atmosphere. Humans also destroy forests, which mean that less carbon dioxide is removed from the atmosphere for photosynthesis. What happens to the extra carbon dioxide in the atmosphere?

- Some of the extra carbon dioxide dissolves in the oceans, making seawater more acidic. This causes problems for living organisms such as shellfish, which have difficulty making their shells.
- Some of the extra carbon dioxide remains in the atmosphere. Most scientists agree that extra carbon dioxide in the atmosphere causes global warming. Global warming causes climate change, increasing the frequency of extreme weather events. It is also making the polar ice caps melt.

H Using gases from the air

The gases in the air have different boiling points. This means that the gases can be separated by fractional distillation. The fractional distillation of air provides:

- nitrogen gas, which is used as a raw material to make fertiliser, and to freeze food
- oxygen gas, for medical treatments
- noble gases, including argon and neon. Argon is used in double glazing. Neon is used in display lighting.

Questions

1 Explain why the oceans are becoming more acidic. Describe one problem this increasing acidity may cause.

2 **H** List three gases that are obtained by the fractional distillation of air, and give a use of each gas.

Questions
Changes in the Earth and its atmosphere

1 Label the different parts of the Earth's structure. Use these words: **mantle, crust, core**.

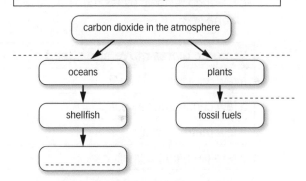

2 In each sentence below, highlight the correct **bold** word or phrase.

   a Tectonic plates consist of huge slabs of the Earth's **crust/crust and upper part of the mantle**.

   b The mantle is mainly **solid/liquid**.

   c The movement of tectonic plates is caused by **convection currents/ocean currents**.

   d The currents that make tectonic plates move are driven by natural **combustion reactions/ radioactive processes**.

3 Complete the table below to show the percentage of each gas in the Earth's atmosphere today.

Gas	Percentage
Nitrogen	
	20
Carbon dioxide, water vapour, noble gases	

4 Complete the sentences below using the words in the box.

> **oxygen   algae   photosynthesis
> carbon dioxide**

Plants and _____ take in _____ gas from the atmosphere. They use this gas in a process called _____. As a result of this process, they produce _____ gas.

5 Tick the boxes next to sources from which humans obtain minerals and other resources.

   a Earth's crust ☐

   b Earth's core ☐

   c Earth's mantle ☐

   d oceans ☐

   e Earth's atmosphere ☐

   f atmosphere of Mars ☐

6 Highlight the sentences below that are true. Then write corrected versions of the statements that are false.

   a Burning fossil fuels increases the amount of carbon dioxide in the atmosphere.

   b Over the past few years, the amount of carbon dioxide absorbed by the oceans has decreased.

   c Most scientists agree that the decreasing amounts of carbon dioxide in the atmosphere are causing global warming.

   d The oceans act as a reservoir, or store, for carbon dioxide.

7 In 1912, Wegener proposed his theory of crustal movement, or continental drift.

   a List three pieces of evidence that Wegener used to support his theory.

   b Give two reasons to explain why other scientists did not at first support the theory.

8 During the first billion years of the Earth's existence, volcanoes released huge amounts of carbon dioxide into the atmosphere. Then, the percentage of carbon dioxide in the atmosphere gradually decreased. Complete the flow diagram below to summarise one theory that explains this decrease. Use the words and phrases in the box.

> **dissolving   photosynthesis
> decay in absence of oxygen
> sedimentary rock**

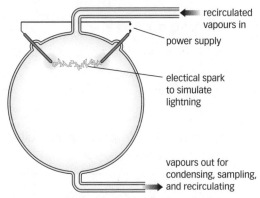

9 Describe the 'primordial soup' theory of the origin of life.

10 This diagram shows part of the apparatus for the Miller–Urey experiment, which was designed to test the 'primordial soup' theory.

   a What does the electrical spark simulate?

   b Name two types of molecule that reacted together in the Miller–Urey experiment.

   c Explain why no-one knows whether or not the 'primordial soup' theory is correct.

11 a Name the process by which the gases of the air can be separated.

   b Give the names of two noble gases that are obtained from the air by this process, and give one use for each gas.

1 In February 2010, there was an earthquake off the coast of Chile. About 500 people died. This map shows the epicentre of the earthquake and the tectonic plates in the region.

a What are tectonic plates made up of? Tick **one** box.

Tectonic plates are made up of . . .	Tick
the Earth's crust.	
the Earth's crust and the whole thickness of the mantle.	
the Earth's crust and the upper part of the mantle.	
the Earth's crust and the upper core.	

(1 mark)

b How fast do tectonic plates move, relative to each other? Tick **one** box.

Tectonic plates move at a speed of . . .	Tick
a few millimetres a year.	
a few centimetres a year.	
a few metres a year.	
a few kilometres a year.	

(1 mark)

c Explain what makes tectonic plates move.

....

....

(2 marks)

d Look at the map above.

Explain why there is a greater risk of earthquakes in Santiago than there is in Brasilia.

....

(1 mark)

e Explain why scientists cannot accurately predict when earthquakes will happen.

....

....

(1 mark)
(Total marks: 6)

2 This table shows the composition of the atmosphere of the planet Mars.

Gas	Percentage in atmosphere of Mars
Carbon dioxide	95
Nitrogen	3
Argon	1.6
Oxygen, methane, water vapour	Very small amounts

a i Sketch a line graph, bar chart, or pie chart to represent the information in the table. Make sure you sketch the most appropriate type of graph or chart.

(2 marks)

ii Use the information in the table, and your own knowledge, to describe one similarity and one difference between the modern atmospheres of Mars and the Earth.

Similarity: ....

Difference: ....
(2 marks)

b There are several theories about how the modern atmosphere of the Earth was formed. One theory suggests that the early atmosphere of the Earth was similar to that of Mars today.

i Where did the carbon dioxide of the Earth's early atmosphere come from?

....
(1 mark)

ii Describe **two** ways by which carbon dioxide was removed from the early atmosphere. Include scientific words in your answer.

....

....
(2 marks)

c The concentration of carbon dioxide in the atmosphere has been increasing for the past 150 years. Give **two** reasons for this increase.

....

....
(2 marks)
(Total marks: 9)

Societal aspects of scientific evidence

This module includes examples of scientific issues that are influenced by the views of a wide range of people and organisations. It also includes examples of the use of scientific knowledge to make technological advances.

You may be asked to link developments in science to ethical, social, economic, or environmental issues. The example below supports you in identifying, explaining, and evaluating these links

Using vegetable oils as vehicle fuels

Skill – Analysing the facts and making deductions

A government asks three scientists to investigate using a fuel made from oilseed rape to replace petrol and diesel in cars. The scientists compare the factors below:
- the energy released on burning the fuels
- the land areas needed to grow and process the oilseed rape, and to obtain petrol and diesel from crude oil
- the waste products made when the fuels burn in cars.

Scientists from several organisations do the research, including:
- a scientist working at an oil company
- a scientist employed by a company that processes oilseed rape plants to make fuel
- a university research scientist funded by an independent charity.

1   Which of the scientists listed may be biased? Give a reason for your choice(s).

To answer this question, you will need to think about who is paying for the research. Would the funder prefer one outcome to another? You also need to consider the organisations the scientists work for – might they profit if the results of the research show one thing rather than another?

There is no one right answer to this question; it is your reasoning that is important here.

2   Suggest one other factor that might influence which scientist's work the government takes most seriously.

Again, there is no one right answer. You could mention things like the scientists' qualifications, experience, or status.

Skill – Understanding the impact of a decision

3   Below are some people's opinions about the two types of fuel. Sort the opinions into four groups depending on whether they are using ethical arguments, environmental arguments, economic arguments, or social arguments.

Georgia – I think that oilseed rape fuel produces more particulate pollution on burning than petrol does.

Hari – It is not right to grow fuel crops on land that could be used to grow food for starving people.

Imogen – Growing and processing oilseed rape in order to make fuel could provide many new jobs.

Julia – Obtaining and processing fossil fuels to get petrol and diesel is very expensive, and is likely to get even more costly in future.

Krishnan – Oilseed rape crops remove carbon dioxide from the atmosphere as they grow. So this fuel contributes less to global warming.

Lydia – I work for an oil company. Our profits will decrease if oilseed rape fuel replaces petrol and diesel.

This part of the question is asking you to identify four types of impact of producing and using the fuels.
- **Environmental impacts** are effects on the surroundings in which plants and animals live.
- **Social impacts** are impacts on people, or groups of people.
- **Economic impacts** are to do with money.
- **Ethical impacts** are to do with morals – is an action right or wrong?

Skill – Applying scientific principles to problems

4   Look again at the opinions of Georgia, Hari, Imogen, Julia, Krishnan, and Lydia. Which of the opinions could be investigated scientifically? Give a reason for your answer.

Here, you need to distinguish between questions that can be answered by doing investigations or studying data, and those that science cannot answer directly.

AQA Upgrade

Answering an extended writing question

In this question you will be assessed on using good English, organising information clearly, and using specialist terms where appropriate.

Identify the benefits and drawbacks of using plant oils to produce vehicle fuels, compared to producing fuels from crude oil. In your answer, you should state whether each benefit and drawback relates to social, economic, or environmental issues.

(6 marks)

QUESTION

G–E

Plant oils are cheeper than crude oil – economic advantige! I think its becoz its easier to grow plants than get oil from under the north see!!!

Examiner: This answer is worth two marks out of six. It is typical of a grade F or G candidate.

The answer includes one economic advantage of plant oils compared to crude oil. There are several spelling and punctuation mistakes.

D–C

Plant oils put carbon dioxide into the atmosfere when you burn them, but the plants take it out wen they grow. This is enviromental.

You grow the plants on land but people are starveing so it wood be better to use the land for food. This is soshal drawback.

Plants oils are reknewable and you can grow them again. This is soshal benifit becoz our grandchilds want fuels for cars two.

Examiner: This answer is worth three marks out of six, and is typical of a grade C or D candidate.

Three impacts of using plant oils have been described, and correctly identified as social, economic, or environmental advantages or disadvantages. The impacts of using plant oils have not been compared to the impacts of using crude oil to produce fuels.

The answer is well organised. There are several spelling mistakes, including words that are given in the question.

B–A*

Some farmers grow plants to make oils for fuel. A social and ethical drawback of this is that the plants grow on land that could be used to grow food. Less land is needed to produce fuels from crude oil.

An environmental benefit is that when the plants grow, they take carbon dioxide from the atmosphere for photosynthesis. But at the same time the tractors for spreading fertilisers put carbon dioxide into the air because they burn diesel. This is an environmental drawback. Both sorts of fuel put carbon dioxide into the air when they burn.

Plants are renewable, but crude oil is not. This is a benefit of making fuels from plant oils.

You can transport both types of fuel easily because they are both liquids. This is a benefit of both.

Examiner: This answer gains six marks out of six, and is typical of an A or A* candidate. All parts of the question are answered, and each benefit or disadvantage is labelled as being a social, economic, or environmental issue.

The answer is logically organised, and includes scientific words. The spelling, punctuation, and grammar are accurate.

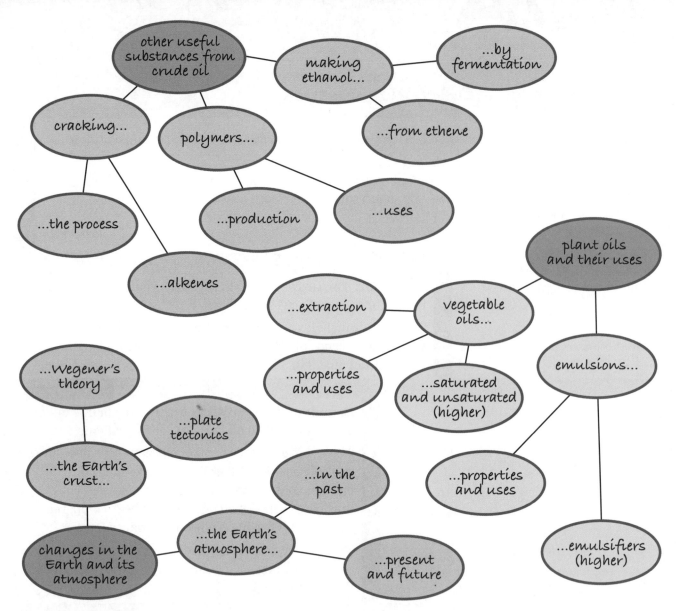

Revision checklist

- Hydrocarbons can be cracked to produce smaller and more useful molecules.
- Unsaturated hydrocarbons called alkenes are produced in cracking reactions.
- Small molecules (monomers) join together in polymerisation reactions to make big molecules (polymers).
- Scientists develop new polymers with properties for particular purposes.
- Ethanol is produced by the hydration of ethene or the fermentation of sugar.
- Vegetable oils are extracted by pressing or distillation from the seeds, fruits, and nuts of some plants.
- Vegetable oils boil at high temperatures and cook food quickly.
- Emulsions are made from vegetable oils and water. They are used in salad dressings, paint, and cosmetics.
- Emulsifiers make emulsions more stable.
- Their molecules have hydrophilic and hydrophobic ends.
- Unsaturated oils have double carbon–carbon bonds. They are better for health than saturated oils.

- Unsaturated oils are hardened by adding hydrogen in the presence of a catalyst at 60 °C.
- The Earth's crust and upper mantle are cracked into tectonic plates.
- Tectonic plates move relative to each other. Sudden movements cause earthquakes at plate boundaries.
- The Earth's atmosphere is about 80% nitrogen and 20% oxygen, with small proportions of carbon dioxide, water vapour, and noble gases.
- One theory suggests the early atmosphere was mainly carbon dioxide from volcanic eruptions.
- Carbon dioxide was removed from the early atmosphere by photosynthesising plants, and by dissolving in the oceans. Carbon from the carbon dioxide became locked up in sedimentary rocks and fossil fuels.
- Burning fossil fuels increases the amount of carbon dioxide in the atmosphere. This causes global warming.

Emitting and absorbing infrared radiation

Energy may be transferred by **infrared radiation** (IR). This is a type of **electromagnetic wave**. It can travel through a vacuum such as space, without the need for any particles.

- All objects emit and absorb infrared radiation.

How much is emitted and absorbed depends on the *temperature* of the material and the *colour of the surface*.

Emission

- Hotter objects emit more infrared radiation than cooler ones.

This is why people show up as bright colours on infrared cameras compared to the darker, cooler surroundings.

- Dark, matt surfaces are *good* **emitters** of infrared radiation.
- Light, shiny surfaces are *poor* emitters of infrared radiation.

Whenever an object emits infrared radiation it gradually cools down. The faster the rate of emission the quicker the object cools. An object designed to reduce the transfer of energy to the surroundings via infrared is often shiny. This reduces the emission of infrared radiation.

Absorption

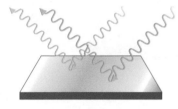 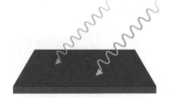

light shiny surface   matt black surface

▲ How infrared radiation is absorbed by different surfaces.

- Dark, matt surfaces are *good* **absorbers** of infrared radiation.
- Light, shiny surfaces are *poor* absorbers of infrared radiation.

A matt black surface is a good absorber of infrared, so heats up quickly. Instead of absorbing infrared radiation, shiny surfaces are good **reflectors**. This means they don't heat up as fast.

Questions

1   Describe how the colour of a surface affects the emission of infrared radiation.

2   Explain why pipes inside solar panels are painted matt black.

Exam tip   AQA

Make sure you can explain why an object might be painted a matt black or shiny silver (either to increase or reduce the rate of energy transfer to its surroundings).

Key words

infrared radiation, electromagnetic wave, emitter, absorber, reflector

Kinetic theory

Everything you see around you is made up of particles.

The particles in **solids**, **liquids**, and **gases** are arranged differently.

Kinetic theory can be used to explain different **states of matter** in terms of particles.

Solids	Liquids	Gases
Particles are regularly arranged, close together, and they are not able to move around, only vibrate.	Particles are a little bit further apart; they are able to move around.	Particles are very far apart and are moving very fast.
solid	liquid	gas

Particle energy

The particles in solids and liquids and gases have different amounts of energy.

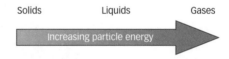

The particles in gases have the most energy as they are moving the fastest. The particles in solids have the lowest energy.

If you increase the **temperature** of a substance, the particles gain energy and move faster. This causes solids to turn to liquids and then eventually into gases.

Questions

1 Draw three diagrams to show how the particles are arranged in solids, liquids, and gases.

2 Explain, in terms of particles, why heating a block of ice causes it to melt and eventually turn into a gas.

Transferring energy

Energy may be transferred from hotter objects to cooler surroundings by **conduction**, **convection**, **evaporation**, and **condensation**. This cools the hotter object, and at the same time warms up the surroundings.

All of these processes involve **particles** and so they cannot take place in a vacuum (like space).

Conduction

Conduction takes place in **solids**. When one end of a solid object is heated the particles in the solid gain energy and vibrate more.

These vibrations are passed on to neighbouring particles and energy is transferred through the solid.

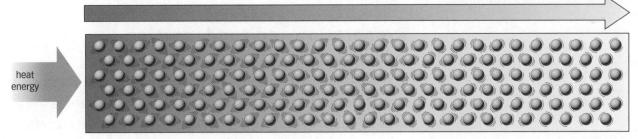

heat energy

▲ Energy can be transferred through a solid via conduction.

Metals are the best **thermal conductors**. Metals contain **free electrons**, which are able to move within the metal. These transfer energy even faster through the metal.

Particles in liquids and gases are too far apart to be good thermal conductors. Liquids and gases are **thermal insulators**.

Convection

Convection can only take place in **fluids** (liquids and gases). In convection particles must be free to move. In a solid the particles are fixed, so convection cannot take place.

Convection occurs when part of the fluid is heated:
- The particles in that region gain kinetic energy and speed up.
- The region expands as the particles move further apart.
- This makes this part of the fluid less dense and it rises.

In convection, hotter regions of fluid rise through colder ones. This transfers energy from hotter regions to cooler ones.

Convection currents can be created. When the hotter fluid has risen, cooler fluid is drawn in to replace it. This is then heated and rises as part of a cycle.

Revision objectives

✔ describe how conduction (including conduction in metals), convection, evaporation, and condensation transfer energy

✔ know the factors that affect the rate of evaporation and condensation

Specification key

✔ P1.1.3 a – b

Student book references

1.3 Conduction

1.4 Convection

1.5 Evaporation and condensation

Exam tip

When describing conduction, don't forget to say that when the particles gain energy they vibrate *more* – not just vibrate (they are always vibrating).
In convection, don't say 'heat rises', instead say 'hotter fluids rise'.

Key words

conduction, convection, evaporation, condensation, particle, solid, thermal conductor, free electrons, thermal insulator, fluid, convection current

The convection current moves through the room. By the time the air reaches here it has lost some of its energy and cooled down slightly.

The air particles gain energy from the radiator. The air becomes less dense than the surrounding air and rises.

The cooler more dense air falls.

Some energy is absorbed by the walls and objects in the room.

▲ Convection currents are used to heat a room.

Convection currents have many uses. For example, the heating element is always placed at the bottom of a kettle. When heated, the hotter water rises – it transfers energy to the rest of the water. The convection current means all the water inside the kettle gets heated.

Evaporation and condensation

Evaporation

Evaporation has a cooling effect on liquid. As a liquid starts to evaporate, the particles with the most energy (those on the surface) leave the liquid and turn into a gas. This transfers energy away from the liquid and so it gets cooler.

This is why we sweat. It helps cool us down by transferring energy from the surface of our skin to the surroundings.

There are three main ways to increase the rate of evaporation from a liquid:
- increase the surface area of the liquid
- pass an air current over the surface (for example, blowing on a hot drink)
- increase the temperature of the liquid.

Condensation

In condensation the reverse happens. When a warm gas strikes a cooler surface the gas turns into a liquid. The temperature of the surface increases as some of the energy from the gas particles is transferred to it.

Questions

1 Explain why metals are the best thermal conductors.

2 Describe how a convection current may form inside a kettle.

3 List the ways to increase the rate of evaporation of a liquid.

Rate of energy transfer

The faster energy is transferred away from an object, the faster it cools.

The bigger the temperature difference between the object and its surroundings, the greater the rate of **energy transfer** by heating. This is why a hot cup of tea cools rapidly at the start, then cools more gradually as it approaches room temperature.

The rate of energy transfer from the object also depends on a number of other factors:

- the object's surface area and volume
- the material from which the object is made
- the nature of the surface that is in contact with the object.

Applications and examples

Cooling fins found in engines are usually metal and painted black. This has three advantages:

- Black: good emitter of infrared radiation – cooling the engine
- Metal: conducts heat away from the engine
- Fins: large surface area, increasing energy transfer through convection and infrared radiation.

Animals in warmer environments have evolved to have larger ears. They have a larger surface area to radiate heat to the surroundings and keep them cool. Animals in cooler environments have small ears. This reduces the transfer of energy to their surroundings, keeping the animal warm.

The vacuum flask is designed to minimise energy transfer. This keeps hot drinks hot and cold drinks cold. It has a number of key features, as listed below.

vacuum layer inside the glass vessel	prevents conduction and convection
shiny silver on both the inside and outside of the glass vessel	poor emitter of IR and good reflector
tight screw cap	reduces convection and evaporation

Questions

1. Produce a summary table showing all the factors that affect the rate of energy transfer away from a hot object. Include a description of the effect each factor has on the rate of energy transfer.

2. Explain how a vacuum flask is able to keep a cold drink cold on a very hot day.

Revision objectives

- ✓ describe how different factors affect the rate of energy transfer by heating, including
- ✓ understand how to vary the rate of energy transfer by heating

Student book references

1.6 Energy transfer by heating

1.7 Comparing energy transfers

Specification key

✓ P1.1.3 c – d

Exam tip AQA

Practise explaining energy transfers with a graph showing how the temperature of a hot drink changes over time.

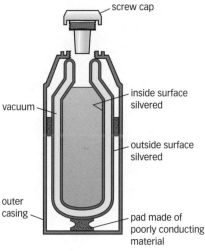

▲ Cross-section of vacuum flask.

Key words

energy transfer

Insulating your home

There are several techniques for insulating homes to reduce energy transferred to the surroundings through conduction, convection, and radiation.

- Cavity-wall **insulation**: a material in between the walls (usually foam) traps air in pockets, reducing conduction and preventing convection.
- Loft insulation: works in the same way as cavity-wall insulation – a material in the loft (usually fibre glass) traps air, reducing conduction and preventing convection.
- Double glazing: conduction is reduced by a layer of air or gas trapped between two panes of glass.
- Draft excluders: energy loss through convection is reduced by making it more difficult to set up convection currents.
- Curtains: reduces energy loss through radiation and conduction, by reducing the energy transfer to the windows.

Each technique reduces the amount of energy needed to heat your home (as less is transferred to the surroundings). This saves money as you do not have to have your heating on for as long or have it set so high (saving on fuel and electricity bills).

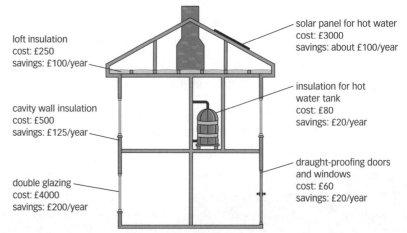

loft insulation
cost: £250
savings: £100/year

cavity wall insulation
cost: £500
savings: £125/year

double glazing
cost: £4000
savings: £200/year

solar panel for hot water
cost: £3000
savings: about £100/year

insulation for hot water tank
cost: £80
savings: £20/year

draught-proofing doors and windows
cost: £60
savings: £20/year

▲ Different ways of reducing your energy consumption.

Exam tip

- Make sure you can explain how a particular method for insulating homes reduces energy transfer (most *trap air* – reducing conduction and convection).
- Remember, solar panels still work on cloudy days, but the water does not get as hot.

U-values

U-values measure how effective a material is as an insulator.
- The lower the U-value the better an insulator.

For example:

Insulator	U-value (relative units)
single glazing	5.0
double glazing	2.9
50-mm loft insulation	0.6
100-mm loft insulation	0.3

Key words

insulation, U-value, payback, solar panel

Payback time

Each technique has a different **payback** time.

This is the time taken before the savings you get each year equal the cost of the materials and installation.

Payback time = cost/savings per year

For example, installing loft insulation may cost £250 but save you £100 per year in heating bills. It has a payback time of 2.5 years.

Heating and solar panels

Some houses have **solar panels** on their roofs. These solar panels contain water that is heated directly by infrared radiation from the Sun.

The infrared radiation is absorbed by the panel and is transferred to the water passing through it. This reduces the cost of heating the water.

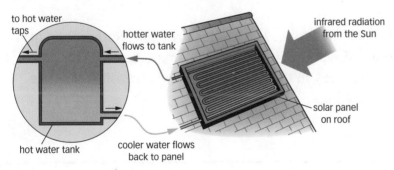

to hot water taps · hotter water flows to tank · infrared radiation from the Sun · solar panel on roof · hot water tank · cooler water flows back to panel

▲ How a solar panel works.

Questions

1 Produce a table to summarise the ways to minimise the energy transfer from a typical home. Explain how each method reduces the energy transfer.

2 Explain how the U-values of different loft insulations may help a home owner purchase the most effective one.

3 Purchasing and installing double glazing costs £1200. After it is installed it saves the home owner £60 per year. Calculate the payback time.

Revision objectives

- ✓ Understand the meaning of the term 'specific heat capacity'
- ✓ Compare the specific heat capacities of different materials
- ✓ Use the equation $E = m \times c \times \theta$

Student book references

1.10 Specific heat capacity

1.11 Uses of specific heat capacity

Specification key

- ✓ P1.1.4 d

Exam tip AQA

- When using the specific heat capacity equation, make sure mass is in kilograms, not grams.
- You may need to rearrange the equation to find the specific heat capacity of a material. Practise doing this before the exam.

Key words

specific heat capacity

What is specific heat capacity?

The **specific heat capacity** of a substance is the amount of energy required to change the temperature of 1 kg of the substance by 1 °C.

Different materials have different specific heat capacities.

An object with low specific heat capacity does not take much energy to increase its temperature. An object with a high specific heat capacity requires more energy to increase the same mass of substance by the same temperature.

Water has a particularly high specific heat capacity, 4200 J/kg°C.

The specific heat capacity equation

$$E = m \times c \times \theta$$

| E | = | m | × | c | × | θ |
| energy transferred (joules, J) | = | mass (kilograms, kg) | × | specific heat capacity (J/kg°C) | × | change in temperature (degrees Celsius, °C) |

Applications of specific heat capacities

Water has a high specific heat capacity and this makes it particularly useful as a coolant in engines. It can absorb a lot of energy before it gets too hot and changes into a gas.

Electrical storage heaters contain large blocks of concrete. These have a high specific heat capacity (although not as high as water). They slowly absorb energy at night (when electricity is cheaper), transferring it to their surroundings during the day.

Oil-filled radiators use the same principle. Rather than heat the air directly, oil inside the radiator is heated. This stores lots of energy in the oil which is slowly transferred to the surroundings.

Questions

1. Explain what is meant by the specific heat capacity of a material.

2. Calculate the energy needed to increase the temperature of 2200 g of water from 20 °C to 90 °C. The specific heat capacity of water is 4200 J/kg°C.

Questions
Energy transfer by heating

1 Highlight the statements below that are **true**. If a statement is **false**, write a corrected version of that statement.
   a All objects emit and absorb infrared radiation.
   b Dark objects are good emitters of infrared radiation.
   c Dark objects are poor emitters of infrared radiation.
   d The particles in a solid are very far apart and move very fast.
   e Conduction takes place in solids. Metals are the best thermal conductors as they contain free electrons.
   f The higher the U-value the better the material is as an insulator.
   g The cost of loft insulation is referred to as payback time.

2 In each sentence below, highlight the correct **bold** word.
   a Shiny surfaces are good **absorbers/reflectors** of infrared radiation.
   b The particles in **liquids/gases** have the most energy.
   c When a liquid evaporates from a surface, the temperature of the surface **increases/decreases.**
   d Water has an unusually **high/low** specific heat capacity.
   e The **bigger/smaller** the temperature difference between an object and its surrounding, the higher the rate of energy transfer.

3 Match the feature of a vacuum flask to the energy transfer it is designed to reduce.

Feature	Reduces energy transfer by...
vacuum	radiation
silvered surface	conduction and convection
tightly fitting lid	convection and evaporation

4 List three techniques to reduce energy transfer from a house.

5 Give two ways to increase the rate of evaporation from a liquid.

6 Draw a diagram to show how energy is transferred through a solid bar by conduction.

7 Complete the sentences below:
   a The rate of energy transfer from warmer objects to _____ objects depends on a number of factors. These include the _____ and _____ _____ of the object, the _____ from which it is made, and the nature of the _____ that is in contact with it.
   b Some animals in warmer climates have _____ ears. This increases the _____ _____ and more energy can be radiated to the _____, keeping the animal cool.

8 The table shows the installation costs and savings made per year for several different home insulation techniques (A, B, and C). For each technique, calculate the payback time.

Technique	Installation cost/£	Savings per year/£	Payback time/year
A	300	50	
B	2000	40	
C	150	15	

9 Explain why the high specific heat capacity of oil makes it useful in oil-filled radiators.

10 An engineering student is designing a component that forms part of a jet engine. She wishes to find out how much energy it would take to heat up the component by 300 °C. The component has a mass of 2.0 kg.
    Complete the table below to find how much energy would be needed for several different materials (A, B, C, and D).
$$E = m \times c \times \theta$$

Material	Specific heat capacity/J/kg°C	Energy required to heat it by 300°C/J
A	900	
B	450	
C	3000	
D	70	

1 This question is about the different techniques used to insulate a typical family home.

a Complete this table to show which energy transfers are reduced by each of the techniques. The first one has been done for you.

Technique	Conduction	Convection	Radiation
Loft insulation	✓	✓	
Cavity-wall insulation			
Double glazing			
Installing curtains			

(3 marks)

b Explain how a home owner might use U-values to determine which type of loft insulation to buy.

....

....

....

(2 marks)

c This table gives information about the costs and savings from some methods of conserving energy in a house.

Technique	Installation cost/£	Savings per year/£
Cavity-wall insulation	200	25
Double glazing	1500	150
100-mm loft insulation	150	10
350-mm loft insulation	300	25

i With a suitable calculation explain which technique should be installed first.

....

....

....

....

(3 marks)

ii Describe what happens to the energy that is 'wasted' from a typical home.

....

....

(2 marks)

d Solar panels could be installed to provide hot water for the house. Explain why the pipes inside most solar panels are painted matt black.

....

....

(2 marks)

(Total marks: 12)

2 Some saucepans have copper bases. Copper is a very good thermal conductor.

a Explain in terms of particles how energy is transferred through the base of the saucepan to its contents when placed on a hot cooking hob.

....

....

....

(2 marks)

b A convection current may form in the water inside the pan. Use the words in the box below to complete the sentences that follow.

You may use each word once, more than once, or not at all.

| faster   energy   rises   less   more   sinks   slower |

When the water is heated the particles gain .... and move .... The particles move

further apart making the water .... dense. The warm water .... and cooler water is

drawn into to replace it.

(4 marks)

c Before the water boils, some of the particles escape from the surface of the liquid and turn into a gas. What is the name given to this process?

....

(1 mark)

d As the water is heated it transfers energy to its surroundings. Describe what happens to the rate at which this energy is transferred as the water gets hotter.

....

(1 mark)

(Total marks: 8)

3 a Explain what is meant by the term 'specific heat capacity'.

....

....

....

(2 marks)

b A kettle is used to heat 1.4 kg of water from 20 °C to 100 °C. Calculate the energy supplied to the kettle and give the unit.

$$E = m \times c \times \theta$$

The specific heat capacity of water is 4200 J/kg °C.

....

....

....

Energy transferred ....

(3 marks)
(Total marks: 5)

Law of conservation of energy

The **law of conservation of energy** is one of the most important rules in all of physics. It states:

- Energy can be *transferred* usefully, stored, or **dissipated** but cannot be *created* or *destroyed*.

There are many different forms of energy:

- **kinetic**
- sound
- light
- heat/thermal
- electrical
- **gravitational potential**
- **elastic potential**
- **chemical**
- **nuclear**

The law of conservation of energy states that energy can be transferred from one form into another. For example, a light bulb transfers electrical energy into heat energy and light energy. But energy can never be created or destroyed.

'Wasting' energy

Energy is often described as being '**wasted**'.

Energy cannot be destroyed; the term 'wasted' refers to energy that has been transferred into a form or forms we no longer require. For example, the heat energy from a light bulb is not usually needed; it can be described as wasted or waste energy.

Waste energy is often transferred to the surroundings as heat. The surroundings become warmer and the energy is slowly dissipated (spread out). As the energy becomes more spread out, it becomes less useful.

Whenever energy is transferred there is always some energy that is wasted.

Revision objectives

- ✔ describe the law of conservation of energy
- ✔ know the meaning of the term 'wasted energy' and describe its effect on an object's surroundings
- ✔ be able to use Sankey diagrams to show energy transfers

Student book references

1.12 Understanding energy

1.13 Useful energy and energy efficiency

Specification key

- ✔ P1.2.1 a – c

Exam tip   AQA

Make sure you can identify which are the **useful** and which are the wasted forms of energy from common devices.

Sankey diagrams

Energy transfers can be represented as special arrowed diagrams called **Sankey diagrams**.

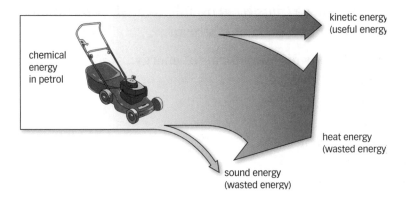

chemical energy in petrol

kinetic energy (useful energy)

heat energy (wasted energy)

sound energy (wasted energy)

▲ Sankey diagram for energy transfers in a petrol mower.

These not only show the energy transfers but how much energy is transferred into each type. The thicker the arrow the greater the proportion of energy transferred into this form.

Remember, energy cannot be created or destroyed so the arrows must not get thinner or thicker. The total energy must stay the same.

Questions

1   Describe the energy changes inside a clockwork radio.

2   Sketch a Sankey diagram for an electric motor.

3   Explain why wasted energy tends to become less useful.

Efficiency

Whenever energy is transferred some of the energy is wasted: not all of the energy can be transferred into useful forms.

- The amount of energy transferred into useful forms, compared to the amount of energy put in, is called the **efficiency**.

Efficiency is measured as a percentage or decimal. For example, a washing machine might be 40% efficient or have an efficiency of 0.4.

This means it transfers 40% of the energy going into it into useful forms. Therefore it wastes 60% of the energy, 60 J for every 100 J supplied.

A more efficient machine transfers a greater proportion of the energy into useful forms. A more efficient washing machine may have an efficiency of 55%.

Appliances and devices can be sorted by their efficiency. A more efficient device wastes a lower proportion of the energy supplied. A device with an efficiency of 80% wastes a lower proportion, and so is more efficient, than a device with an efficiency of 65%. However, no machine can ever be 100% efficient.

Calculating efficiency

The key equation for working out efficiency is

$$\text{efficiency} = \frac{\text{useful energy transferred}}{\text{total energy supplied}}$$

You need to multiply the answer by 100 to get the answer as a percentage.

For example, a light bulb supplied with 300 J of energy transfers 60 J into light and wastes 240 J as heat. Its efficiency is given by:

$$\text{efficiency} = \frac{\text{useful energy transferred (60 J)}}{\text{total energy supplied (300 J)}}$$

efficiency = 0.2 (or 20%)

Exam tip

- When calculating efficiency, be careful to work out which energy is useful and which energy is wasted.
- Remember, the efficiency can never be more than 100% or, if you write it as a ratio, never greater than 1.

Sankey diagram and efficiency

You can compare the efficiency of devices using the information in a Sankey diagram.

The greater the size of the useful arrow, the more efficient the device.

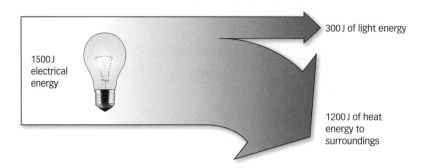

1500 J electrical energy

300 J of light energy

1200 J of heat energy to surroundings

▲ Sankey diagram for a filament lightbulb.

A more efficient light source (like an LED or compact fluorescent tube) will transfer a greater proportional of the electrical energy into light – the arrow showing the useful light output will be wider.

Questions

1 Calculate the efficiency of:

a an electric heater that transfers 1300 J into heat and 700 J into light for every 2000 J supplied

b a petrol engine that wastes 900 J of heat energy for every 1500 J supplied.

2 Calculate the efficiency of the lightbulb shown in the Sankey diagram above.

3 Sketch a Sankey diagram to show the energy transfer by a more efficient light bulb.

Working to Grade E

1 Highlight which of the following are **forms of energy**:

friction vacuum chemical convection elastic potential heat/thermal lift nuclear gravitational potential gravity light sound kinetic generator electrical

2 Complete the sentences below:
   a The law of conservation of energy states that _____ cannot be _____ or _____ but it can be _____ usefully, stored, or _____
   b Energy that has been transferred into a form we no longer need is called .... energy. This energy is usually transferred to the surroundings as .... It becomes more and more spread out, making it less useful.

3 Match the device or situation to the main energy transfers that take place.

Device
kettle
lightbulb
wind-up radio
ball dropped from a height

Main energy transfers
electrical → heat
electrical → heat and light
gravitational potential → kinetic
elastic potential → electrical → sound

4 Highlight the statements below that are **true**. Then write corrected versions of the statements that are **false**.
   a Energy cannot be created or destroyed.
   b Energy is measured in watts.
   c When wasted energy is transferred to the surroundings, the surroundings get cooler.
   d The more efficient a device is, the lower the proportion of energy it wastes.
   e In a Sankey diagram, the greater the size of the useful arrow, the more efficient the device.

Working to Grade C

5 Draw a Sankey diagram to show the energy transfers that take place inside a petrol engine.

6 The table shows the energy transfers for each 200 J supplied to five different light bulbs.

Bulb	Energy transferred into light/J	Energy transferred into heat/J
A	50	150
B	180	
C	120	
D		100
E		60

   a Complete the table (the first row has been done for you).
   b Draw Sankey diagrams for each of the bulbs.
   c Calculate the efficiency of bulb C.
   d Without calculation explain how you can tell which bulb is the most efficient.

7 a Describe the energy changes when a ball is dropped from 1 m above the ground and bounces back up to a height of 70 cm.
   b Explain why the ball does not bounce back up to its original height.

8 An electrical lift is supplied with 5000 J of energy. As it lifts a concrete block it wastes 3500 J as heat and sound.
   a How much energy is transferred usefully by the lift?
   b Describe what happens to the wasted energy.
   c Calculate the efficiency of the lift.

9 A company claims its new kettles are 120% efficient.
   a Explain why this is not possible.
   b Explain why the claims from any company about one of their products should always be supported with evidence collected by independent scientists.

1 a State the law of conservation of energy.

....

....

....

(2 marks)

b Describe the useful energy transfers that take place in the following devices. There may be more than one form of useful energy in each case. This first one has been done for you.

Electric kettle: *Electrical to heat*

Petrol engine: ....

TV: ....

Car battery: ....

(3 marks)

c i Draw a Sankey diagram to show the energy transfers for a typical electric filament lamp. You should consider the relative sizes of the arrows on your diagram.

(2 marks)

ii Explain how your diagram would be different for an energy-efficient lamp.

....

....

....

(2 marks)

(Total marks: 9)

2 a i Explain what is meant by the term 'wasted energy'.

....

....

(2 marks)

ii When wasted energy is transferred to the surroundings it becomes less useful. Explain why.

....

(1 mark)

b i A radio is supplied with 300 kJ of electrical energy. It transfers 50 kJ into sound. Assuming there are no other energy transfers, how much energy is wasted as heat?

....

Wasted energy .... kJ

(1 mark)

ii Calculate the percentage efficiency of the radio.

$$\text{efficiency} = \frac{\text{useful energy out}}{\text{total energy in}} (\times 100)$$

....

....

Efficiency .... %

(2 marks)
(Total marks: 6)

Revision objectives

- ✔ give examples of energy transfers from common electrical devices
- ✔ compare the advantages and disadvantages of different electrical devices
- ✔ calculate the energy transferred by electrical devices

Student book references

1.14 Using electricity

Specification key

✔ P1.3.1 a – c

Exam tip　AQA

Power can be expressed in **kilowatts**. Remember to convert this into watts (1 kW = 1000 W).

Electrical devices

Electrical devices are incredibly useful. Electricity can be transferred into most other forms of energy. Some examples are given in the table below:

Device	Energy in	Main forms of energy out
Kettle	electrical	heat, kinetic
Toaster	electrical	heat, light
Electric motor	electrical	heat, sound, kinetic
Speaker	electrical	sound, kinetic
Computer	electrical	heat, light, sound, kinetic

Different electrical devices have advantages and disadvantages. For example, a battery-powered radio will run for a long time but eventually the batteries will need to be replaced. A mains-electricity-powered radio will run for even longer, but cannot be used on the move.

Electrical energy transfers

The amount of electrical energy transferred by an electrical device depends on two factors:

- how long the device is used for
- the **power** of the device.

A more powerful device may be used for a shorter time and so may use less energy than a less powerful device, which has to be used for longer.

You can calculate the power of an device using the equation below:

$$E = P \times t$$

electrical energy transferred (**joules**, J) = power of device (**watts**, W) × time used for (**seconds**, s)

Reducing energy consumption

It is important to try to reduce our energy consumption. This not only saves us money, but it also conserves our natural resources and means less electricity needs to be generated.

There are several different methods to do this:
- Replace inefficient filament lightbulbs with low-energy lighting (compact fluorescent bulbs or LEDs).
- Consider replacing older electrical devices with more modern, energy-efficient ones (for example, replacing an old oven with a new one).

Different electric ovens may have different efficiencies. In general, cheaper ovens are less efficient: they waste a greater proportion of the energy supplied to them. However, it is important to consider payback time when purchasing new electrical devices.

Device	Cost	Savings per year	Payback time to the nearest full year
Oven A	£1000	£75	13
Oven B	£800	£45	18
Oven C	£650	£40	16
Oven D	£500	£25	20

Key words

kilowatt, power, joule, watt

Questions

1 List three different electrical devices and describe the energy transfers that take place when they are being used.

2 Which of the following uses more energy? (Include a calculation.)

   a 20 W light bulb used for 10 hours.

   b 2.2 kW kettle used for 250 seconds.

3 Explain why it might be a good idea to replace filament lightbulbs with more modern, energy-efficient alternatives.

10: Paying for electricity

Revision objectives

- ✔ know that kilowatt-hours (kWh) is a unit of energy
- ✔ calculate the energy transferred by electrical devices in kWh
- ✔ calculate the cost of running common electrical devices

The kilowatt-hour

Energy is usually measured in joules. However, one joule is quite a small amount of energy. So an alternative **unit** of energy is the **kilowatt-hour** (kWh).

- The kilowatt-hour is a unit of energy.

One kWh is the same as 3.6 million joules!

Calculating energy in kilowatt-hours

It is useful to calculate the energy transferred by an device in kilowatt-hours. This is sometimes referred to as the number of *units*.

We use the same equation $E = P \times t$, but there are two key differences.

To calculate energy in kilowatt-hours

- P (power) must be measured in kilowatts
- t (time) must be measured in hours.

$$E = P \times t$$

E	$=$	P	$\times$	t
electrical energy transferred (kilowatt-hours, kWh)		power of device (kilowatts, kW)		time used for (hours, h)

1 kilowatt is 1000 watts, 500 watts is 0.5 kilowatts, 300 watts is 0.3 kilowatts, and so on.

Exam tip

- You need to be able to calculate energy in kilowatt-hours (kWh). Take care when converting power to kilowatts and time into hours.
- Practise using readings from electricity meters to find the cost of the electricity used.

Paying for electricity

We calculate the cost of electrical devices in pence using the energy transferred in kWh.

Cost	= Cost per kWh	× Energy transferred
(pence, p)	(pence per kilowatt-hour, p/kWh)	(kilowatt-hour, kWh)

Key words

unit, kilowatt-hour

The electricity meter

Every house in the UK has an electricity meter. This is a device that records the number of units used (this is energy transferred by all the devices inside the house, measured in kilowatt-hours).

This is used by electricity companies to calculate your electricity bill.

Month	Meter reading
January	40568
March	41589

The number of units used between January and March is:

Energy transferred = 41589 kWh – 40568 kWh
Energy transferred = 1021 kWh

If each unit costs 12p then the cost for this quarter would be

Cost = cost per kWh × energy transferred
Cost = 12p × 1021 kWh
Cost = 12252p or £122.52

Questions

1 Calculate the energy used in kilowatt-hours by the following:

    a   3 kW heater used for 6 hours

    b   9.2 kW shower used for 30 minutes

    c   2000 W electric pump used for 4 hours

2 If each unit of electricity costs 11p, calculate how much it costs to run a 4000 W boiler for 90 minutes.

Questions
The use and cost of electricity

Working to Grade E

1   Complete the table below to show the main forms of energy from each electrical device.

Device	Energy in	Main forms of energy out
kettle	electrical	
TV	electrical	
radio	electrical	
escalator	electrical	

2   Use either the word **increases** or **decreases** to complete each sentence below:
    a   The amount of energy transferred by an electrical device _____ the longer you use it for.
    b   If you use a more powerful electrical device for the same period of time, the total amount of electrical energy transferred _____ .
    c   In general, when comparing electrical devices, as the cost of the device decreases the efficiency _____ .
    d   The cost of electrical energy _____ as the number of units you use increases.

3   In each sentence below, highlight the **one bold** word that is correct.
    a   Power is usually measured in **joules/watts.**
    b   The kilowatt-hour is a unit of **power/energy**.
    c   Compact fluorescent tubes used in lighting are usually **more/less** efficient than filament lightbulbs.
    d   Replacing older electrical devices with more modern ones normally **reduces/increases** our energy consumptions as more modern devices tend to be more efficient.

4   Complete the table below to give the power of several different devices in both W and kW.

Power of device/W	Power of device/kW
1000	
5500	
800	
	1.2
	0.5
20	

Working to Grade C

5   Give two reasons why it is important to reduce our energy consumption.

6   An office block uses 1200 compact fluorescent tubes for lighting. Each tube has a power output of 15 W and is used for 10 hours each day. Use the equation below to calculate the electrical energy transferred in joules:
$$E = P \times t$$
    a   by each tube
    b   in total.

7   A heater has a power output of 3000 W. It is used for 30 minutes. Use the equation below to calculate the energy transferred:
$$E = P \times t$$
    a   in J
    b   in kWh.

8   An electricity company takes meter readings from three different houses. The first reading was taken in March, with a second reading taken in June.

House	March reading (units of electricity)	June reading (units of electricity)
1	88451	89326
2	45321	51630
3	98015	102576

    a   Which house used the most units between March and June?
    b   If each unit costs 12p calculate the electricity bill for each house.

9   A 12 kW power shower is used for 15 minutes a day for 28 days. Calculate:
    a   The length of time, in hours, the shower is in use over this period.
    b   The number of 'units' used in this time.
    c   The cost of running the shower over that period if each unit costs 11p.

10 Compare the advantages and disadvantages of using a battery-powered radio with a mains-powered one.

1 a An electric kettle has a power rating of 2.2 kW. It takes 2 minutes to boil. Calculate the energy transferred in joules.

energy transferred = power × time

....

....

....

Energy transferred ....

(3 marks)

b If a more powerful kettle was used for the same time, what effect would this have on the amount of energy transferred?

....

(1 mark)

(Total marks: 4)

2 An electricity company takes a reading from an electricity meter in January and again in March. The meter readings can be seen below:

January reading: 35 658   March reading: 35 978

a Calculate the number of units consumed between the two readings.

....

(1 mark)

b Each unit costs 12p. Calculate the cost of the units consumed and give the unit.

....

....

Cost ....

(3 marks)

(Total marks: 4)

Factors affecting the rate of energy transfer by heating

There are a number of factors that affect how fast an object transfers energy to its surroundings (the rate of energy transfer by heating).These include:

- the temperature difference between the object and its surroundings
- the surface area and volume of the object
- the material from which the object is made
- the nature of the surface that is in contact with the object (this includes whether or not the object is insulated)

There are several different investigations you might be asked to carry out that look into these different factors. For each investigation you should consider the variables carefully. A variable is a quantity in an experiment that can be measured (for example, the temperature of the object, the volume of the object, the type of insulation used). Different variables are given special names:

- **Independent variable:** this is the variable you change as part of your investigation.
- **Dependent variable:** this is the variable you measure after changing the independent variable. The dependent variable *depends on* the independent variable.
- **Control variable:** a control variable is another quantity that would affect the dependent variable if not kept the same for the experiment. In order to be a **fair test**, control variables must be kept constant.

A class conducts two different investigations into the rate of energy transfer by heating. The greater the rate of energy transfer to the surroundings the faster a hot object will cool down.

Investigation One

Hypothesis: different insulating materials affect how fast an object transfers energy to its surroundings.

For this investigation a pupil put 300 cm³ of water at 70 °C into four identical beakers wrapped in different types of insulating material (A, B, C, and D). She left them for 10 minutes and then recorded how much the temperature had fallen.

Material	Start temperature/ °C	End temperature/ °C	Change in temperature/ °C
A	70	62	
B	70	50	
C	70	34	
D	70	64	

Investigation Two

Hypothesis: different volumes of water transfer energy to their surroundings at different rates: the greater the volume the lower the rate.

For this investigation a pupil put different volumes of water at 70 °C into five identical containers. He left them for five minutes and then recorded how much the temperature had fallen.

Volume/ cm³	Start temperature/ °C	End temperature/ °C	Change in temperature/ °C
100	70	38	
200	70	50	
300	70	55	
400	70	62	
500	70	65	

1 For each experiment:
   a Complete the table by calculating the change in temperature.
   b Name the independent variable.
   c Name three control variables.
   d Explain why the control variables must be kept constant.

Depending on the nature of the variable it can be described as either categoric or as continuous.

Categoric: this type of variable has values that are labels. If either the independent or dependent variable is a category, results must be presented in a bar graph.

Continuous: this type of variable can have any value (a number). When both the independent and the dependent variables are continuous they should be plotted on a line graph, normally with a line of best fit (this can be straight or curved).

2 For each experiment:
   a Identify whether the independent and dependent variables are categoric or continuous.
   b Plot an appropriate graph for each investigation.
   c Discuss your findings and whether or not the experiment supports the hypothesis.

AQA Upgrade

Answering a question with data response

QUESTION

Solar panels are a frequent sight in Mediterranean countries and are increasingly common in some parts of the UK. They provide homes with hot water. However, they can be expensive to install and have a payback time of between 15 and 20 years.

1 Explain the meaning of the term 'payback time' in terms of solar panels. *(1 mark)*

2 Describe how solar panels are used to produce hot water and why this reduces the energy bills of home owners with solar panels on their roof.

In this question you will be assessed on using good English, organising information clearly, and using specialist terms where appropriate. *(6 marks)*

G–E

1 It is the time they are working. They don't work at night.

2 They absorb heat from the Sun and heat water in pipes. On sunny days the water gets very hot, but it does not work at night or when it is cloudy outside. They also generate electricity and you don't have to buy any as it is all free.

Examiner: The candidate has given an incorrect answer. They have not understood the term 'payback time'.

The answer is very vague and lacks key terms like *infra-red radiation* and *absorbed*. They have also confused solar panels with solar cells which are used to generate electricity. A maximum of one mark would have been awarded for a simplistic explanation of water in the pipes being heated from the Sun.

D–C

1 It the amount of money you save each year from installing the solar panel.

2 Money is saved as you don't need to pay to heat up water. The solar panels heat up the water by absorbing heat and light from the Sun. They are black as this is the best colour for absorbing heat. Water is stored in a tank and heated all the time.

Examiner: The candidate has made the link between installing solar panels and saving money, but they have not answered the question by explaining the meaning of 'payback time'.

A rather disjointed answer, but with some good use of key terms and a sound description of how the solar panel works. They should have mentioned infrared radiation rather than just heat and light from the Sun. They have outlined how the home owner is able to save money on their energy bills, but in a simplistic way. Some energy will still be needed to heat water; solar panels reduce the energy needed to warm the water and so savings can be made.

B–A*

1 Payback time is the time taken for the savings made by installing solar panels to cover the cost of purchasing and installing them.

2 During the day infrared radiation from the Sun is absorbed by the pipes inside the solar panel. The pipes are painted black as black is the best absorber of infrared radiation and so they get very hot. This energy is conducted through the pipes to the water inside. This increases the temperature of the water. The water is then stored in a hot water tank. Home owners with solar panels installed use less energy to heat up water, as their water has already been warmed by the Sun. This reduces the amount of energy they use and so they don't pay as much.

Examiner: Clear and correct.

An excellent answer that answers both parts of the question, using all of the correct technical terms. They have explained in detail how solar panels work and how a home owner saves money by having them installed on their roof.

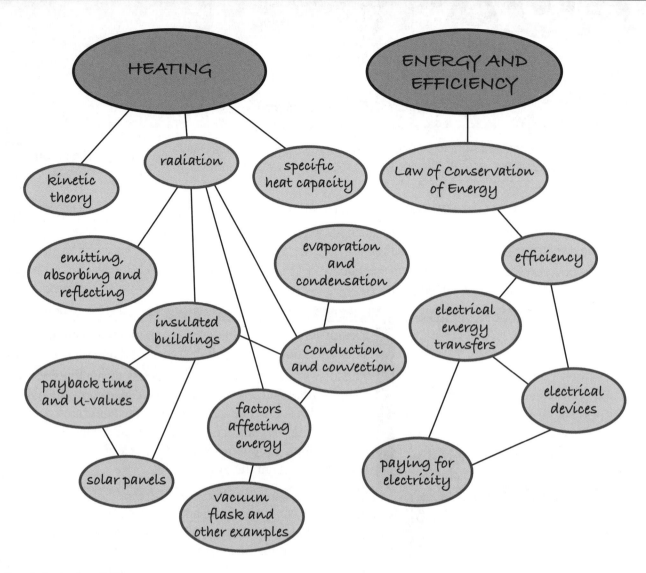

Revision checklist

- All objects emit infrared radiation (IR). Hotter objects emit more IR than cooler ones.
- Black, matt objects are the best emitters and absorbers of IR. Shiny, white surfaces reflect IR and are poor emitters and absorbers.
- Particles are arranged differently in solids, liquids, and gases.
- Particles in solids have less energy than those in liquids, which have less energy than those in gases.
- Energy can be transferred by heating through conduction, convection, evaporation, and condensation.
- Conduction happens in solids; energy is passed from one vibrating particle to the next. Metals are the best conductors because they also contain free electrons.
- Convection happens in fluids (liquids and gases). In convection a region of fluid is heated. The particles gain energy, move faster, and so the region expands. This makes it less dense and it rises.
- Convection currents form when cooler fluid is drawn in to replace the warmer fluid. It is then heated and rises in a cycle.
- Evaporation (when a liquid turns into a gas) has a cooling effect as the particles leaving the liquid transfer energy away with them. Condensation (when a gas turns into a liquid) is the reverse of evaporation.
- The rate of energy transfer from hotter objects to cooler ones depends on: surface area and volume, construction material, and surface in contact.
- The bigger the temperature difference, the greater the rate of energy transfer.
- When comparing techniques to insulate your home, you should consider payback time and U-value (lower U-values mean a better insulator).
- Specific heat capacity is the energy required to raise the temperature of 1 kg of a substance by 1 °C.
- Energy cannot be created or destroyed, just stored or transferred from one form into another.
- Sankey diagrams can be used to represent energy transfers.
- Efficiency is a measure of the amount of useful energy transferred compared with the total energy supplied.
- Electrical devices vary in their efficiency and the amount of energy they use.
- The kilowatt-hour is a unit of electrical energy. The cost of electricity depends on the number of kWh used.

Generating electricity

In order to generate electricity, one form of energy has to be transferred into electrical energy.

A **generator** is a special device that converts kinetic energy into electrical energy. To generate electricity all you need to do is make a generator spin.

Thermal power stations

There are many different kinds of **thermal power station** but they all generate electricity in the same way.

The only difference between different thermal power stations is the source of energy used to heat the water.

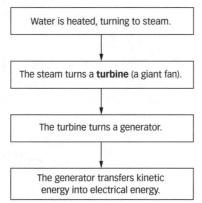

Water is heated, turning to steam.

↓

The steam turns a **turbine** (a giant fan).

↓

The turbine turns a generator.

↓

The generator transfers kinetic energy into electrical energy.

Matching supply with demand

Demand for electricity varies depending the time of day, the time of year, weather conditions, and even what's on the TV.

Different types of power station have different **start-up times**. This is how quickly they can increase or reduce the amount of electricity they are generating. Nuclear and coal have very slow start-up times but natural gas and hydroelectric power are much quicker.

Electricity cannot be stored in large quantities so when there is a sudden surge in demand a **pumped storage** station is used. This is a special type of hydroelectric power only used for changes in demand. At peak demand it starts generating very quickly and at times of low demand it can be used to store energy for later use, by using electricity to pump water back uphill.

Questions

1. Describe how electricity is generated in a thermal power station (include details of the energy transfers that take place).

2. Explain what is meant by the start-up time of a power station.

3. Describe how a pumped storage power station might be used to meet sudden increases in demand.

Revision objectives

- ✔ know how electricity is distributed through the National Grid and the role transformers play in this process
- ✔ compare the advantages and disadvantage of overhead pylons and underground cables

Student book references

1.22 The National Grid

Specification key

✔ P1.4.2

Exam tip AQA

Make sure you can explain *why* transformers are used.

The National Grid

The electricity generated at power stations needs to be distributed to homes and business all around the country.

In the UK we have a **National Grid**. This is a huge network of underground cables and overhead power lines linking houses to power stations, which are sometimes hundreds of miles away.

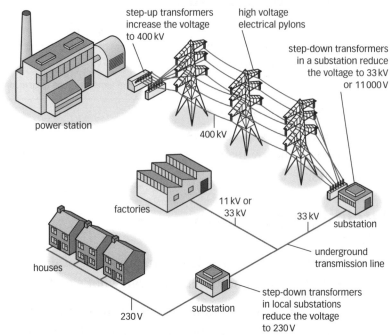

step-up transformers increase the voltage to 400 kV

high voltage electrical pylons

step-down transformers in a substation reduce the voltage to 33 kV or 11 000 V

power station

400 kV

factories

11 kV or 33 kV

33 kV

substation

underground transmission line

houses

230 V

substation

step-down transformers in local substations reduce the voltage to 230 V

▲ The National Grid.

Transmitting at high voltages

The electricity is transmitted at very high voltages. When you increase the voltage (keeping the power the same), the current drops. A lower current means the wires don't get as hot. This means less energy is wasted in transmission.

Transformers are special devices that can increase or reduce the **voltage**. **Step-up transformers** are used to increase the voltage before it is distributed through the grid (up to 400 000 V). **Step-down transformers** are then used in **substations** to reduce the voltage to a safer level to be used in the home (230 V).

Pylons versus underground cables

Some power lines are buried in the ground; others are suspended high in the air on pylons. Burying cables has a number of advantages and disadvantages when compared to using pylons.

Advantages of underground cables	Disadvantages of underground cables
The cables are not an eyesore, unlike large pylons. They can be used in areas of outstanding natural beauty and in national parks.	It is much more expensive to bury cables.
The cables are protected from severe weather and storms.	The cables have to be insulated and waterproofed; this means the cables get warmer, wasting more energy.
	It is very costly and disruptive to repair or renew damaged cables.
	The voltage used cannot be as high as in pylon lines, so more energy is wasted as heat.

Questions

1. Describe how electricity is distributed through the National Grid from power stations to homes. Include a description of each of the key parts.

2. Explain why it is more efficient to transmit electricity at high voltages.

3. Give two advantages and disadvantages of using pylons rather than burying cables underground.

Revision objectives

- ✔ describe how fossil fuels are used to generate electricity
- ✔ outline the advantages and disadvantages of using fossil fuels to generate electricity
- ✔ know how the process of carbon capture may be used to prevent carbon dioxide building up in the atmosphere

Student book references

1.17 Fossil fuels and carbon capture

Specification key

✔ P1.4.1 a and f

Key words

non-renewable, carbon capture

Questions

1 Give two advantages and two disadvantages of using fossil fuels to generate electricity.

2 Outline the differences between the use of coal, oil, and natural gas to generate electricity.

3 Describe what is meant by carbon capture and explain why it might be beneficial to develop this technology.

Using fossil fuels

Fossil fuels include coal, oil, and natural gas. They were all formed from the remains of living plants or animals that died millions of years ago. They are a **non-renewable** energy resource as they will eventually be used up.

Fossil fuels are burnt in large quantities in order to generate electricity. Burning fossil fuels can produce huge amounts of electricity. The fuels are relatively cheap and the technology is well established. However, there are a number of disadvantages:

- Burning fossil fuel releases carbon dioxide (CO_2) into the atmosphere (in varying amounts). This increases global warming and leads to climate change.
- The fuels have to be mined/extracted and then transported. This damages wildlife habitats and there is the added risk of spills or leaks.
- The power stations and the mines/rigs are often very ugly and noisy.

Different fossil fuels are used in slightly different ways. In some natural gas power stations the exhaust gases from the burning gas are used to spin the turbine. This gives this type of power station a short start-up time, allowing it to increase rapidly the amount of electricity it generates if there is a surge in demand.

Fossil fuel	Substance heated	CO_2 production	Start-up time
coal	water	very high	long
oil	water	high	long
natural gas	exhaust gas	medium	short

Carbon capture

Carbon capture is a rapidly evolving technology, which in the future may dramatically reduce the amount of CO_2 that enters the atmosphere from the burning of fossil fuels.

Instead of travelling into the air, the CO_2 is trapped and stored underground (perhaps in old oil or gas fields). One day this may reduce the CO_2 released by a typical plant by as much as 80%.

Exam tip
AQA

You need to be able to describe the differences between how the three fossil fuels are used during energy production.

Generating electricity from nuclear power

Electricity may be generated from **nuclear reactors**. Inside this reactor the nuclear fuel undergoes a nuclear reaction called **nuclear fission**. This reaction releases heat.

The heat released is then used to turn water to steam, which turns a turbine then a generator (in the same way as other thermal power stations).

The fuel used is either uranium or plutonium. We have plenty of this kind of fuel; however, it will eventually run out, so nuclear power is another non-renewable resource (like fossil fuels).

Advantages and disadvantages of nuclear power

Using nuclear power offers a number of advantages and disadvantages.

Advantages	Disadvantages
Huge amounts of electricity can be generated per kilogram of fuel.	Nuclear reactors produce highly **radioactive waste**. This is very dangerous and harmful. It needs to be stored carefully.
The fuel is not burnt, so there is no carbon dioxide released. Nuclear power does not contribute to global warming.	There is the risk of a nuclear accident releasing radioactive waste into the environment.
The fuel is relatively cheap and easily available – it will not run out for many years.	Nuclear reactors have a very slow start-up time. They can't react to sudden changes in demand.
	The power stations contribute to both noise and visual pollution.
	Nuclear power stations can be very expensive to build and even more expensive to **decommission** (dismantle) at the end of their useful life.

Revision objectives

- ✓ describe how nuclear power is used to generate electricity
- ✓ outline the advantages and disadvantages of using nuclear power to generate electricity

Student book references

1.18 Nuclear power

Specification key

✓ P1.4.1 a and f

Exam tip

Remember to stress that an advantage of nuclear power is that it can generate more electricity *per kilogram* of fuel than alternative sources.

Questions

1 Describe how electricity is produced using a nuclear reactor.

2 Explain why nuclear power stations do not contribute to manmade global warming.

3 What is meant by decommission? Explain why this is often a costly process.

Key words

nuclear reactor, nuclear fission, radioactive waste, decommission

Renewable energy sources

Along with fossil fuels and nuclear power there are a number of other energy resources we can use to generate electricity.

Each resource is used in a slightly different way but most turn turbines, which turn generators in order to generate electricity.

All of these sources are classified as **renewable**. They don't use a fuel that will run out and so can be used over and over again.

Questions

1   Describe how geothermal power is used to generate electricity and outline one advantage and one disadvantage of this method.

2   Which two renewable energy resources are most useful for the production of small-scale local electricity in remote areas?

3   Explain why, despite releasing CO_2 when biofuels are burnt, biomass is a carbon-neutral energy resource.

Advantages and disadvantages of renewables

	How electricity is generated	No atmospheric pollution (including no carbon dioxide). They don't contribute to global warming.	There are no fuel costs (only maintenance and construction costs).	Advantages	Disadvantages
Wind	The wind turns large **wind turbines** directly.			Can be built offshore.	Visual and noise pollution. Only generates electricity when it is windy.
Wave	There are several different kinds of wave generator. They all use the up and down motion of the waves to turn turbines.				Visual and noise pollution (can also be a danger to shipping). Unreliable/untested technology.
Tidal	As the tides move in and out they turn turbines directly. There are different types of tidal power, including large **tidal barrages** (dams) across estuaries, or smaller tidal lagoons.			Reliable and predictable electricity generation.	Affects marine habitats. Can be very expensive to build. Limited number of suitable sites. Can only generate power for a short period of 6–8 hours per day.
Hydroelectric power (HEP)	A large dam is built across a valley. The water builds up behind the dam. As it falls through pipes large turbines are turned by the falling water.			Large quantities of electricity can be generated. Short start-up time and can be used as pumped storage. Can be used (in small scale) in remote areas.	Building dams can be very expensive. The dam floods valleys upstream and can have other environmental effects. Only a few suitable locations.
Solar (cells)	Energy from the sun is directly transferred into electrical energy using special **solar cells**. No turbines or generators are needed. Alternatively, sunlight is reflected off hundreds of mirrors and focused on a **solar thermal tower**. Inside the tower, water is heated and turns to steam (this is used to turn turbines).			Very useful in remote locations (away from National Grid), such as roadsigns. Works very well on the small scale.	Solar cells are very expensive to produce. Output depends on the light level.
Geothermal	In some volcanic regions of the world there are hot rocks near the surface. Water and steam rises to the surface. This steam is collected and piped to a **thermal power station** to turn turbines directly.			Relatively cheap to build.	Only a few suitable locations around the world.
Biomass	**Biofuels** (specially grown crops or organic waste products) are burnt. The heat released turns water to steam – this turns turbines.			Uses waste products (fuel costs are low). **Carbon neutral** (no overall increase in CO_2 as the amount released by burning is absorbed by growing the biofuel).	Visual and noise pollution. In some countries land need for food is used to grow biofuels instead.

Questions
Generating power

1 Read the statements below. Highlight the ones that are **true** and re-write corrected versions of the statements that are **false**.
  - **a** Nuclear power is a form of renewable energy.
  - **b** In thermal power stations heat is used to turn water to steam; this steam turns turbines, which turn generators to generate electricity.
  - **c** Non-renewable energy resources use fuels that will never run out.
  - **d** Solar power is very useful in remote locations.
  - **e** A hydroelectric power station has a long start-up time.
  - **f** Natural gas produces more carbon dioxide than other fossil fuels.

2 Draw lines to match each renewable energy resource to its description.

Energy resource	Brief description
wind	The up-and-down motion of the sea is transferred into electrical energy.
wave	Biofuels are burnt; the heat is used to turn water to steam.
tidal	Large dams are built across river valleys.
hydroelectric power	Wind is used to turn large turbines.
geothermal	Hot rocks turn water to steam – this is used to turn turbines.
biomass	This may include tidal lagoons or larger tidal barrages.
solar (cells)	Energy from the Sun is transferred into electrical energy.

3 Give two ways in which electricity may be distributed through the National Grid.

4 List three examples of non-renewable energy resources.

Working to Grade C

5 Using the word **increases** or **decreases**, complete the sentences on transformers below:
  - **a** A step-up transformer _____ the voltage. This _____ the current.
  - **b** Transmitting electrical energy at high voltages _____ the amount of energy wasted, as the current is lower so the wires do not get as hot.
  - **c** A step-down transformer _____ the voltage, making it safer for use in the home.
  - **d** A step-down transformer _____ the current.

6 Sort the following methods of generating electricity in order of start-up time (from the longest start-up time to the shortest).

coal	natural gas	HEP	nuclear

7 Describe how electricity is generated in a nuclear power station.

8 Outline the advantages and disadvantages of using wave power and tidal power to generate electricity.

9 Draw a labelled diagram to show how carbon-capture technology may be used in the future.

10 The chart below shows how demand for electrical energy varies over the course of a typical day.

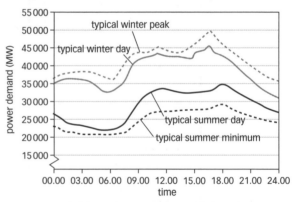

  - **a** Explain the differences in demand between a typical summer day and a typical winter day.
  - **b** Suggest why there is an increase in demand at around:
    - **i** 08.30
    - **ii** 17.00

Examination questions
Generating power

1 There are many different types of thermal power station. They all generate electricity in a similar way.

    a The following statements outline the process of electricity generation in thermal power plants. Sort them into order from first to last.

A	The steam turns a turbine.
B	The turbine turns a generator.
C	Water is heated, turning to steam.
D	The generator transfers kinetic energy into electrical energy.

       First .... Last

(2 marks)

    b **i** Explain the meaning of the term 'start-up time'.

          ....

(1 mark)

      ii Along with coal-fired and oil-fired power stations, which other non-renewable energy resource has a long start-up time?

          ....

(1 mark)

    c Explain how pumped storage stations are used to ensure the supply of electricity always matches demand.

    ....

    ....

    ....

    ....

    ....

(3 marks)
(Total marks: 7)

2 The National Grid is used to transmit electricity energy from power stations to homes and businesses all over the country.

a Use words from the box below to complete the sentences that follow.

Each word may be used once, more than once, or not at all.

| step-up   energy   step-down   voltage   current |

Electricity is transmitted through the National Grid at very high voltages. A .... transformer

increases the .... and reduces the .... The lower .... means less

.... is lost in transmission as the wires do not get as hot.

(5 marks)

b The National Grid is made from wires that are either suspended by pylons or buried underground. Give **two** disadvantages of burying cables underground to transmit electrical energy.

1 ....

2 ....

(2 marks)

(Total marks: 7)

3 In this question you will be assessed on using good English, organising information clearly, and using specialist terms where appropriate.

Describe the advantages and disadvantages of using wind power to generate electricity.

....

....

....

....

....

....

....

....

(Total marks: 6)

What are waves?

Waves are a series of **vibrations** or **oscillations**. They are around us all the time.

There are many different types of wave but all *transfer energy* from one place to another.

Types of wave

There are two main types of wave:

- **transverse**
- **longitudinal**.

They both transfer energy but the oscillations that make up the waves are different.

Transverse waves

In transverse waves the oscillations are at right angles to the direction of energy transfer.

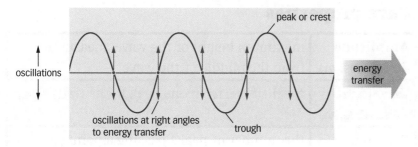

▲ A transverse wave.

Transverse waves look like ripples on water. They are made up of a number of *peaks* and *troughs*.

Examples of transverse waves include:

- light (all electromagnetic waves: radio, microwaves, infrared radiation, ultraviolet radiation, X-rays, gamma rays)
- some mechanical waves on springs or strings.

Revision objectives

- ✓ know that waves transfer energy but not matter
- ✓ describe the two different types of wave and give examples of each
- ✓ explain the meaning of the terms 'wavelength', 'frequency', and 'amplitude'

Student book references

1.24 Waves all around us

1.25 Transverse and longitudinal waves

Specification key

- ✓ P1.5.1 a, b, c, f and j

Longitudinal waves

In longitudinal waves the oscillations are parallel to the direction of energy transfer.

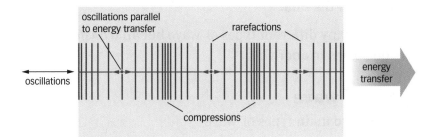

▲ A longitudinal wave.

A longitudinal wave is made up of **compressions** (where the particles are bunched up, closer together) and **rarefactions** (where the particles are further apart).

Examples of longitudinal waves include:

*   sound
*   some mechanical waves on springs.

Wave properties

Amplitude (in metres, m)	maximum height of the wave, measured from the middle of the wave
Wavelength (in metres, m)	the distance from one peak to the next
Frequency (in hertz, Hz)	the number of peaks passing a point per second

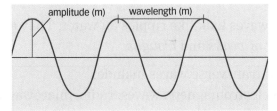

▲ Key features of a wave.

Questions

1   Describe the differences between transverse and longitudinal waves and give an example of each.

2   Draw a labelled diagram to show the wavelength and amplitude of a water wave.

3   If 30 wave peaks pass a point in 1 minute, what is the frequency of the wave?

Reflection

When waves bounce off a surface they are said to be reflected. All waves can be reflected.

To draw **reflection** we often draw ray diagrams, these always include a **normal line**. This is a line at 90° to the surface.

The **law of reflection** states:
- *The **angle of incidence** = the **angle of reflection***.

Refraction

When waves travel from one **medium** to another they can be refracted.

If the speed of the wave changes, the wave changes direction. This is called **refraction**.

Light can be refracted when it passes from air into a glass block. Light travels slower in the glass so the ray bends towards the normal.

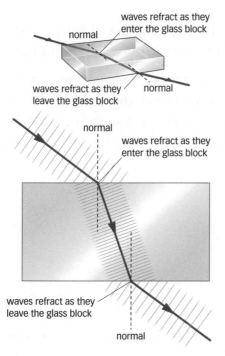

▲ Waves can be refracted.

If the wave travels along the normal then no refraction takes place.

All waves can be refracted, including sound.

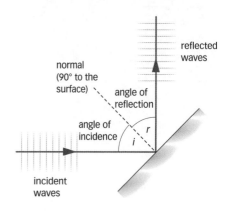

▲ Reflection of a wave.

Exam tip

Practise drawing diagrams for reflection, refraction, and diffraction. Make sure you can label the key features.

Key words

reflection, normal line, law of
reflection, angle of incidence,
angle of reflection, medium,
refraction, diffraction

Diffraction

When waves pass through a gap or around an obstacle they spread out. This is called **diffraction**.

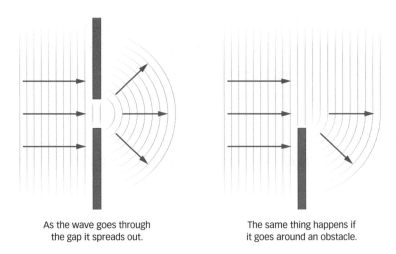

As the wave goes through the gap it spreads out.

The same thing happens if it goes around an obstacle.

▲ Waves are diffracted when they pass through gaps and around obstacles.

There is a significant amount of diffraction when the wavelength of the wave is the same size as the gap.

To diffract light a tiny gap is needed (its wavelength is very small). Sound diffracts well through open doors because it has a wavelength that is bigger than the doorway. This allows you to hear what's going on outside without necessarily seeing it.

Questions

1 What is meant by the law of reflection?

2 a Draw a diagram to show light being refracted through a glass block.

   b Describe what happens if the light enters the glass block along the normal line.

3 Describe what is meant by diffraction and state the conditions required for significant diffraction to take place.

Electromagnetic waves

Electromagnetic (EM) waves are a special kind of transverse wave. Unlike other waves they don't need particles; they can travel through a **vacuum** like space.

Light is an example of an electromagnetic wave. It travels through space from the Sun to the Earth.

The electromagnetic spectrum

There are seven different electromagnetic waves that together form the **electromagnetic spectrum**. They can all travel through a vacuum but they have different frequencies and wavelengths.

Radio waves are the EM waves with the longest wavelength (lowest frequency). They can have wavelengths over 10 km.

Gamma waves are at the other end of the spectrum. They have the highest frequency and the shortest wavelength (down to 10^{-15} m).

Electromagnetic waves form a continuous (there are no gaps) spectrum. Radio waves are at one end and gamma waves are at the other.

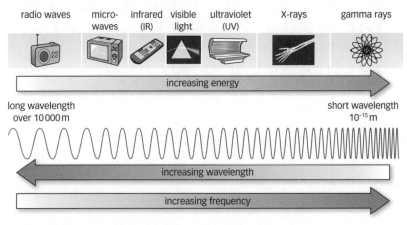

▲ The electromagnetic spectrum.

The higher the frequency, the higher the energy, so radio waves have the lowest energy and gamma rays the most.

Our eyes can only detect visible light, but other sensors can detect the other parts of the spectrum.

All electromagnetic waves travel at the same speed through a vacuum. This is the speed of light (300 000 000 m/s).

Revision objectives

- ✔ list the order of the electromagnetic spectrum in terms of frequency, energy or wavelength
- ✔ describe the properties of electromagnetic waves
- ✔ give examples of how some electromagnetic waves are used in communications

Student book references

1.27 The electromagnetic spectrum

1.28 Communications and optics

Specification key

✔ P1.5.1 d and e

Exam tip

- Make sure you can list all seven electromagnetic waves in order of frequency, energy, and wavelength.
- Remember, despite having different frequencies, energies, and wavelengths, all electromagnetic waves travel at the *same speed* through a vacuum.

Key words

electromagnetic wave, vacuum, electromagnetic spectrum

Electromagnetic waves and communication

As electromagnetic waves travel so fast they are very useful for communication. There are some examples listed below:

Radio waves	TV, radio, and wireless communications
Microwaves	mobile phones and satellite TV
Infrared	remote controls and some cable Internet connections
Visible light	photography and some cable Internet connections

The radio waves used for radio stations have a longer wavelength than those used for TV signals. This means they *diffract* more than TV signals. This allows radio signals to be picked up in places where TV signals can't reach, for example, at the bottom of some valleys.

Mobile phones and microwaves

Mobile phones are very useful for communication and can be especially helpful in emergencies.

All mobile phones use microwaves to send and receive information. Some people are concerned about the effect they have on the body. Research has shown they have a small heating effect on living tissue.

Scientists are not sure whether this is a serious health risk and if it will cause any long-term damage. There is no clear evidence either way; people must balance the possible risks of using mobile phones with the benefits.

Questions

1   List the electromagnetic spectrum from shortest wavelength to longest wavelength.

2   Give an example of how radio waves might be used for communication.

3   Describe the possible risks in using a mobile phone.

4   **H** Give an example for a typical wavelength of radio wave and a gamma ray.

The wave equation

The **speed** of a wave, its **frequency**, and its **wavelength** are all linked together in the wave equation:

$$v = f \times \lambda$$

wave speed = frequency × wavelength
(metres per second, m/s)   (hertz, Hz)   (metres, m)

For example, if a sound wave has a frequency of 6600 Hz and a wavelength of 0.05 m, we can find its speed.

$v = f \times \lambda$

$v = 6600\,Hz \times 0.05\,m$

$v = 330\,m/s$

H Electromagnetic waves

The wave equation can be used with all types of wave, including electromagnetic waves.

All electromagnetic waves travel at the same speed through a vacuum: 300 000 000 m/s.

We can use the wave equation to find the frequency of a radio wave that has a wavelength of 200 m.

$v = f \times \lambda$ so $f = v/\lambda$

$f = v/\lambda$

$f = \dfrac{300\,000\,000\,m/s}{200\,m}$

$f = 1\,500\,000\,Hz$ or 1.5 MHz

Revision objectives

✔ explain and use the wave equation $v = f \times \lambda$

Student book references

1.24 Waves all around us

Specification key

✔ P1.5.1 i

Exam tip

When using the wave equation, frequency must be measured in hertz (Hz) and wavelength in metres (m).

Questions

1 Calculate the wave speeds of the following waves:

   a   water wave with a frequency of 0.5 Hz and a wavelength of 4 m

   b   sound wave with a wavelength of 60 cm and a frequency of 500 Hz

   c   wave with a frequency of 1.2 kHz and a wavelength of 80 cm

2 **H** Calculate the wavelength of an electromagnetic wave with a frequency of $3 \times 10^{10}\,Hz$.

Key words

speed, frequency, wavelength

Revision objectives

✔ describe the properties of an image formed inside a plane mirror

Student book references

1.28 Communications and optics

Specification key

✔ P1.5.2

Exam tip AQA

On ray diagrams, remember that all angles are measured to the **normal** line.

Reflection and images

When light is reflected off a mirror is must obey the **law of reflection**.

- *The **angle of incidence** = the **angle of reflection**.*

We see objects because the light they give off, or the light reflected off them, enters our eyes.

When we look into a mirror we see an image of ourselves. This image is formed by the light reflecting off the mirror. These images have three key properties:

Upright	The image is the right way up.
Laterally inverted	The image is flipped around horizontally.
Virtual	The image is not really there; it can't be projected onto a screen.

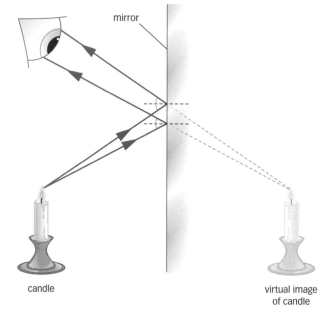

candle   virtual image of candle

▲ A plane mirror produces an upright, laterally inverted, virtual image.

Key words

normal, law of reflection, angle of incidence, angle of reflection, upright, laterally inverted, virtual

Questions

1 Explain why the word FIRE is written backwards on the front of fire engines.

2 Describe the three key properties of an image formed behind a mirror.

3 Draw a diagram to show how an image is formed inside a plane mirror.

Sound waves

Sound waves are produced whenever an object *vibrates*. These vibrations cause neighbouring air particles to vibrate and the sound waves travel through the air.

Sound waves are *longitudinal waves*. The oscillations are parallel to the direction of energy transfer.

Like all waves, sound waves can be reflected, refracted, and diffracted. A reflection of a sound wave is called an **echo**.

Pitch and volume

If an object vibrates faster it will create more sound waves per second. This creates a sound wave with a higher frequency; it sounds higher in **pitch**. *The higher the frequency, the higher the pitch.*

Some sound waves are too high pitched for humans to hear. They have a frequency above human hearing (above 20 000 Hz). These kinds of sound waves are called **ultrasound**.

A louder sound (one with a higher **volume**) is created when the particles vibrate further. This gives the sound wave a larger amplitude. *The larger the amplitude, the louder the sound.*

Oscilloscopes

Oscilloscopes can be used to produce pictures of sound waves. Higher-pitched, louder sounds have a higher frequency (the waves are closer together) and a greater amplitude (they are taller).

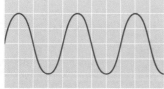
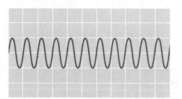

a low-pitch, low-frequency, loud sound   a higher-pitch, higher-frequency, quiet sound

▲ Different sound waves shown on an oscilloscope.

Revision objectives

✓ describe the key features of sound waves

✓ relate the pitch of a sound to its frequency and its loudness to its amplitude

✓ know that echoes are reflections of sound

Student book references

1.29 Sound waves

Specification key

✔ P1.5.3

Key words

sound waves, echo, pitch, ultrasound, volume

Questions

1 Describe how a sound wave is formed.

2 Describe how the pitch of a sound is affected by its frequency.

3 Draw diagrams to show two sound waves of the same pitch, but with different volumes.

Revision objectives

✓ describe the Doppler effect

Student book references

1.30 The Doppler effect

Specification key

✓ P1.5.4 a

Wave sources

Any object that emits a wave can be described as a **wave source**.

Type of wave	Examples of wave sources
sound	speaker, police siren, car engine
light	lightbulb, galaxy
microwaves	satellite, microwave oven

The Doppler effect

When a wave source moves this affects the frequency and wavelength of the wave detected by stationary observers. This is called the **Doppler effect**.

- When the wave source moves *away* from the observer, the waves get stretched out. The wavelength *increases* and the frequency *decreases*.
- When the wave source moves *towards* the observer the waves get all bunched up. The wavelength *decreases* and the frequency *increases*.

This effect can be heard when race cars or police sirens move past an observer. The sound appears higher pitched when the car is moving towards the observer and lower pitched when it has gone past.

Key words

wave source, Doppler effect

Questions

1   Give an example of a wave source for light, sound, and microwaves.

2   Explain why a race car makes the distinctive 'neeee-awwww' sound when it races passed a stationary observer.

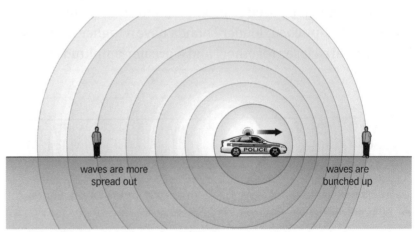

waves are more spread out

waves are bunched up

▲ The Doppler effect can be heard when a police car passes by with its siren sounding.

The Big Bang theory

The **Big Bang theory** is the current scientific description for the origin of the Universe. It states:

- The Universe began around 14 billion years ago.
- The Universe started from a very small, incredibly hot initial point.
- The Universe then exploded outwards and has been expanding ever since.

▲ Most scientists think the Universe was created in a Big Bang.

Evidence

There are two key pieces of evidence in support of this theory:

- The Universe is expanding: rewind time and the galaxies would all get closer together as the Universe got smaller and smaller until its initial creation.
- **Cosmic microwave background radiation**: scientists are able to detect the heat left over from the Big Bang.

Revision objectives

- ✓ describe the key features of the Big Bang theory
- ✓ outline the evidence for the Big Bang theory, including red-shift/expanding Universe and cosmic microwave background radiation (CMBR)

Student book references

1.31 Red-shift

1.32 The Big Bang theory

Specification key

- ✓ P1.5.4 b – e

Exam tip

Make sure you can explain *how* observations of red-shift lead to the idea of an expanding Universe.

The expanding Universe and red-shift

Scientists use the Doppler effect applied to light to show the Universe is expanding.

When galaxies move away from us the light they emit is stretched: its wavelength increases. As red has the longest wavelength of all the colours this effect is called **red-shift**.

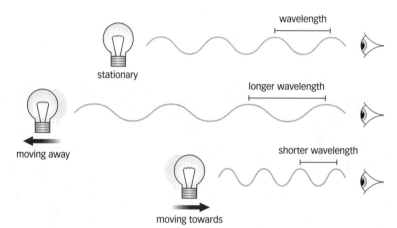

stationary

wavelength

moving away

longer wavelength

moving towards

shorter wavelength

▲ The wavelength of light changes, depending on the motion of the source.

When you look at the light from distant galaxies there are two key observations:

- Most galaxies show a red-shift – they are moving away from us.
- The further a galaxy is away, the greater the red-shift – the faster it is moving.

These two observations allow scientists to conclude that the Universe is expanding.

Cosmic microwave background radiation

The second key piece of evidence is cosmic microwave background radiation (CMBR).

Cosmic microwave background radiation is a form of radiation that fills the entire Universe; it is the same everywhere you look. It is the 'heat' left over from the Big Bang. As the Universe expanded, it cooled. This initial heat is now in the microwave part of the electromagnetic spectrum.

The Big Bang theory is currently the only theory that can explain the existence of the cosmic microwave background radiation.

Questions

1. Describe the key features of the Big Bang theory.

2. Explain how the observation of red-shift supports the idea of a Big Bang.

3. What is meant by cosmic microwave background radiation and why is it important to the Big Bang theory?

1   In each sentence below, highlight the correct **bold**.
   a   Waves transfer **matter**/**energy** from one place to another.
   b   Light is an example of a **transverse**/ **longitudinal** wave.
   c   The law of reflection states the angle of incidence is equal to the angle of **refraction**/ **reflection**.
   d   Radio waves have the **shortest**/**longest** wavelength of all electromagnetic waves.
   e   Gamma rays have the **most**/**least** energy of all electromagnetic waves.
   f   **Infrared**/**microwaves** are used by most TV remote controls.
   g   The higher the pitch of a sound the **higher**/ **lower** its frequency.
   h   Most galaxies are moving **towards**/**away** from us.

2   List all seven types of electromagnetic waves, from highest frequency to the lowest frequency.

3   Draw a labelled diagram to show how a single ray of light is reflected off a plane mirror. Your diagram should include the following labels:
   a   ray of incidence
   b   angle of incidence
   c   normal
   d   ray of reflection
   e   angle of reflection

4   Electromagnetic waves are useful for communications. Name one example of how the following might be used in communications:
   a   radio waves
   b   microwaves
   c   infrared
   d   visible light

5   Highlight the statements below that are **true**. Write corrected versions of the statements that are **false**.
   a   Gamma rays have a higher frequency than radio waves.
   b   Gamma rays travel faster through a vacuum than radio waves.
   c   When waves spread out as they pass through a gap this is called refraction.
   d   The best diffraction occurs when the wavelength of the wave is the same size as the gap.
   e   The amplitude of a wave is the height of the wave from the top of the peak to the bottom of the trough.
   f   Sound waves are examples of transverse waves.
   g   A reflection of sound is called an echo.
   h   A louder sound has a smaller amplitude.

   i   When a sound source moves towards you the wavelength decreases.
   j   The light emitted by distant galaxies is stretched as they move away from us. This is called blue-shift.

6   Use wave equation below to find the speed of the following waves:

   wave speed = frequency × wavelength

Wave speed	Frequency	Wavelength
	1000 Hz	2 m
	3.2 kHz	0.5 m
	300 Hz	40 cm
	0.9 kHz	12 cm

7   Write definitions for the following wave terms:
   a   wavelength
   b   frequency
   c   amplitude

8   Match the following terms describing the image formed by a plane mirror.

Upright	The image cannot be projected onto a screen.
Laterally inverted	The image is the right way up.
Virtual	The image is flipped around horizontally.

9   Name two pieces of evidence in support of the Big Bang theory.

10   Copy and complete the following sentences about the Big Bang theory.
   a   The Universe began about 14 _____ years ago.
   b   It started from a very_____, very hot, very dense initial point.
   c   It then _____ outwards and has been _____ ever since.

11   Classify the following waves as either transverse, longitudinal, or could be either.

sound	radio waves	mechanical waves on springs
light	infrared	water waves
X-rays	microwaves	gamma rays

12 Draw a labelled diagram of a transverse wave. Your diagram should include the following labels:
   a amplitude
   b wavelength.

13 Draw a labelled diagram of a longitudinal wave. Your diagram should include the following labels:
   a compression
   b rarefaction
   c wavelength.

14 Explain why sound diffracts through an open doorway but light does not.

15 Complete the following sentences about the Doppler Effect. Your answers should include the following terms: wavelength, frequency, increases, and decreases.
   a When a wave source moves towards an observer _____
   b When a wave source moves away from an observer _____

Working to Grade A*

16 Use your answer above to explain why the engine noise from a race car appears to change pitch as it races past a stationary observer.

17 Using the terms in the box below describe the two different sounds as shown on an oscilloscope screen. You may use the terms more than once.

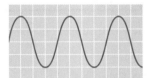 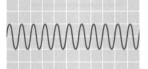

  a low pitch, low frequency,   a higher pitch, higher
       loud sound   frequency, quieter sound

> pitch   frequency loud quiet higher
> lower amplitude

18 In terms of vibrations, describe the differences between transverse and longitudinal waves.

19 Complete the following sentences on sound waves.
   a A sound wave is produced whenever an object _____
   b These _____ cause neighbouring particles to _____
   c Sound waves are examples of _____ waves, so these _____ are _____ to the direction of energy transfer.

20 Draw a diagram showing how radio waves are diffracted as they pass over a hill (an obstacle). Use your diagram to explain why it may be possible to receive a radio signal behind the hill but not a mobile phone signal.

21 Complete the table below using the wave equation.
wave speed = frequency × wavelength

Wave speed (m/s)	Frequency (Hz)	Wavelength (m)
3500	75	
340		0.2
12 000		60
3×10^8	150 000 000	

1 This question is about waves.

a What do all waves transfer from one place to another?

....
(1 mark)

b Draw straight lines to link each term to its description.

Term		Description
amplitude		the number of peaks passing a point per second
wavelength		the minimum distance from one peak to another
frequency		the maximum height of the wave, from the middle to the peak

(3 marks)

c i Describe the oscillations in a transverse wave.

....

....
(2 marks)

ii Give **two** examples of transverse waves.

1 ....

2 ....
(2 marks)
(Total marks: 8)

2 a Complete the sentences on reflection below.

When waves bounce off surfaces this is called reflection. The law of reflection states that the angle of

.... is equal to the angle of .... All angles are measured to the .... line.
(3 marks)

b i Complete the diagrams below to show how waves are diffracted when they pass through gaps of
different sizes.

(3 marks)

    ii   Under what conditions does significant diffraction occur?

....

....

(1 mark)

(Total marks: 7)

3 A flute produces a note with a frequency of 1.2 kHz and a wavelength of 30 cm.

    a   Calculate the speed of sound and give the unit.

$$\text{wave speed} = \text{frequency} \times \text{wavelength}$$

....

....

Wave speed ....

(3 marks)

    b   The flute is used to play the same note at the same volume whilst on a train moving towards a stationary observer.

What effect, if any, does this have on the amplitude and wavelength of the sound heard by the observer in front of the train?

Amplitude: ....

Wavelength: ....

(2 marks)

(Total marks: 5)

4 In this question you will be assessed on using good English, organising information clearly, and using specialist terms where appropriate.

Describe the **two** key pieces of evidence for the Big Bang theory of the origin of the Universe.

....

....

....

....

....

....

....

(6 marks)

(Total marks: 6)

How Science Works
Electrical energy and waves

Law of reflection

There are a number of key terms you must be familiar with when discussing any scientific investigation.

In terms of experimental data you might be asked whether it is:

- **Accurate** – meaning close to the true value.
- **Precise** – meaning there is very little spread around the average (mean) value.
- **Repeatable** – meaning that if the experiment was completed again it would produce the same results.
- **Reproducible** – meaning if the investigation was completed by another person or using a different method (different equipment or techniques) it would produce the same results.

The exam might include questions about data collected as part of an investigation. Any investigation will contain errors (or uncertainties). They could be caused by tiny differences in the experiment or limitations caused by things like the resolution of the scale on the equipment, or human errors in things like timings. An experimental error will affect the data collected, moving it away from the true value, reducing its accuracy. There are three types of error:

Random errors	These cause results to be spread above and below the true value. They are unpredictable and cannot be corrected.
	Repeating measurements and taking an average can reduce the effects of random errors.
Systematic errors	These cause results to differ from the true value by a consistent amount (either always above or always below the true value).
	Repeating measurements and taking an average does not reduce the effects of systematic errors; instead a different piece of equipment or an alternative technique should be used.
Zero errors	This is an example of a systematic error and it occurs when a piece of equipment does not give a value of zero when it should, for example, if a voltmeter reads 0.2 V when it should read 0 V. All results will be 0.2 V too high.
	To correct for zero errors, the zero value should be added or subtracted from each reading.

A student investigates how the angle of reflection varies when a ray of light is reflected off a mirror at different angles of incidence.

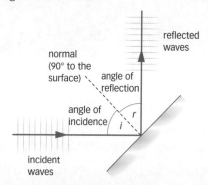

Angle of incidence (°)	Angle of reflection (°)			
	1	2	3	Average
15	15	14	16	15
30	30	35	29	
45	45	45	45	
60	62	65	62	
75	69	75	76	

The law of reflection states:

angle of incidence = angle of reflection

1 Complete the table by calculating the averages (give your answer to the nearest whole degree).

2 Plot an appropriate graph of angle of incidence against the average angle of reflection. Explain whether or not the data supports the law of reflection.

3 Discuss whether or not you think the results are:
   a accurate
   b precise
   c repeatable
   d reproducible

4 a What type of error causes the readings to vary in an unpredictable way (both above and below the true value)?
   b Name two possible sources of error in this investigation.

5 Another student conducted the same experiment but they drew their normal line incorrectly – it was not at 90° to the surface of the mirror. What type of error would this introduce into the results?

6 Explain why it is important for the data produced by a company selling products to be reproducible by independent scientists.

AQA *Upgrade*

Answering a question with data response

In the UK, electricity is generated using a mixture of renewable and non-renewable energy resources.

1 What does the term 'renewable energy resource' mean? *(1 mark)*

2 These piecharts show the relative proportion of electricity generated from different energy sources.

Describe the key changes from 1970 to 2010. *(3 marks)*

1970   2010

- Coal
- Oil
- National gas
- Nuclear
- Wind
- Renewables

3 The changes in the proportion of different energy sources have altered the risk from manmade global warming. Explain, as fully as you can, how this has changed. *(3 marks)*

G–E

1 It will run out.

2 The sources used have changed. There is now more natural gas.

3 Global warming is caused by sulfur dioxide and this has changed.

Examiner: The candidate has confused non-renewable with renewable. No mark is awarded.

The answer is very vague. The candidate only mentions one energy resource. However, one mark may be awarded as they have noticed the increase in natural gas.

The candidate incorrectly links sulfur dioxide to manmade global warming. No marks are awarded.

D–C

1 You can use it again and again. It will not run out.

2 The amount from coal has dropped. The amount from natural gas has increased a lot.

3 Global warming is caused by the release of CO_2. Less coal is burnt so the amount of CO_2 released has gone down. This reduces the risk.

Examiner: The answer given is not very clear, although it may be awarded a mark. Renewable energy resources can be used again and again as they do not use a fuel which will run out.

Both points are correct and so two marks may be awarded. However, the candidate has not discussed any of the other energy resources. They need to mention all of them to gain all the marks.

The candidate has got a mark for recognising that manmade global warming is due to the release of CO_2 and that this may have dropped as a lower proportion of our electricity comes from burning coal. However, they have not discussed that it has been replaced by energy resources that either do not produce CO_2 (nuclear, wind, and renewables,) or produce less CO_2 (natural gas).

B–A*

1 This type of energy resource does not use a fuel that will run out.

2 There has been an increase in the proportion of electricity generated from wind, other renewables, nuclear and natural gas. There has been a decline in coal and a significant drop in oil.

3 The risk from manmade global warming may have been reduced as a smaller proportion of the electricity comes from burning coal or oil. These both produce large quantities of CO_2. In their place we now use more nuclear, wind, and other renewables, which do not produce CO_2. We also use more natural gas, which produces less CO_2 than coal and oil.

Examiner: Good clear answer.

An excellent answer. Each energy resource is mentioned.

The student has given a clear answer to the question. They clearly identify that the proportion of electricity from sources producing lots of CO_2 has dropped. They have also made it clear that although natural gas does produce CO_2, it is less than other fossil fuels.

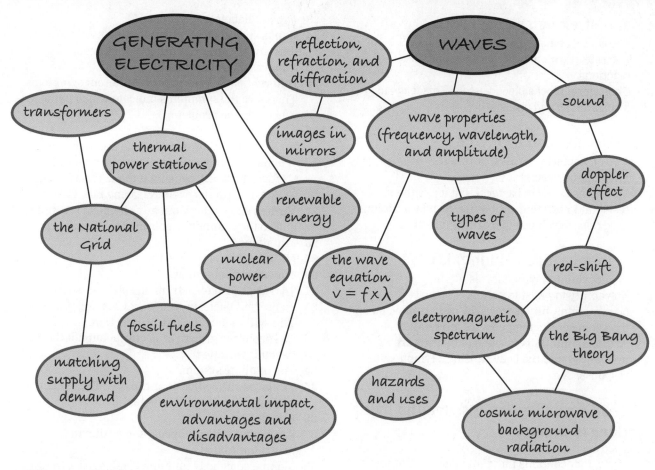

Revision checklist

- In thermal power stations heat is used to turn water to steam. This turns a turbine, which turns a generator to generate electricity.
- Different power stations have different start-up times. Nuclear and coal have the longest, HEP and natural gas have the shortest.
- Electricity is distributed using the National Grid. This connects power stations to homes and businesses.
- Transformers allow electricity to be transmitted at high voltages. This means a lower current can be used, the wires don't get as hot, and so less energy is wasted.
- Fossil fuels produce most of the electricity in the UK. They are a non-renewable energy resource (they will eventually run out).
- Nuclear power can be used to generate electricity. Inside nuclear reactors, nuclear fission takes place releasing heat.
- Renewables do not use a fuel that will run out. Examples include: wind, wave, tidal, solar, biomass, and geothermal.
- All methods of electricity generation offer a number of different advantages and disadvantages.
- Waves transfer energy. There are two types: transverse (oscillations at right angles to energy transfer, for example, light, radio waves, water waves) and longitudinal (oscillations parallel to energy transfer, for example, sound and some mechanical waves on springs). Longitudinal waves contain compressions and rarefactions.
- All waves have an amplitude, wavelength, and frequency.
- The wave equation states:

    wave speed = frequency × wavelength

- Waves can be reflected, refracted, and diffracted (significant diffraction: wavelength = size of gap).
- The law of reflection states:
  angle of incidence = the angle of reflection
  (measured from the normal line).
- Images formed in plane mirrors are virtual, upright, and laterally inverted.
- Electromagnetic waves can travel through a vacuum. The electromagnetic spectrum (from longest to shortest wavelength is: radio waves, microwaves, infrared, visible, ultraviolet, X-rays, and gamma rays.
- Electromagnetic waves can be used for communication.
- Sound is a longitudinal wave. High frequency means high pitch. Large amplitude means a loud sound. A reflection of sound is called an echo.
- The Doppler effect is the observed change in wavelength when a wave source moves towards or away from an observer. When the source moves towards an observer the wavelength reduces (waves are squashed up); when the source moves away the wavelength increases (waves are stretched out).
- The Big Bang theory states that around 14 billion years ago the Universe exploded from a very small, very hot initial point.
- Evidence includes red-shift (galaxies are moving away from us; the furthest away are moving faster – indicating that the Universe is expanding) and cosmic microwave background radiation (heat left over from the Big Bang).

Answers

B1 1: Diet, exercise, and health

1 The correct balance of foods and energy.
2 The rate at which cells carry out chemical reactions.
3 Cholesterol blocks blood vessels. This leads to heart attacks and strokes.

B1 2: Disease and medicine

1 Two of: bacteria, viruses, or fungi.
2 They kill bacteria.
3 Mutations occur in bacteria that make them resistant to existing antibiotics. So new antibiotics need to be developed to treat the infection.

B1 3: Immunity and immunisation

1 Phagocytes and lymphocytes.
2 The ability to resist infection.
3 Natural immunity is when the body is infected and then some of the lymphocytes are retained. Artificial immunity is when pathogens are introduced into the body causing a lymphocyte response.

B1 1–3 Levelled questions: Healthy living

Working to Grade E

1 Food such as sugar.
2 A diet that contains the right amount of different foods and the right amount of energy.
3 A person is malnourished if their diet is not balanced.
4 Obese
5 Energy
6 Energy
7 Build cells and repair tissue.
8 Any microbe that can cause an infectious disease.
9 A poison produced by a microorganism.
10 Bacteria
11 Either of: make us unwell or cause disease.
12 A drug that kills harmful bacteria in the body.
13 Paracetamol or codeine.
14 No
15 MRSA
16 Any three from: skin; mucus in the airways; stomach acid; blood clots as scabs.
17 a The lymphocyte is the cell with large rounded nucleus; the phagocyte has the lobed nucleus.
   b Ingests and digests pathogens.
18 Harmless (inactivated) or dead pathogen.
19 Measles, mumps, and rubella.

Working to Grade C

20 Amount of activity; proportion of muscle to fat; inherited factors.
21 In the cells.
22 More muscle and less fat results in higher metabolic rate.

23 Type II diabetes.
24 Hands spread many microorganisms because we touch many different things. Washing hands removes microorganisms.
25 Different pathogens produce different symptoms. Therefore the symptoms indicate which pathogen is causing the problem.
26 a C, B, A, D.
   b Virus attaches to cell; virus injects genetic material into cell; viral genetic material takes over host cell, causing it to make new viruses; host cell splits open, releasing new viruses.
27 Viruses do not carry out any chemical reactions, and so they cannot be poisoned by antibiotics.
28 Mutations
29 No living bacteria present.
30 To reduce contamination.
31 To transfer bacteria from one place to another.
32 To prevent bacteria entering or leaving the dishes. This will reduce the risk of infection.
33 To encourage growth of bacteria, but not the harmful varieties.
34 The immune system.
35 Produces antibodies or antitoxins. These kill the pathogen or neutralise the toxin.
36 Protein
37 Antibodies kill pathogens, and antitoxins neutralise toxins.
38 Making somebody immune to (able to resist) an infection.

Working to Grade A*

39 Reduces fat and increases muscle.
40 Cholesterol builds up in the walls of blood vessels. It can block the blood vessels, resulting in a heart attack.
41 Microorganisms multiply in the body and produce toxins that make us unwell.
42 Antibiotics kill many bacteria, but one or two may survive due to a mutation. The surviving bacteria will be resistant to the antibiotic and will multiply. They pass the resistance on to the next generation.
43 It produces bacteria that cannot be treated by antibiotics.
44 Use antibiotics less (for serious infections only) and ensure the full course of antibiotics is taken.
45 Each type of pathogen has a particular shaped antigen on its surface. The antibodies made by the lymphocyte have a specific shape that can only lock onto a particular shaped antigen.
46 A person receives a harmless or dead version of the pathogen. There is an immune response and the person's body makes antibodies. The body then has the ability to make these antibodies again rapidly if a real infection occurs. The antibodies destroy the pathogen before it can make the person ill.

B1 1–3 Examination questions: Healthy living

1 **a** White chocolate bar (1).
  b Carbohydrates and fats (1).
  c **i** Raisin cereal bar (1).
    ii Because it contains the least fat (1) and the least sugar (1).

2 **a** Variable until about 1970, then a gradual decrease (1).
  b **i** Between 1968 and 1970 (1).
    ii There was a sudden decrease in number of cases recorded after this time (1).
  c A dead or inactive virus is injected (1); this triggers lymphocytes to divide (1); some are retained (as memory cells) (1); these will respond/produce antibodies quicker if an active pathogen is introduced (1).

B1 4: Human control systems

1 Selecting the appropriate behaviour for a stimulus.
2 A receptor is a cell or organ that can detect stimuli.
3 Nervous systems act more quickly than hormonal systems. Hormonal responses last longer.

B1 5: Hormones and reproduction

1 The timing or the release of the egg, and the preparation of the womb for pregnancy.
2 To stimulate egg release, or to prevent egg release.
3 IVF is a medical procedure where fertilisation occurs in a test tube and the embryo is implanted into the female.

B1 4–5 Levelled questions: Controlling the human body

Working to Grade E

1 Any three of: light; sound; change in position; chemicals; pressure; pain; temperature.
2 Light
3 Skin
4 Nose and tongue
5 An electrical message that travels along a nerve.
6 **a** A: Nucleus; B: Insulating sheath; C: Nerve fibre; D: Synaptic end bulbs; E: Muscle.
  b Motor neurone
  c Impulse travels away from cell body toward the muscle.
7 A junction between two neurones.
8 Central nervous system and peripheral nervous system.
9 Knee jerk, hand withdrawal, or any sensible alternative.
10 Picking up an object, or any sensible alternative.
11 Glands
12 Kidney
13 37 °C
14 The changes in the body that result in a person reaching sexual maturity.

15 Oestrogen and progesterone.
16 Luteinising hormone (LH).
17 The pituitary gland.
18 *In vitro* fertilisation.
19 The release of a mature egg from the ovary.

Working to Grade C

20 Takes impulses from receptors to the CNS.
21 Takes impulses from the CNS to the effector.
22 As a chemical message.
23 A rapid, protective, automatic response.
24 Stimulus → receptor → sensory neurone → relay neurone → motor neurone → effector → response.
25 Central nervous system.
26 Contracts
27 In the bloodstream.
28 In sweat, in urine, or when we breathe out.
29 Skin releases sweat, which evaporates, taking heat from the body.
30 Chemical reactions/muscle contraction.
31 Lost in sweat/in urine.
32 Source of energy.
33 Target organs
34 Maturation of the egg in the ovary.
35 Oestrogen and progesterone.
36 FSH and LH.
37 Blood clots (leading to heart attacks and strokes).
38 The part of the menstrual cycle when the wall of the womb is shed together with some blood.

Working to Grade A*

39 To maintain enzyme function.
40 Oestrogen and progesterone.
41 High levels of progesterone (low oestrogen).
42 To cause several eggs to mature and be released.
43 Families can control when they will start a family; it allows infertile couples to have children; embryos can be screened for disorders.

B1 4–5 Examination questions: Controlling the human body

1 Eye – Light (1); Ear – Sound (1); Tongue – Chemicals (1); Skin – Temperature (1).
2 Brain (1) and spinal cord (1).
3 **a** A chemical messenger made in one part of the body (1) that acts in another part of the body (the target organ) (1).
  b **i** Folicle stimulating hormone/FSH (1).
    ii Luteinising hormone/LH (1).
  c They contain progesterone and oestrogen (1). These prevent the release of follicle stimulating hormone (FSH) (1), which prevents the maturation of eggs (1).
4 **a** **i** – B (1); **ii** – A (1); **iii** – C (1); **iv** – E (1).
  b Your answer should include six of these points in a logical order. 1 mark is awarded for each point up to a maximum of 6:
    • The sensory nerve ending detects the stimulus.

- An impulse is sent along the sensory neurone.
- Into the CNS/spinal cord.
- The impulse passes across a synapse.
- Into the relay neurone.
- The nerve impulse passes into a motor neurone.
- Passes out of the CNS/spinal cord.
- Impulse reaches a muscle.
- Arm is withdrawn.

  c Picking up a hot object (or any other logical alternative) (1).

5 a The reaction time gets quicker with more tests (1).

  b Eye (1).

  c i Used the computer to do the timing to milliseconds (1).

      ii The stimulus was repeated at least 10 times in each test (1).

  d i Her last result was slower than the previous value (1).

      ii Your answer could be either yes or no if it is well-reasoned: Yes, because the last does not follow the trend (it was significant); No, the last result was anomalous and not significant (1).

  e Select a group of at least five people who play computer games (1). Select a second group of five who do not play the computer games (1). Both groups carry out the test five times and in exactly the same way (1). Compare the results (1).

B1 6: Control in plants

1 A growth movement.

2 Hormones/auxin.

3 The auxin moves to the shaded side of the plant shoot.

B1 7: Use and abuse of drugs

1 They become addicted.

2 To give more reliable results.

3 Laboratory trials check that the drug is not toxic before it is given to a patient.

B1 6–7 Levelled questions: Control in plants and drugs

Working to Grade E

1 Light, gravity, and moisture.

2 Change in the environment.

3 Auxin

4 A chemical that affects our body chemistry.

5 Painkillers, antibiotics, and statins.

6 To ensure that the drugs work, and that they are not dangerous.

7 Tested on cells, tissues, and live animals.

8 Scientific testing of a new drug on human volunteers.

9 A dummy pill without the active drug.

10 a Sleeping pill, and to prevent morning sickness.

    b Treatment for leprosy.

11 Reduce blood cholesterol level.

12 a Taking drugs for no medical reason.

    b When a person needs a particular drug to maintain a functioning lifestyle.

    c Unpleasant sensations that occur when the body's chemical reactions do not function fully.

13 a To increase muscle development and to enhance performance.

    b Problems with reproductive cycle, and heart problems.

Working to Grade C

14 Growth movements called tropisms.

15 a Shoot should grow further up, roots should grow further down.

    b The shoot

    c Phototropism

16 a The shoot should turn up, the root will turn down.

    b Gravity

    c Gravitropism

17 Rooting hormones

18 a They avoid bias.

    b Neither the patients nor the doctors know who has the real drug.

19 An unwanted effect from a drug.

20 Cardiovascular diseases

21 a The greater the alcohol concentration, the greater the average braking time.

    b Alcohol slows people's reaction times.

    c Allows laws to be introduced to limit alcohol consumption for drivers.

    d Introduce a greater range of alcohol concentrations, and look for a point or concentration when the reaction time starts to decrease.

    e Have two drinks that look and taste the same; one will contain alcohol and one won't. Then repeat the tests.

22 They give the athletes an unfair advantage.

Working to Grade A*

23 Auxins cause plant cells in the shoot to elongate.

24 Auxins cause the shoots of broad-leafed plants to grow rapidly but not the roots, causing them to die.

25 The auxins move (by diffusion) to the shaded side of the shoot (away from the light). This causes the cells on the shaded side to elongate, which causes the shoot to bend toward the light.

26 a They will have grown straight up.

    b They all received equal light all round, therefore they do not bend.

    c The seedlings would begin to grow towards the light.

27 a No clear growth patterns.

    b No directional stimulus, such as gravity or light.

28 Shine light from one side only.

29 a Limb abnormalities in developing babies of pregnant women.
  b They did not test the drug on enough types of animals or any pregnant women.
  c Make sure the patient is not pregnant.
30 Tends to lead to people taking more powerful drugs, and can cause mental illness. However, it can be used to treat chronic pain.
31 No/disagree – because legal drugs are used by more people.
32 If they need to keep taking the drug. If they stop taking the drug to maintain a functioning lifestyle, they will suffer withdrawal symptoms.

B1 6–7 Examination questions: Control in plants and drugs

1 a A drug is a chemical that affects a person's body chemistry (1).
  b Painkillers, antibiotics and statins (or any other sensible answer) (1).
  c Alcohol, caffeine, nicotine, cannabis, steroids, cocaine and heroin (or any other sensible answer) (1).
  d Most people use legal recreational drugs (1).
  e Where people need a drug to maintain a functioning lifestyle. If they try to give up the drug, they suffer withdrawal symptoms (1).
2 a Gravitropism (1).
  b They grow toward the light (1) and they can use the light for photosynthesis (1).
  c Any four of the following points in a logical order. 1 mark will be awarded for each point up to a maximum of 4:
  - The plant produces a hormone called auxin.
  - In the shoot tips.
  - This diffuses back along the shoot.
  - The auxin moves away from the light to the shaded side of the shoot.
  - This causes the cells on the shaded side to elongate (get longer).
  - This bends the shoot toward the light.

How Science Works: Diet, exercise, hormones, genes, and drugs

1

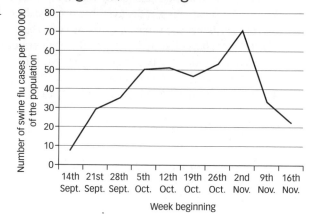

1 mark will be awarded for equidistant spacing with ascending scales for both axes.
1 mark will be awarded for correct labels and units, and axes placed the correct way round.
2 marks will be awarded for accurate plotting of points (a tolerance of +/– 1 small square is allowed by the examiner). 1 mark will be deducted for one error; maximum deduction 2 marks.
1 mark will be awarded for joining the line from point to point.
2 The trend is upward until 2nd November – gains 1 mark. After 2nd November the trend falls – gains 1 mark.
3 Recognising either the slight rise on 5th October, or the slight dip on 19th October will gain 1 mark.
4 9th November as there the trend begins to fall.
5 10 cases (a tolerance of +/– 5 is allowed by the examiner).

B1 8: Adaptations of organisms

1 Any feature that aids survival and reproduction.
2 High temperatures and lack of water.
3 Cold. Adaptations include: thicker fur, smaller ears and nose, rounded body shape, insulating fat.

B1 9: Distribution in the environment

1 Where two or more groups of species compete with each other for the same resources.
2 Availability of resources such as food, light, carbon dioxide, predators, prey.
3 Most populations will reduce because pollutants or air affect the quality of the habitat, for example by changing pH levels or oxygen levels in water, or by the presence of toxic chemicals that poison the organisms. Some species (indicator species) are able to survive in such conditions and will increase.

B1 10: Energy and biomass

1 The mass of living material.
2 The total dry mass of all the individuals in the link of the food chain.
3 By keeping food chains short – fewer links mean smaller energy losses. Animals are kept warm and in small enclosures to reduce energy loss through movement and heat. By reducing pests, which compete with the organism for its energy.

B1 11: Natural cycles

1 The breakdown of the bodies, or wastes, of organisms.
2 The constant cycling of the element carbon between the living and the non-living world.
3 Detritivores eat bits of dead body such as dead leaves and digest them, releasing the elements in their wastes. This speeds up the process of decay.

B1 8–11 Levelled questions: Organisms and their environment

Working to Grade E

1 Fins/tail for swimming, gills for gas exchange.
2 Swollen stems to store water; leaves reduced to spines to reduce water loss; extensive root systems to absorb water.
3 High temperatures, but also extremes of salt and pressure.
4 Body shape designed to reduce water resistance to a minimum.
5 Light; space; water; minerals; carbon dioxide.
6 The release of harmful substances into the environment by humans.
7 Sulfur dioxide from burning fuels, or any other sensible answer.
8 Has a straw-like tail that can obtain oxygen from the air.
9 At the base.
10 Biomass
11 A link in the food chain.
12 An organism that feeds on dead organisms, such as an earthworm eating dead leaves.
13 Bacteria and fungi.
14 Respiration
15 Carbohydrates, fats, and proteins.
16 Via the food chain.

Working to Grade C

17 They can swim faster to catch prey or escape predators.
18 a Dive to great depths.
   b To find food.
19 Makes the body lighter for flight.
20 The colder the habitat, the thicker the fur, or vice versa.
21 a Plant A – the cactus lives in a hot dry environment; Plant B – the broad-leafed plant lives in a wetter environment.
   b Swollen stems; leaves reduced to spines; extensive root systems.
   c Swollen stems store water; leaves reduced to spines reduce water loss; extensive root systems absorb water.
22 Indicator species
23 a B
   b Oxygen is low because large numbers of bacteria/microorganisms respire, using up the oxygen.
24 Chemical energy in sugars.
25 Photosynthesis
26 The animals use less energy due to restricted movement and being kept warm due to heat loss.
27 Numbers of organisms at each tropic level and the typical mass of an organism at each level.
28 a Sketch should show: pyramid shape, three blocks, widest at base, narrowest at top.
   b Small numbers giving small biomass. Only a few foxes can be sustained by the number of rabbits in the habitat.
   c Heat; faeces; movement.
   d The amount of energy falls at each link in the chain. There will not be sufficient energy to sustain too long a chain.
29 They must be equal.
30 Fossilisation: organisms die and are buried, or sink to the bottom of water; the organisms are covered by soils and exposed to high pressures; the bodies of the organisms turn into fossil fuels.
31 It releases large amounts of carbon dioxide into the atmosphere, at a faster rate that it is being removed from the atmosphere by plants.
32 a Wet and warm.
   b Microorganisms need both warmth and moisture to survive and function well. This condition was dry, so decay was slow.
   c Repeat the experiment several times.

Working to Grade A*

33 Plant B would die. This is because water loss would be more than water uptake.
34 a Thermophile bacteria
   b Because the human gut bacteria could not survive well at 50 °C.
35 Mayfly larvae are present because there is plenty of oxygen (and food), but there are few rat-tailed maggots as they are poor competitors.
36 The numbers of the two types of squirrels; the habitats in which they are both living; the types of food they both eat.
37 a The type of lichens in an area indicates the air pollution.
   b Answers should include reasons such as lichens are used because they live for a long time, and give an indication of the long term pollution levels.
38 a It is best to store bread in cool and dry conditions.
   b Conduct the experiment as above but use a range of different temperatures.
   c Any two from: the type of bread used; light; age of bread; amount of bread.
39 Trees will absorb carbon dioxide for photosynthesis, which will counter the amount of carbon dioxide being released by human activity.
40 When the animal dies, it decays; this is caused by microorganisms; the microorganisms respire, releasing carbon dioxide back into the atmosphere; the carbon dioxide is absorbed by the plant for photosynthesis; carbon compounds such as carbohydrates are made into the body of the plant.

B1 8–11 Examination questions: Organisms and their environment

1 a One from: grasping hands; tail for balance; grasping feet (1).

b They feed at different times of the day (1) and they eat different foods (1).

c They can make observations of similarities (1); organisms in the same group share many common features (1).

d They share a common ancestor (1).

2 a A – photosynthesis (1); B – combustion/burning (1); C – respiration (1).

b Bacteria (1) and fungi (1).

c 1 mark per factor is awarded, up to a total of 2 marks. 1 mark per explanation is awarded up to a total of 2 marks. (Total question score: 4.) These could include:
- Temperature – decay microorganisms are more active in warm (not hot) conditions.
- Moisture – decay microorganisms are more active in moist conditions.
- Oxygen – decay microorganisms are more active in aerobic conditions.

3 a They are spreading out from the south east of the UK towards the north and west (1).

b They can fly long distances (1); they have a longer period of reproduction, so are active for longer in the year (1), and their numbers increase more so they can spread more per year (1).

c They compete with other ladybird species for food (aphids) (1); they eat other species of ladybird (1); they eat ladybird eggs (1).

d i Large sample of results (1).

ii To make results accurate; it avoids mis-identification (1).

B1 12: Variation and reproduction

1 Variation

2 Genes, the environment, or a combination of both.

3 Sexual reproduction requires sex cells (gametes) produced by two parents to join; all offspring are genetically different from each parent. Asexual reproduction requires no fusion of gametes so only one parent is needed; all offspring are genetically identical to (clones of) the parent

B1 13: Engineering organisms

1 Two of: tissue culture, embryo transplants, adult cell cloning.

2 To make new products, e.g. hormones such as insulin, drugs, antibodies.

3 The process of transferring a gene from one organism to another. Ethical concerns include: superbugs, interfering with natural organisms.

B1 14: Genetically modified organisms

1 Crop plants that have had their genetic code altered by adding genes from other organisms.

2 They have an additional useful characteristic, such as pest resistance, herbicide resistance, increased vitamin content, or longer shelf life.

3 Any from: plants might escape and become more successful – superweeds; they might disrupt the natural food chain; uncertainty about the effects of eating GM crops; the seeds might be too expensive for some farmers.

B1 15: Evolution

1 The scientist who proposed the theory of evolution by natural selection.

2 The process by which those individuals with features best adapted to their environment (the 'fittest' animals in a generation) survive to reproduce and pass on their useful characteristics.

3 Darwin's theory suggests that variation between individuals occurs by chance (mutations) over several generations. Lamarck suggested that the changes occur in an individual of a species during its lifetime, rather than over several generations.

B1 12–15 Levelled questions: Genetics and evolution

Working to Grade E

1 Variation is the differences between individuals.

2 a Genes

b Combination of genes and the environment.

c Genes

d Combination of genes and the environment.

3 Deoxyribonucleic acid – DNA.

4 The nucleus

5 Gametes/sex cells/eggs and sperm.

6 The process where two gametes meet and fuse.

7 Bacteria, plants, and many single-celled organisms.

8 A genetically identical organism.

9 Any one from: hormones such as insulin, drugs, antibodies.

10 Special enzymes

11 To include genes that kill insect pests.

12 No, for example the UK doesn't.

13 Any two arguments from: crops may escape, and out-compete wild flowers; disruption of food chains if insect-resistant plants are grown; uncertainty about the effects on human health; cost of testing, development and seeds; time taken for testing.

14 A chance change in an organism's genes.

15 Charles Darwin

16 Plants, animals, and microorganisms.

17 Plants: oak tree, daffodil; Animals: human, fish, crab; Microorganism: *E. coli, salmonella*.

Working to Grade C

18 a D

b The manufacture of proteins, which affect how a cell works.

19 During reproduction. In sexual reproduction, genes are passed on in the eggs and sperm (or gametes).

20 Genes are passed to us from our parents: half from the father in the sperm cell, and half from the mother in the egg cell.

21 We are a mix of characteristics from our mother and our father, as the genes come from both parents.

22 All the new plants are identical, with the desired characteristics, and it is cheap.

23 B → D → A → C → E.

24 A host mother into which an embryo is implanted.

25 To produce large numbers of identical animals with the desired characteristics.

26 A sheep (Dolly).

27 They give an electric shock/use an electric current.

28 a   i B; ii A; iii C.
   b   Because it is a closer match, and there is no risk of disease transmission.

29 The crops can be sprayed with weedkiller, which will destroy the weeds but not the soya, and stop the competition from weed plants.

30 The process produces crops with the desired characteristic far quicker than selective breeding.

31 a   It reduces the need for pesticides so there would be less pollution in the environment.
   b   GM food has been eaten in some countries for 10 years with no ill-effects noted.
   c   GM crops have a higher yield so can feed larger populations.

32 They make observations about the structure of the organisms and look for similarities and differences; organisms with more similarities are grouped together.

33 They share a common ancestor.

34 Humans and dogs share more similarities with each other than they do with fish, so humans and dogs have a closer common ancestor.

35 They live in similar environments, and share a feature which helps them survive in that environment. This is an ecological link.

36 Two from: the theory disagreed with religious ideas; there was not much evidence at the time; scientists didn't know about genes at the time, so couldn't explain any mechanism for evolution.

37 Because organisms cannot alter their genotype during their lifetime.

38 Over three billion years ago.

Working to Grade A*

39 The gene would code for the manufacture of a protein. This protein would have a certain pigmentation/colour. The cells in the (iris of the) eye would make large amounts of this protein.

40 Thousands of different proteins are needed to make a human body.

41 In asexual reproduction, only one parent is needed; there are no sex cells involved so no mixing of genetic information; all the offspring are genetically identical. In sexual reproduction, sex cells (gametes) combine from two parents (the mother and father); the offspring shares half its genetic material with the father and half with the mother; all offspring are genetically different from each parent.

42 Advantages include: quick, no need to find a mate. Disadvantages include lack of variation.

43 The new individuals are all genetically identical to, or clones of, the parent plant.

44 Any one from: all the offspring have the desired characteristic, large numbers can be produced.

45 The loop of DNA would be inserted into a fertilised sheep's egg.

46 a   Variation in the peppered moth species: there is always a struggle to survive; the darker variation is more suited to the environment/it is 'fitter'; the darker variety survives and breeds; over time there will be more dark variety, as they are more successful.
   b   It would be seen more easily by predators such as birds and eaten.
   c   A mutation
   d   The moth had an 'inner need' to change its body to a darker colour; it changed (so the genes must have changed); then the dark variety survived.
   e   The environmental change happened quickly because their life cycle is short.

B1 12–15 Examination questions: Genetics and evolution

1 a   Clones (1).
   b   Grow on agar jelly (1), which contains plant hormones (1).
   c   Any two from the following list – 1 mark for each: plants will have known characteristics, such as flower colour; all plants will be identical; the technique is faster.

2 Any four from the following list in a logical order, earning 1 mark each up to a maximum of 4:
   • Variation exists within the species.
   • Some variations are produced by mutations.
   • Some variations (long snouts) provide an advantage.
   • There is a struggle to survive.
   • The animals with the advantage are the 'fittest' and survive.
   • These pass the gene for the advantage (long snout) on to the next generation.
   • Gradually all animals tend to have long snouts.

3 5 marks available. 2 marks will be awarded for two positive points; 2 marks will be awarded for two negative points; the final mark will be awarded for a satisfactory evaluation of the pros and cons and a concluding judgement.
   Positives include: the technique produces more food, which can feed people in areas of famine; the increase in food production is because the food is engineered not to decay quickly, and is not affected by pests or pesticides; foods can be engineered to be enriched and more nutritious, e.g. with vitamins to improve health.

Negative include: genes could escape, creating superweeds that are resistant to pesticides; the technology itself – any long-term health problems of the engineered plants are not known to the consumer; the process is expensive, and so some poorer countries (which have the greatest need to feed their population) might not be able to afford the seeds.

How Science Works: Surviving and changing in the environment

1 a Accuracy is achieved by using a digital oxygen probe, which is very accurate; or counting the rat-tailed maggots in 1 square metre.
   b Reliable results are achieved by doing repeat readings of oxygen levels to calculate an average. Alternatively, a large number of quadrat readings would ensure reliability.

2 More rat-tailed maggots are found at point A because of higher pollution; higher nitrate levels; which result in low oxygen levels. One mark for each of these three points.
3 a Oxygen levels are low because the oxygen has been used up by aerobic organisms.
   b Nitrates

C1 1: Atoms and the periodic table

1 Proton +1, neutron 0, electron –1.

2

3 Atomic number = 9, mass number = 9 + 10 = 19.

C1 2: Chemical reactions

1 Nitrogen dioxide – covalent; iron oxide – ionic.
2 sodium + chlorine → sodium chloride
3 $2Li + F_2 → 2LiF$

C1 1–2 Levelled questions: The fundamental ideas in chemistry

Working to Grade E

1 a O
  b Iron
  c Five from: chlorine – Cl; cobalt – Co; cadmium – Cd; carbon – C; calcium – Ca; caesium – Cs; chromium – Cr; copper – Cu.
  d Four from: helium, neon, argon, krypton, xenon, radon.
  e Four from: Li, Na, K, Rb, Cs, Fr.
2 Protons and neutrons.
3 100, groups.
4

Name of element	Number of electrons	Electronic structure
lithium	3	2.1
sodium	11	2.8.1
potassium	19	2.8.8.1

5 One from: they react vigorously with water to form a hydroxide and hydrogen gas; they react vigorously with oxygen from the air to form oxides.

6

carbon   silicon

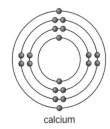

calcium

Working to Grade C

7 a 8
  b Helium
  c The noble gases have the maximum number of electrons in their highest energy level/ outermost shell. This electronic structure makes the noble gases particularly stable.
8 a 5
  b 5 + 6 = 11
9 45 – 21 = 24
10

Name of element	Number of protons	Number of neutrons	Number of electrons
hydrogen	1	0	1
oxygen	8	8	8
sodium	11	12	11
aluminium	13	14	13
boron	5	6	5
calcium	20	20	20

11 one electron is transferred from the highest energy level of the sodium atom to the highest energy level of the chlorine atom

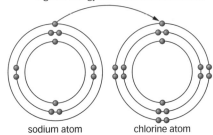

sodium atom   chlorine atom

12 Covalent bonding.
13 Ions
14 a carbon + oxygen → carbon dioxide
  b magnesium + chlorine → magnesium chloride
  c iron + sulfur → iron sulfide
  d sulfuric acid + sodium hydroxide → sodium sulfate + water
  e lead carbonate → lead oxide + carbon dioxide
15 6.4 g – 3.2 g = 3.2 g

Working to Grade A*

16 a Oxygen: $2Mg + O_2 → 2MgO$
  b Balanced
  c Sodium and hydrogen:
    $H_2SO_4 + 2NaOH → Na_2SO_4 + 2H_2O$
  d Balanced
  e Balanced
  f Oxygen and hydrogen: $CH_4 + 2O_2 → CO_2 + 2H_2O$

C1 1–2 Examination questions: The fundamental ideas in chemistry

1 a i The atom of the element has 6 electrons in its highest energy level. (1)
    ii 8 (1)
  b i 9 (1)
    ii 9 + 10 = 19 (1)

iii Fluorine (1); F (1).

iv

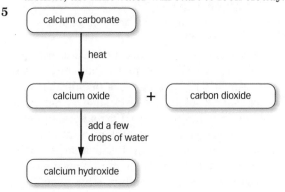

(2)

2 a i lithium + oxygen → lithium oxide (1)

   ii $4Li + O_2 → 2Li_2O$ (1)

 b 60 g (2)

 c i metal (1); loses (1); positive (1)

   ii 2 (1)

 d Helium (1)

 e Number of protons = 3 (1);
Number of neutrons = 4 (1)

C1 3: Limestone and building materials

1 Mortar – cement and sand; concrete – cement, sand, aggregate.

2 A suspension of calcium carbonate in water.

3 a calcium oxide + water → calcium hydroxide

 b magnesium carbonate + nitric acid → magnesium nitrate + carbon dioxide + water

C1 3 Levelled questions: Limestone and building materials

Working to Grade E

1 a One from: limestone makes buildings and cement, quarries provide jobs.

 b Quarries create extra traffic.

 c Old quarries can be made into lakes.

 d Tourists may stop visiting an area with a new quarry.

2 clay, mortar, concrete.

3 potassium carbonate

4 Take a sample of colourless limewater. Bubble the gas through the limewater. If the gas is carbon dioxide, the limewater will start to look cloudy.

5

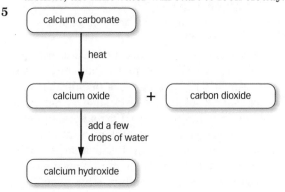

Working to Grade C

6 Calcium carbonate → calcium oxide + carbon dioxide

7 a zinc carbonate → zinc oxide + carbon dioxide

 b lead carbonate → lead oxide + carbon dioxide

8 a Copper sulfate

 b Zinc chloride

 c Calcium nitrate

 d Magnesium chloride

 e Sodium sulfate

9 a → sodium nitrate + carbon dioxide + water

 b → magnesium nitrate + carbon dioxide + water

 c → calcium chloride + carbon dioxide + water

 d → zinc sulfate + carbon dioxide + water

10 a Mild steel

 b Oak wood and limestone conduct heat least well. This means they are good insulators of heat, which helps to prevent heat loss from buildings made of these materials.

 c There is no data for the limestone, and the high strength concrete cracks if it is pulled.

Working to Grade A*

11 $ZnCO_3 → ZnO + CO_2$

12 $Ca(OH)_2 + CO_2 → CaCO_3 + H_2O$

13 a $MgCO_3 + 2HNO_3 → Mg(NO_3)_2 + CO_2 + H_2O$

 b $ZnCO_3 + 2HCl → ZnCl_2 + CO_2 + H_2O$

 c $Na_2CO_3 + HCl → 2NaCl + CO_2 + H_2O$

 d Balanced.

 e $CaCO_3 + 2HNO_3 → Ca(NO_3)_2 + CO_2 + H_2O$

C1 3 Examination questions: Limestone and building materials

1 a i Quarry companies can sell the limestone (1).

   ii Quarries make the land unavailable for other purposes (1).

 b i calcium carbonate → calcium oxide + carbon dioxide (1)

   ii Traditional lime kilns were open to the air so that the carbon dioxide produced in the decomposition reaction could escape (1).

   iii Calcium hydroxide solution is also known as limewater. It is used to test for carbon dioxide gas. It is also used to neutralise acids, for example in lakes whose pH is too low (1 mark for each correct answer).

 c Calcium sulfate (1) and magnesium sulfate (1).

 d $CaCO_3 + 2HCl → CaCl_2 + CO_2 + H_2O$ (1)

2 a i Distance of Bunsen flame from bottom of test tube (1); amount of limewater (1).

   ii Time for limewater to begin to look cloudy (1).

 b Zinc carbonate → zinc oxide + carbon dioxide (1)

 c magnesium oxide (1) + carbon dioxide (1)

 d calcium hydroxide + carbon dioxide → calcium carbonate + water (1)

C1 4: Extracting metals

1 Mine the ore; concentrate the ore to separate its metal compounds from waste rock; extract the metal from its compounds; purify the metal.

2 Aluminium is more reactive than carbon so it cannot be extracted by reduction with carbon. Instead, an electric current is passed through molten aluminium oxide.

3   Phytomining – planting certain plants on low-grade copper ores. The plants absorb copper compounds. Burn the plants. The ash is rich in copper compounds.
Bioleaching – use bacteria to make solutions of copper compounds. Use electrolysis or displacement reactions to extract copper from these solutions.

C1 5: Metals: recycling, properties, alloys, and uses

1   Reasons for recycling metals – some ores are in short supply; extracting metals from ores creates waste that may damage the environment; extracting metals from ores requires electrical energy or heat energy.
2   Low carbon steel is easily shaped and is used for food cans and car body panels. High carbon steel is hard and is used to make tools. Stainless steel is resistant to corrosion and is used to make cutlery and surgical instruments.
3   Titanium is suitable for aeroplanes because it has a low density and does not corrode. Titanium is suitable for artificial hip bones because it does not corrode.

C1 4–5 Levelled questions: Metals and their uses

Working to Grade E

1   Gold
2   b, c, d, a.
3   Molybdenum, manganese, scandium, titanium.
4   Recycling produces smaller amounts of waste materials, and requires less energy.
5

Type of steel	Properties
Stainless steel	Resistant to corrosion
High carbon steel	Very hard
Low carbon steel	Easily shaped

6   brittle, cast iron, compression.
7   a   It has a low density and is resistant to corrosion.
    b   It resists corrosion, even in salty water.
8   Reduced means that oxygen has been removed from a compound. Reducing iron oxide with carbon produces iron and carbon monoxide and/or carbon dioxide.

Working to Grade C

9   a   tin, lead.
    b   Two from: calcium, magnesium, aluminium.
    c   Gold
10 It is expensive to extract titanium from its ore because the extraction has many stages and requires much energy.

11 Obtaining copper by phytomining or bioleaching creates less waste and requires less energy than extracting copper from low-grade ores by smelting.
12 a   Electrode A.
    b   The negative electrode, electrode B.
13 copper sulfate + iron → copper + iron sulfate
14 a   Aluminium alloy 7075.
    b   This alloy is harder than the other two materials in the table, and has the greatest tensile strength.
    c   Pure aluminium has a slightly lower density than aluminium alloy 7075, so aluminium alloy 7075 is heavier than pure aluminium per unit volume.

C1 4–5 Examination questions: Metals and their uses

1   a   2 marks from: copper can easily be bent into different shapes without cracking (1); it is hard enough to make pipes and tanks (1); it does not react with water (1).
    b   i   Nickel brass and naval brass. (1)
        ii Nickel brass is an alloy of copper, so it is probably harder than pure copper (1).
    c   i   This method creates large amounts of waste (1); requires a great deal of energy (1).
        ii Particular species of plant are planted on low-grade copper ore. The plants take in copper compounds (1). The plants are harvested and burnt. Copper is extracted from their ash (1).
2   a   i   The scientists found the total mass of indium in samples 2–6. They then divided this value by the number of samples (5). The answer was 100 g. They decided not include the value from sample 1, since it is anomalous (1).
        ii   40 tonnes (2).
        iii 399 960 tonnes (1).
        iv   The waste may produce a large and unsightly heap (1).
    b   Any reasoned answer acceptable, for example: I recommend that the mine should be allowed to reopen. The advantages of opening the mine are that 400 jobs could be created. A compound made from indium is used to make solar cells, for which demand is increasing. I think these advantages outweigh the disadvantages such as the fact that indium is harmful if swallowed or breathed in, and that pollution has been linked to the extraction of indium metal in China, but the mine owners must take precautions to minimise the risks from these hazards. (1 mark for each reasoned point made that supports the recommendation.)

C1 6: Crude oil and hydrocarbons

1 A hydrocarbon is a compound made up of hydrogen and carbon only; a mixture consists of two or more elements or compounds that are not chemically joined together; a fraction is a mixture of hydrocarbons whose molecules have a similar number of carbon atoms; an alkane is a hydrocarbon that is saturated.

2 A mixture consists of two or more elements or compounds that are not chemically joined together. Each of the substances in a mixture has its own properties, and being part of a mixture does not affect these properties. You can separate mixtures by physical means such as filtration and distillation.

3 CH_4, C_2H_6, C_3H_8.

C1 7: Hydrocarbon fuels

1 As molecule size increases, boiling point and viscosity increase and flammability decreases.

2

Substance	Produced as a result of ...	Causes these problems ...
Carbon dioxide	The combustion of hydrocarbon fuels	Global warming
Carbon monoxide	Partial combustion of hydrocarbon fuels	Poisonous – can cause death if breathed in
Sulfur dioxide	Combustion of fuels that contain sulfur	Acid rain
Oxides of nitrogen	Combustion of hydrocarbons in air at high temperatures	Acid rain
Particulates	Partial combustion of hydrocarbons	Global dimming

C1 8: Biofuels and hydrogen fuel

1 Biodiesel and diesel both produce carbon dioxide on burning. The plants from which the biofuels were made removed carbon dioxide from the atmosphere during photosynthesis whilst they were growing. But growing biofuel crops require inputs such as fertilisers. The production of fertilisers results in carbon dioxide gas emissions. Overall, biofuels are likely to result in smaller carbon dioxide emissions than diesel.

2 Benefits – only one product, water vapour, which is non-polluting; can be produced from renewable resources, such as methane from animal waste. Drawbacks – since hydrogen gas is explosive with air, it is difficult and dangerous to store and transport.

C1 6–8 Levelled questions: Crude oil and fuels

Working to Grade E

1 a False – crude oil is a mixture of compounds.
 b False – a mixture consists of two or more elements or compounds that are not chemically combined.
 c False – when substances are mixed together, their chemical properties remain unchanged.
 d True
 e True

2 a hydrocarbons
 b hydrogen
 c alkanes
 d saturated

3 d, a, b, e, c, f.

4 Nitrogen dioxide – formed when hydrocarbons burn in air at high temperatures.
 Carbon monoxide – formed when hydrocarbons burn in a poor supply of air.
 Sulfur dioxide – formed when a sulfur-containing fuel burns.

5 a Global warming.
 b Acid rain.
 c Acid rain.
 d Global dimming.

Working to Grade C

6

Name of alkane	Molecular formula	Structural formula
Methane	CH_4	
Ethane	C_2H_6	
Propane	C_3H_8	
Butane	C_4H_{10}	

7 a increases
 b decreases
 c decreases

8 a carbon dioxide + water.
 b methane + oxygen → carbon dioxide + carbon monoxide + water.

9 a $72 - 20 = 52\,°C$
 b Methane
 c They are oxidised.

	Ethanol	Petrol
Use of renewable resources	Pro: Plants from which ethanol obtained can be grown each year. Con: Growing the plants from which ethanol is made requires inputs of fertilisers which are made from non-renewable resources.	Pro: None as petrol is non-renewable. Con: Obtained from non-renewable crude oil.
Fuel storage and use	Pro: Relatively safe and easy to store. Con: Storage tanks and fuel pumps not yet widespread at filling stations.	Pro: Relatively safe and easy to store. Con: Because filling stations can only store enough fuel to last a few days, customers are vulnerable if supplies are threatened.
Combustion products	Pro: Produces water on burning. Con: Produces carbon dioxide on burning.	Pro: Produces water on burning. Con: Produces carbon dioxide on burning.

C1 6–8 Examination questions: Crude oil and fuels

1 **a** Carbon dioxide – global warming (1);
sulfur dioxide and oxides of nitrogen – acid rain (2);
solid particles – global dimming (1).

   b **i** Methane + oxygen → carbon dioxide + water (2)

      ii Carbon monoxide. (1)

2 **a** evaporate (1); condense (1); cool (1).

   b

	Letter	
The place where a mixture of vapours enters the column.	E	(1)
The hottest part of the column.	D or F	(1)
The place where the fraction containing substances with the highest boiling points leaves the column.	F	(1)
The place where the fraction containing the most flammable substances leaves the column.	A	(1)
The place where methane gas leaves the column.	A	(1)

3 **a**

H—C—C—C—H (structure with H atoms on each carbon) (2)

   b **i** As the molecule size increases from methane to hexane, so the boiling point increases (1).

      ii One from: pentane, hexane (1).

4 Marks are awarded for using good English, organising information clearly and using specialist terms where appropriate. 6 marks available. Points to include:
- Hydrogen can be produced from renewable sources, such as methane from animal waste.
- Petrol and diesel are produced from non-renewable crude oil.
- Burning hydrogen produces just one waste product – water vapour.
- Burning petrol and diesel produces carbon dioxide gas, which causes global warming.
- Burning petrol and diesel produces oxides of nitrogen, which causes acid rain.
- Hydrogen is an explosive gas, so the risks associated with storing and transporting it are greater than the risks associated with storing and transporting liquid petrol and diesel.

How Science Works: atoms, rocks, metals, and fuels

1 Independent variable – fuel; dependent variable – temperature change.

2 Volume of water, mass of oil burned, distance between top of flame and bottom of water container.

3 The resolution of the thermometer that can detect a temperature change of 0.5 °C is greater, so smaller changes in temperature can be detected.

4 Yes, the results support the hypothesis, because the temperature change of the water on burning 1 g of each fuel increases as the number of carbon atoms in a molecule of the fuel increases. The increasing temperature change of the water is a measure of the energy released on burning a fuel.

5 Any value between 46 and 50 °C.

6 To find out how close together the repeated values are – the closer together they are, the closer they are likely to be to the true value; to spot any anomalous data.

C1 9: Obtaining useful substances from crude oil

1 Cracking the naphtha fraction of crude oil produces alkanes with smaller molecules that can be added to the petrol fraction, for which there is a high demand.

2 Conditions – the hydrocarbons must be vapourised and then passed over a hot catalyst, or mixed with steam and then heated to a high temperature. Products – alkanes (with smaller molecules than those of the reactants) and alkenes such as ethene.

3 Ethene C_2H_4 and propene C_3H_6.

4 Bubble the alkene through orange bromine water, which will become colourless.

C1 10: Polymers

1 Dental polymers are white, hard and tough. They are poor conductors of heat. The fact that they are poor conductors of heat mean that it is not uncomfortable to eat very hot or cold foods. The fact that they are white means that they match the colour of the teeth. The fact that they are hard and tough means that they will be hard-wearing and not need replacing for many years, if at all.

2 Hydrogels absorb huge volumes of liquids. This means they are suitable for nappies, which must absorb large volumes of urine.

3 Environmental advantage – cornstarch bags are biodegradable, whereas poly(ethene) bags persist in the environment for many years; economic advantage – growers of corn and producers of cornstarch bags have products to sell; social – cornstarch is renewable, so it does not take supplies from future generations. Poly(ethene) is produced from products obtained from crude oil, which is a non-renewable resource.

C1 11: Ethanol

1

	From ethene by hydration	From glucose by fermentation
Raw materials	Crude oil (ethene) and water (steam)	Plants (sugars)
Conditions	Catalyst 300 °C	Enzymes from yeast catalyse the reaction 37 °C
Products	Ethanol	Ethanol and carbon dioxide

2 Making ethanol from ethene uses up a non-renewable resource – crude oil. This is a disadvantage. Another disadvantage is that the energy costs of producing ethanol from ethene are relatively high, since the reaction takes place at a high temperature. The raw materials for making ethanol by the fermentation of plant sugars are renewable, which is an advantage. The energy costs of this process are relatively low, which is also an advantage.

C1 9–11: Levelled questions: Other useful substances from crude oil

Working to Grade E

1 Poly(ethene), petrol, diesel.

2 Dental fillings – hard and tough and a poor conductor of heat; disposable nappies – absorbs large volumes of liquid; breathable waterproof fabrics – allows water vapour to pass through its tiny pores, but not liquid water; to make mattresses that mould to the body – changes shape in response to warming or pressure.

3 a True

b A molecule of poly(ethene) is made by joining together thousands of ethene molecules.

c True

d The monomer propene makes poly(propene).

4 smaller, vapourise, vapours, catalyst, steam, decomposition.

Working to Grade C

5 C_2H_4, ethene

C_3H_6, propene

6 C_4H_8 and C_7H_{14} are alkenes.

7

Name of hydrocarbon	Results
Ethane	Bromine water does not change colour
Propene	Colour change from orange to colourless
Ethene	Colour change from orange to colourless
Butane	Bromine water does not change colour

8

9 The relative demand for the petrol fraction is greater than its typical relative proportion in crude oil. Cracking the naphtha fraction produces hydrocarbons in the petrol fraction, so increasing the amount of petrol an oil company has available to sell.

10

Starting materials	Type of reaction	Conditions
Glucose	Fermentation	Needs natural catalyst from yeast; 37 °C
Ethene and water	Hydration	Needs catalyst; 300 °C

11

	Advantages	Disadvantages
From ethene	No fertilisers are required, so water pollution is unlikely.	Takes place at a higher temperature, so requires more energy, resulting in more pollution.
From glucose	Takes place at a lower temperature, so requires less energy, resulting in less pollution (for example CO_2 emissions if the heat is supplied by burning a hydrocarbon).	Plants are the raw material for this process. Growing the crops may require inputs of fertilisers, which may cause water pollution.

12 A benefit of plastic recycling is that reserves of non-renewable crude oil are not being used up to produce the plastic. If plastics are recycled, then less plastics are taken to landfill, or incinerated. Incineration produces polluting gases. A problem of plastic recycling is collecting the plastics, which is time-consuming and requires energy inputs for the transporting plastics to a central collection point. A second problem is the sorting of the plastics into different types, which is labour-intensive and so expensive.

C1 9–11 Examination questions: Other useful substances from crude oil

1 a Thermal decomposition (1).
  b The aluminium oxide acts as a catalyst (1).
  c i C_2H_4 (1)
    ii Bubble the ethene through orange bromine water (1). The orange bromine water will become colourless (1). This shows that the ethene has a double bond (1).
2 a The bags are not biodegradable, which means they are not broken down by microbes (1).
  b Jute is made from a plant material, which is renewable, unlike the raw material for making poly(ethene), which is non-renewable crude oil (1).
    Jute bags are biodegradable, so can be broken down by microbes when they are disposed of, unlike poly(ethene) bags, which are non-renewable (1).
3 a

  b i Two from: poly(butene) does not react with most things that may be mixed with the water, for example detergents and oils. It is flexible, so is easy to put into place under roads and so on. It is elastic, so stretches if the water in the pipes freezes and expands. (1 mark for each)

    ii The material of the pipe may react with the chlorine or its compounds that are dissolved in the water (1). The reaction may lead to the pipe being damaged (1).

C1 12: Plant oils and their uses

1 Plant oils can be extracted from seeds, fruits and nuts.
2 The olives are crushed and pressed. The oil is then separated from water and other impurities.
3 Vegetable oils can be used as vehicle fuels since they release large amounts of energy on burning.

C1 13: Emulsions and saturated and unsaturated fats

1 An emulsion is a mixture of oil and water than does not separate out.
2 Add bromine water to the oil in a test tube. Place a bung in the test tube. Shake. If the oil is unsaturated, the mixture will change colour from orange to colourless.
3 Unsaturated vegetable oils can be hardened by adding hydrogen gas to them. The reaction happens at a temperature of about 60 °C. A nickel catalyst is required.

C1 12–13 Levelled questions: Plant oils and their uses

Working to Grade E

1 seeds, nuts, fruit.
2 b, d, a, c
3 a Oils do not dissolve well in water.
  b True
  c Emulsifiers make emulsions more stable.
  d A student shakes a mixture of oil, vinegar, and sugar. Afterwards, he sees two layers of liquid. This shows that the sugar is not an emulsifier.
4 a D
  b A
  c E
  d B

Working to Grade C

5 a Coconut oil and palm oil.
  b Coconut oil and palm oil.
6 a Catherine, because more energy is released on eating the potatoes cooked by this method. The extra energy comes from the oil absorbed by the potatoes on cooking.
  b The advantages of cooking potatoes in oil compared to cooking them in water are that the potatoes cook more quickly in oil, and have a flavour that some people prefer.
  c The disadvantage of cooking potatoes in oil is that the resulting food releases more energy on digestion than potatoes cooked in water. Eating lots of oil-rich foods can lead to weight gain.

7 a Eating too much fat can lead to weight gain. Cutting down on fats eaten can help to stabilise or reduce weight.

b Saturated fats can raise blood cholesterol, which increases the risk of heart disease. Unsaturated fats are better for health.

8 a Independent variable – type of plant oil; dependent variable – temperature increase of water.

b Control variables – distance of flame from water, volume of water.

c The oil which causes the greatest water temperature increase per gram of oil is the oil which releases the most energy on burning.

Working to Grade A*

9 End A is hydrophilic, since it is in the water.

10 a Hydrogen

b Nickel catalyst, 60 °C.

c The hardened oil boils at a higher temperature than the unsaturated oil from which it is made.

d Hardened oils are used for spreads and to make cakes and pastries. The fact that they are solid at room temperature makes them suitable for these purposes.

C1 12–13 Examination questions: Plant oils and their uses

1 a Detergent, mustard powder, egg yolk. (1)

b i It is a viscous liquid with a good coating ability (1).

ii Two from: paints, cosmetics, ice creams. (2)

c End A is hydrophobic (1), since it is in the oil (1).

2 Advantages of cooking in oil – cook more quickly (1), taste that many people prefer (1); disadvantage – eating too much oil can cause weight gain (1).

3 a i C and D (1).

ii zero (1)

b i Hydrogen is added to the unsaturated vegetable oil (1). A nickel catalyst is required (1), and a temperature of 60 °C (1).

ii Spreads for bread and as an ingredient for cakes and pastries (1). They are suitable for these purposes because they are solids at room temperature (1).

C1 14: Changes in the Earth

1 The Earth's crust, the atmosphere, and the oceans.

2 Tectonic plates move at speeds of a few centimetres a year.

3 The Earth's mantle moves because, deep inside the Earth, natural radioactive processes heat the mantle. The heat drives convection currents within the mantle.

4 The shapes of Africa and South America look as if they might once have fitted together; there are fossils of the same plants on both continents. There

are rocks of the same type at the edges of the two continents where they might once have been joined.

C1 15: The Earth's atmosphere 1

1 Nitrogen – about 80%; oxygen – about 20%, smaller proportions of carbon dioxide, water vapour, the noble gases.

2 Plants removed carbon dioxide from the atmosphere in photosynthesis; carbon dioxide gas dissolved in the oceans.

3 No one was around to make observations at the time.

C1 16: The Earth's atmosphere 2

1 There is more carbon dioxide in the atmosphere as a result of humans burning fossil fuels. This leads to more carbon dioxide dissolving in the oceans, and the pH of the oceans decreasing. The increasing acidity makes it difficult for shellfish to make their shells.

2 Nitrogen – raw material for fertiliser manufacture and to freeze food; oxygen – medical treatments; argon – double glazing; neon – display lighting.

C1 14–16 Levelled questions: Changes in the Earth and its atmosphere

Working to Grade E

1 Outwards, from centre – core, mantle, crust.

2 a crust and upper part of the mantle;

b solid;

c convection currents;

d radioactive processes.

3

Gas	Percentage
Nitrogen	80
Oxygen	20
Carbon dioxide, water vapour, noble gases	small proportion

4 algae; carbon dioxide; photosynthesis; oxygen.

5 a, d, e

Working to Grade C

6 a True

b Over the past few years, the amount of carbon dioxide absorbed by the oceans has increased.

c Most scientists agree that the increasing amounts of carbon dioxide in the atmosphere are causing global warming.

d True

7 a The shapes of Africa and South America look as if they might once have fitted together; there are fossils of the same plants on both continents; there are rocks of the same type at the edges of the two continents where they might once have been joined.

b Wegener was not a geologist; no one could work out how the continents might have moved.

8

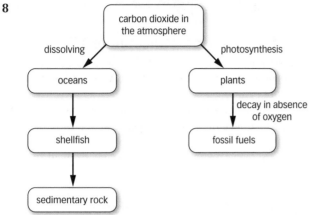

Working to Grade A*

9 Gases in the early atmosphere reacted with each other in the presence of sunlight, or lightning, to make the complex molecules that are the basis of life.

10 **a** Lightning
   b Two from: water vapour, carbon monoxide, hydrogen, hydrocarbon molecules and ammonia.
   c No one was around at the time to make observations.

11 **a** Fractional distillation.
   b Argon – double glazing; neon – display lighting.

C1 14–16 Examination questions: Changes in the Earth and its atmosphere

1 **a** The Earth's crust and the upper part of the mantle (1).
   b A few centimetres a year (1).
   c Radioactive process deep inside the Earth release heat (1). The heat causes convection currents within the mantle (1). These make the tectonic plates move.
   d Santiago is on a plate boundary, whereas Brasilia is not (1).
   e Earthquakes happen at plate boundaries when tectonic plates suddenly move relative to each other. No one can predict exactly when these movements will happen, so no one can predict exactly when earthquakes can happen (1).

2 **a i**

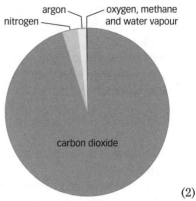

(2)

A pie chart is best, but bar chart is also acceptable.

   ii Similarity – both atmospheres include nitrogen, carbon dioxide and argon gases (1). Difference – the percentage of carbon dioxide in the Martian atmosphere is much greater than the percentage of this gas in the atmosphere of the Earth (1). *There are several other acceptable differences such as the significantly lower percentages of oxygen and nitrogen in the Martian atmosphere.*

   b i Erupting volcanoes (1).
   ii Carbon dioxide was removed by early plants and algae photosynthesising (1), and also by dissolving in the oceans (1).

   c Humans have been burning fossil fuels in increasing amounts (1); humans also destroy forests, so less carbon dioxide is removed from the atmosphere by photosynthesis (1).

How Science Works – Polymers, plant oils, the Earth, and its atmosphere

1 The scientists working at an oil company and at the oilseed rape company might be biased because they are being paid by organisations that earn their money by selling one of the products under investigation.

2 The scientist's qualifications, or experience, or status within the scientific community.

3 Ethical arguments – Hari; Environmental arguments – Georgia, Krishnan; Economic arguments – Julia, Lydia; Social arguments – Imogen (and Hari).

4 Arguments that could be investigated scientifically – Georgia and Krishnan. Scientists can do investigations to collect evidence to help answer the questions.

P1 1: Infrared radiation

1 Darker/matt surfaces emit more infrared than light/shiny surfaces.
2 Black is a better absorber of infrared, so the pipes (and the water inside) heats up quicker.

P1 2: Kinetic theory

1

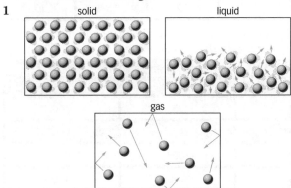

2 As the ice is heated, the particles gain energy and vibrate more. Eventually they have enough energy to move out of the regular arrangement and the block changes state to a liquid. The particles in the liquid gain energy and move faster. Eventually they move fast enough to break free from the liquid and so the liquid turns into a gas.

P1 3: Energy transfer by heating

1 They contain free electrons which can move through the metal, transferring the energy more quickly.
2 When the water is heated by the element in the base, the water particles gain energy and move faster. The hotter region expands and so becomes less dense. It rises through the cooler water. More water is drawn in to replace the water which has risen and the process repeats created a convection current.
3 Increase the surface area of the liquid; pass an air current over the liquid (e.g. blow on it); increase the temperature of the liquid.

P1 4: Comparing energy transfers

1

Factor	Effect
Temperature difference between object and surroundings	The greater the temperature difference, the greater the rate of energy transfer.
Surface area and volume	In general; the greater the surface area compared to the volume, the greater the rate of energy transfer.
Material	Some materials transfer energy more quickly than others (e.g. metals). The colour and finish of the material also affects the infrared radiation it emits (the darker and less shiny the material the more infrared radiation it emits).
Nature of the surface it is in contact with	Some materials transfer energy more quickly than others (e.g. metals).

2 Energy is unable to get into the flask to warm the liquid inside. The vacuum flask reduces the energy transfer into the flask.

Vacuum layer inside the glass vessel	Prevents conduction and convection.
Shiny silver on both the inside and outside of the glass vessel	Poor emitter of infrared radiation and good reflector.
Tight screw cap	Reduces convection and evaporation.

P1 5: Heating and insulating buildings

1

Cavity wall insulation	A material in between the walls (usually foam) traps air in pockets. Reducing conduction and preventing convection.
Loft insulation	Works in the same way as cavity wall insulation – a material in the loft (usually fibre glass) traps air. Reducing conduction and preventing convection.
Double glazing	Conduction is reduced by a layer of air trapped between two panes of glass.
Draft excluders	Energy loss through convection is reduced by making it more difficult to set up convection currents
Curtains	Reduces energy loss through radiation and conduction, by reducing the energy transfer to the windows.

2 The lower the U-value, the better the object is as an insulator.

3 Payback time $= \dfrac{\text{cost}}{\text{savings per year}}$

$= \dfrac{1200}{60}$

$= 20$ years

P1 6: Specific heat capacity

1   The energy required to increase the temperature of 1 kg of a substance by 1 °C.

2   $E = m \times c \times \theta$
$= 2.2 \times 4200 \times 70$
$= 646\,800\,\text{J}$

P1 1–6 Levelled questions: Energy transfer by heating

1   a   True
    b   True
    c   Dark objects are good emitters of infrared radiation.
    d   The particles in a gas are very far apart and move very fast.
    e   True
    f   The lower the U-value, the better the material is as an insulator.
    g   The time taken for the saving made each year to pay for the purchase and installation of a type of insulation is called the payback time.

2   a   reflectors
    b   gases
    c   decreases
    d   high
    e   bigger

3

Feature	Reduces energy transfer by...
vacuum	conduction and convection
silvered surface	radiation
tightly fitting lid	convection and evaporation

4   Three from:
Cavity wall insulation: A material in between the walls (usually foam) traps air in pockets. Reduces conduction and prevents convection.
Loft insulation: Works in the same way as cavity wall insulation – a material in the loft (usually fibre glass) traps air. Reduces conduction and prevents convection.
Double glazing: Conduction is reduced by a layer of air trapped between two panes of glass.
Draft excluders: Energy loss through convection is reduced by making it more difficult to set up convection currents.
Curtains: Reduces energy loss through radiation and conduction, by reducing the energy transfer to the windows.

5   Two from: Increase the surface area of the liquid; pass an air current over the surface (for example, blowing on a hot drink); increase the temperature of the liquid.

6

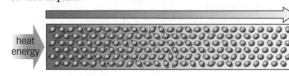

heat energy

7   a   cooler; volume; surface area; material; material
    b   larger; surface area; surroundings

8

Technique	Installation cost/£	Savings per year/£	Payback time/yr
A	300	50	6
B	2000	40	50
C	150	15	10

9   It can store a great deal of energy and then slowly transfer it to the surroundings.

10

Material	Specific heat capacity/J/kg °C	Energy required to heat it by 300 °C/J
A	900	540 000
B	450	270 000
C	3000	1 800 000
D	70	42 000

P1 1–6 Examination questions: Energy transfer by heating

1   a   You will gain 1 mark for each row.

Technique	Conduction	Convection	Radiation
Loft insulation	✓	✓	
Cavity wall insulation	✓	✓	
Double glazing	✓	✓	
Installing curtains		✓	✓

b   Different U-values means the material is a better/worse insulator (1); The lower the U-value the better the material is an insulator (1).

c   i   You will gain 1 mark for correct calculations, 1 mark for identifying the correct technique to install first, and 1 mark for explaining why.

$$Payback\ time = \frac{cost}{savings\ per\ year}$$

Cavity wall insulation $= \dfrac{200}{25} = 8$ years

Double glazing $= \dfrac{1500}{150} = 10$ years

Loft insulation 100 mm $= \dfrac{150}{10} = 15$ years

Loft insulation 350 mm $= \dfrac{300}{25} = 12$ years (1)

Cavity wall insulation should be installed first (1). It has the shortest payback time (1).

ii It is transferred to surroundings/
  atmosphere (1); increasing the temperature/
  warming the surroundings (1).

d Matt black is a good absorber of infrared
  radiation (1); so the pipes and the water inside
  them, heats up quicker (1).

2 a Particles gain energy and so vibrate more (1).
  The vibrations make their neighbouring
  particles vibrate more, and the energy is
  transferred through the material (1).

b energy; faster; less; rises (1 mark for each word
  in correct order).

c Evaporation.

d It increases.

3 a Energy required to increase the temperature of
  a substance. (You would gain 1 mark for this
  answer.)
  Energy required to increase the temperature
  of 1 kg of a substance by 1 °C. (You would gain
  2 marks for this more detailed answer.)

b Energy supplied $= m \times C \times \theta$
  or
  $\qquad = 1.4 \times 4200 \times 80$ (1)
  $\qquad = 470\,400\,J$ (1) for answer;
  $\qquad$ (1) for units.

P1 7: Conservation of energy

1 Elastic potential energy (in the spring/clockwork)
  → kinetic energy → electrical energy (via a
  generator) → light and sound energy.

2

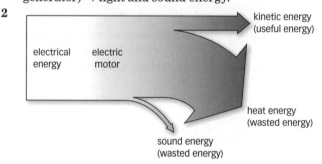

3 It spreads out (dissipates).

P1 8: Energy efficiency

1 a Efficiency $= \dfrac{\text{useful energy transferred}}{\text{total energy supplied}}$

  efficiency $= \dfrac{1300\,J}{1500\,J}$

  efficiency $= 0.65$ (or 65%)

b Efficiency $= \dfrac{\text{useful energy transferred}}{\text{total energy supplied}}$

  efficiency $= \dfrac{600\,J}{1500\,J}$

  efficiency $= 0.4$ (or 40%)

2 Efficiency $= \dfrac{\text{useful energy transferred}}{\text{total energy supplied}}$

  efficiency $= \dfrac{300\,J}{1500\,J}$

  efficiency $= 0.2$ (or 20%)

3

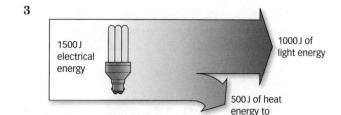

P1 7–8 Levelled questions: Energy conservation and efficiency

1 chemical; elastic potential; heat/thermal; nuclear;
  gravitational potential; light; sound; kinetic;
  electrical.

2 a energy; created; destroyed; transferred;
  dissipated.

b wasted; heat.

3

Device	Main energy transfers
Kettle	electrical → heat
Light bulb	electrical → heat and light
Wind-up radio	elastic potential → electrical → sound
A ball dropped from a height	gravitational potential → kinetic

4 a True

b Energy is measured in joules.

c When wasted energy is transferred to the
  surroundings, the surroundings get warmer.

d True

e True

5

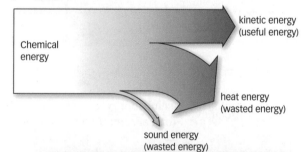

6 a

Bulb	Energy transferred into light/J	Energy transferred into heat/J
A	50	150
B	180	20
C	120	80
D	100	100
E	140	60

b

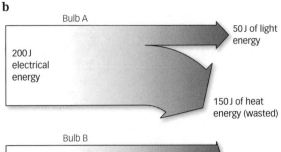

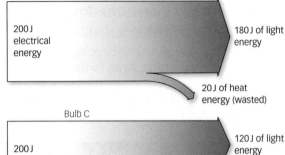

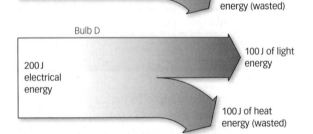

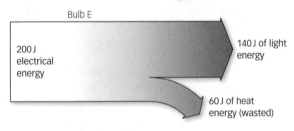

Bulb E

200 J electrical energy → 140 J of light energy / 60 J of heat energy (wasted)

c Efficiency = $\dfrac{\text{useful energy}}{\text{total energy}}$

$= \dfrac{120}{200}$

$= 0.6 \text{ (or 60\%)}$

d B – most energy transferred into light (or least energy transferred into heat).

7 a Gravitational potential energy → kinetic energy → heat, sound and elastic potential (as it hit the ground) → kinetic energy → gravitational potential energy

b Some energy is lost (as heat and sound) when the ball hits the ground, so not all the kinetic energy is converted back into gravitational potential energy.

8 a 1500 J

b Transferred to surroundings (which get warmer).

c Efficiency = $\dfrac{\text{useful energy}}{\text{total energy}}$

$= \dfrac{1500}{5000}$

$= 0.3 \text{ (or 30\%)}$

9 a Efficiency cannot be more than 100%, as this would mean energy is being created.

b To ensure there is no bias in the results/presentation/analysis of the results.

P1 7–8 Examination questions: Energy conservation and efficiency

1 a Energy cannot be created or destroyed (1); but it can be transferred usefully, stored, and dissipated (1).

b Petrol engine: Chemical → kinetic (1)
TV: Electrical → light and sound (1)
Car battery: Chemical → electrical (1)

c i Your diagram must show electrical energy being transferred into heat and light (1). The heat arrow must be wider than the light arrow (1).

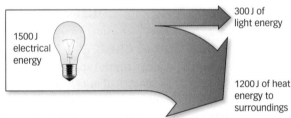

ii Light would be a greater proportion of the energy, shown by a thicker arrow (2).

2 a i Energy transferred into a form we do not want/need (2).

ii It spreads outs/dissipates (1).

b i 250 kJ (1)

ii Efficiency $= \dfrac{50\,000}{300\,000}$

$= 0.17 \text{ (or 17\%) (2)}$

P1 9: Using electrical devices

1 Any three of:

Appliance	Energy in	Main forms of energy out
Kettle	Electrical	Heat, kinetic
Toaster	Electrical	Heat, light
Electric motor	Electrical	Heat, sound, kinetic
Speaker	Electrical	Sound, kinetic
Computer	Electrical	Heat, light, sound, kinetic

2 a Energy = power × time = 20 × (10 × 60 × 60)
$= 720\,000$ J

b Energy = power × time = 2200 × 250 = 550 000 J
So the light bulb transfers more energy.

3 Less energy is wasted as heat (therefore conserves resources and saves the owner money).

P1 10: Paying for electricity

1　a　Energy = power × time = 3 × 6 = 18 kWh
　　b　Energy = power × time = 9.2 × 0.5 = 4.6 kWh
　　c　Energy = power × time 2 × 4 = 8 kWh
2　Cost = price × energy

$$= 11 \times \left(4 \times \frac{90}{60}\right)$$
$$= 11 \times 6$$
$$= 66p$$

P1 9–10 Levelled questions: The use and cost of electricity

1

Appliance	Energy in	Main forms of energy out
Kettle	Electrical	Heat, sound, kinetic
TV	Electrical	Heat, sound, light
Radio	Electrical	Heat, sound
Escalator	Electrical	Heat, sound, kinetic, gravitational potential energy

2　a　increases
　　b　increases
　　c　decreases
　　d　increases
3　a　watts
　　b　energy
　　c　more
　　d　reduces
4

Power of appliance/W	Power of appliance/kW
1000	1
5500	5.5
800	0.8
1200	1.2
500	0.5
20	0.02

5　Conserve natural resources (including fossil fuels as less electrical energy is needed); saves you money.
6　a　Energy = power × time = 15 × (10 × 60 × 60)
　　　　　　　　　　= 540 000 J
　　b　Energy = 540 000 × 1200
　　　　　　　　= 648 000 000 J or 648 MJ
7　a　Energy = 3000 × (30 × 60)
　　　　　　　= 540 000 J
　　b　Energy = 3 × 0.5
　　　　　　　= 1.5 kWh
8　a　House 1 = 875 units; House 2 = 6309 units; House 3 = 4561 units.
　　　House 2 used the most units
　　b　House 1 = £105.00; House 2 = £757.08; House 3 = £547.32

9　a　7 hours.
　　b　Energy = power × time = 12 × 7 = 84 kWh
　　c　Cost = £9.24
10　Battery one is portable, but the batteries may run out.

P1 9–10 Examination questions: The use and cost of electricity

1　a　Energy = power × time
　　　　　　　　= 2200 × 120
　　　　　　　　= 264 000 J (2 marks for answer; 1 mark for units)
　　　　(An answer of 264 or 4400 (multiplying 2200 by 2 instead of 120) gives 1 mark.)
　　b　It would increase (1).
2　a　320 units (1).
　　b　Cost = 320 × 0.12 = £38.40 (2)
　　　Unit = kWh (1)

How Science Works: Energy and efficiency

1　Experiment 1
　　a

Material	Start temperature (°C)	End temperature (°C)	Change in temperature (°C)
A	70	62	8
B	70	50	20
C	70	34	36
D	70	64	6

　　b　Type of insulating material.
　　c　Starting temperature; volume of water; time; surface; material of beaker.
　　d　Otherwise it would not be a fair test as one of the control variables may have an effect on the dependent variable, making the experiment invalid.

Experiment 2
　　a

Volume (cm³)	Start temperature (°C)	End temperature (°C)	Change in temperature (°C)
100	70	38	32
200	70	50	20
300	70	55	15
400	70	62	8
500	70	65	5

　　b　Volume of water.
　　c　Starting temperature; time; surface; material of beaker.
　　d　Otherwise it would not be a fair test as one of the control variables may have an effect on the dependent variable, making the experiment invalid.

2 **Experiment 1**
  a Independent – type of insulating material – categoric.
     Dependent – temperature change – continuous.
  b Bar chart: axis labelled (including units for the temperature change), bars correct length.
  c The results support the hypothesis. Different materials led to different temperature drops, so energy must be transferred to surroundings at different rates.

Experiment 2
  a Independent – volume – continuous.
     Dependent – temperature change – continuous.
  b Line graph: axis labelled (including units), sensible scale and graph takes up at least 1/3 of the graph paper, points plotted in the correct place, line of best fit (curve) drawn.
  c The results support the hypothesis. Different volumes led to different temperature drops, so energy must be transferred to surroundings at different rates. The greater the volume the lower the rate of energy transfer and so the lower the temperature drop.

P1 11: Generating electricity and matching supply with demand

1 Fuel is burnt (or a nuclear reaction takes place): chemical or nuclear energy → heat energy.
   The heat is used to turn water to steam, the steam turns a turbine: heat energy → kinetic energy.
   As the turbine turns, it turns a generator that generates electricity: kinetic energy → electrical energy.
2 How quickly it can increase the amount of electrical energy it is generating.
3 When there is a sudden increase in demand, gates are opened and water from the reservoir rushes through them. This water turns turbines, which turn generators and produce electricity. When demand reduces the gates are closed again.

P1 12: The National Grid

1 Electricity is generated in power stations. Transformers are used to step-up the voltage (this reduces the current and so less energy is lost in transmission). The electricity is transmitted via a series of pylons or underground cables. Another transformer is used to step down the voltage (to a safer level for homes). Cables run into every home.
2 The current can be lower, so the wires do not get as warm. Much less energy is wasted as heat.
3 Advantages: higher voltages can be used (less energy is wasted); generally cheaper to install and maintain.
   Disadvantages: the pylons are ugly; pylons can be easily damaged in extreme weather.

P1 13: Fossil fuels

1 Advantages: large amounts of electricity can be generated; it is an established technology; fossil fuels are relatively cheap (per kW of power generated).
   Disadvantages: the fuels have to be mined/extracted and transported; burning fuels releases atmospheric pollutants (such as CO_2 which contributes to man-made global warming); the power plants are often very ugly and noisy.

2

Fossil fuel	Substance heated	CO_2 production	Start-up time
Coal	Water	Very high	Long
Oil	Water	High	Long
Natural gas	Water or air	Medium	Short

3 The CO_2 released in burning the fuel is captured and prevented from entering the atmosphere. It is stored underground. This would reduce the amount of CO_2 released and so reduce man-made global warming.

P1 14: Nuclear power

1 A nuclear reaction (the splitting of a uranium or plutonium nucleus) releases heat. This heat turns water to steam. The steam turns a turbine, which turns a generator that generates electricity.
2 They do not produce CO_2 as no fuel is burnt.
3 The dismantling of a nuclear power station when it reaches the end of its useful life. This is costly because of the radioactive waste in the nuclear reactor. This needs to be handed very carefully.

P1 15: Renewables

1 Water is pumped into the ground in areas where there are hot rock close the surface (or in some cases steam rises naturally). The steam is used to turn turbines that turn a generator, which generates electricity.
   Advantages: cheap to build; no fuel costs; will not run out.
   Disadvantages: can only be built in certain areas; plants can be very ugly and noisy.
2 Solar and hydroelectric power.
3 The CO_2 released by burning biofuels is the same as the plants (used to make the biofuels) absorbed while they were growing. So there is no change in the amount of CO_2 in the atmosphere.

P1 11–15 Levelled questions: Generating power

1 a Nuclear power is a form of non-renewable energy.
   b True
   c Non-renewable energy resources use fuels which will run out.
   d True
   e A hydroelectric power station has a short start-up time.
   f Natural gas produces less carbon dioxide than other fossil fuels.

2

Energy resource	Brief description
Wind	Wind is used to turn large turbines
Wave	The up-and-down motion of the sea is transferred into electrical energy
Tidal	This may include tidal lagoons or larger tidal barrages
Hydroelectric power (HEP)	Large dams are built across river valleys
Geothermal	Hot rocks turn water to steam – this is used to turn turbines
Biomass	Biofuels are burnt; the heat is used to turn water to steam
Solar (cells)	Energy from the Sun is transferred into electrical energy

3 Pylon or underground cables.
4 Coal, oil, natural gas or nuclear.
5 a increases; decreases
   b decreases
   c decreases.
   d increases
6 nuclear – coal – natural gas – HEP
7 A nuclear reaction (the splitting of a uranium or plutonium nucleus) releases heat. This heat turns water to steam. The steam turns a turbine that turns a generator, which generates electricity.

8

	Advantages	Disadvantages
Wave	Renewable, no CO_2 released, no fuel costs.	Visual and noise pollution (can also be a danger to shipping). Unreliable/untested technology.
Tidal	Renewable, no CO_2 released, no fuel costs, and reliable and predictable electricity generation.	Affects marine habitats. Can be very expensive to build. Limited number of suitable sites.

9

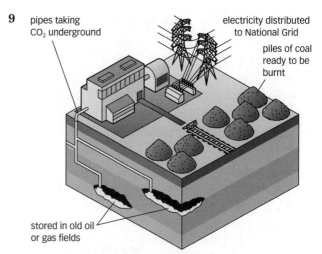

pipes taking CO_2 underground

electricity distributed to National Grid

piles of coal ready to be burnt

stored in old oil or gas fields

10 a In winter electricity is used for heating, so there is great demand.
    b i People are waking up and having breakfast (using kettles, toasters, etc).
       ii People are returning from work and starting to cook dinner.

P1 11–15 Examination questions: Generating power

1 a C – A – B – D (2 marks if all in correct order; 1 mark if two in correct order).
   b i How quickly a power station can increase the amount of electricity it generates. (1)
      ii Nuclear (1)
   c When demand is high, the pump storage station can start to generate electricity very quickly by opening the lock gates so water from the reservoir drives the turbines (2). When demand is low, electricity from the National Grid is used to pump water back up to the reservoir (1).

2 a step-up; voltage; current; current; energy (1 mark for each word in correct order).
   b Two from: voltage cannot be as high; expensive to install; difficult to maintain; more energy is wasted (2).

3 Your answer should be well-structured, with few spelling and grammatical errors. 6 points available. Answer might include:
   Advantages: No fuel costs; no CO_2 released; renewable.
   Disadvantages: Unreliable; ugly; noisy.

P1 16: Introduction to waves

1 In transverse waves the oscillations are at right angles to the direction of energy transfer. In longitudinal waves the oscillations are parallel to the direction of energy transfer.

Transverse	Longitudinal
Water waves, light (all electromagnetic waves: radio, microwaves, infra-red radiation, ultraviolet radiation, x-rays, gamma rays) and some mechanical waves on springs or strings.	Sound and some mechanical waves on springs.

2

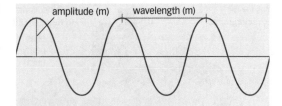

3   0.5 Hz (1 wave every 2 seconds).

P1 17: Wave experiments
1   The angle of incidence = the angle of reflection.
2   **a**

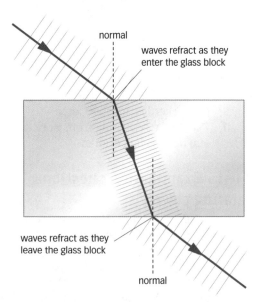

waves refract as they enter the glass block

waves refract as they leave the glass block

b   The light will slow down, but it does not change direction. Instead it passes straight through the glass block.

3   When a wave spreads out as it passes through a gap or around an obstacle. The best diffraction occurs when the size of the gap is the same as the wavelength of the wave.

P1 18: The electromagnetic spectrum
1   Gamma – X-rays – Ultraviolet – Visible light – Infrared – Microwave – Radio waves
2   TV, radio, and wireless communications (like Bluetooth).
3   Research has shown they have a small heating effect on living tissue. Scientists are not sure whether this is a serious health risk and if it will cause any long term damage.
4   Radio up to 10 km/gamma 10^{-15} m

P1 19: The wave equation
1   Using the formula: $v = f \times \lambda$
    a $v = 0.5\,\text{Hz} \times 4\,\text{m} = 2\,\text{m/s}$
    b $v = 500\,\text{Hz} \times 0.60\,\text{m} = 300\,\text{m/s}$
    c $v = 1200\,\text{Hz} \times 0.80\,\text{m} = 960\,\text{m/s}$
2 $v = f \times \lambda$

so $\lambda = \dfrac{v}{f}$,

$$\lambda = \frac{3 \times 10^8}{3 \times 10^{10}},$$

$$= 0.01\,\text{m}$$

P1 20: Images
1   When seen in a rear view mirror the image is laterally inverted and so appears normal.
2   Upright: The image is the right way up.
Laterally inverted: The image is flipped around horizontally.
Virtual: The image is not really there; it can't be projected onto a screen.
3

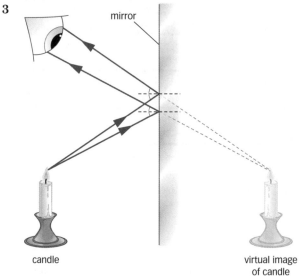

candle   virtual image of candle

P1 21: Sound
1   Whenever an object vibrates (the air/medium around it vibrates and these vibrations travel through the medium).
2   Higher frequency = higher pitch; lower frequency = lower pitch.
3

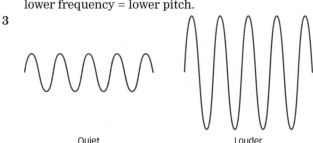

Quiet   Louder

P1 22: Wave sources and the Doppler effect

1 Sound: Speaker, police siren, car engine
   Light: Light bulb, galaxy
   Microwaves: Satellite, microwave oven
2 As it approaches the observer the waves are compressed (increasing the frequency and reducing the wavelength) so it sounds higher pitched. As it moves away from the observer the waves are stretched out (reducing the frequency and increasing the wavelength) and it sounds lower pitched.

P1 23: The Big Bang theory

1 The Big Bang theory states:
   • The Universe began around 14 billion years ago.
   • It started from a very small, incredibly hot initial point.
   • It then exploded outwards and has been expanding ever since.
2 Red shift shows most galaxies are moving away from us and the ones further away are moving faster. So the Universe must be expanding. In the past it must have been much smaller (as the Big Bang theory states).
3 Cosmic microwave background radiation is a form of radiation which fills the entire Universe. It is the 'heat' left over from the Big Bang. The Big Bang theory is currently the only theory that can explain the existence of the cosmic microwave background radiation.

P1 16–23 Levelled questions: Waves

1 **a** energy
  b transverse
  c reflection
  d longest
  e most
  f Infrared
  g higher
  h away
2 Gamma – X-rays – Ultraviolet – Visible light – Infrared – Microwaves – Radio waves
3

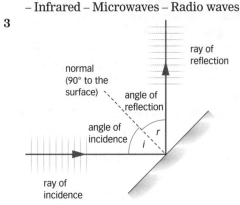

4 **a** Radio waves: TV, radio and wireless communications (like Bluetooth).

b Microwaves: Mobile phones and satellite TV.
c Infrared: Remote controls and some cable Internet connections.
d Visible light: Photography and some cable Internet connections.
5 **a** True
  b All electromagnetic waves travel at the same speed through a vacuum.
  c When waves spread out as they pass through a gap this is called diffraction.
  d True
  e The amplitude of a wave is the height of the wave from the top of the peak to the middle of the wave.
  f Sound waves are examples of longitudinal waves.
  g True
  h A louder sound has a greater amplitude.
  i True
  j The light emitted by distant galaxies is stretched as they move away from us. This is called red-shift.
6

Wave speed	Frequency	Wavelength
2000 m/s	1000 Hz	2 m
1600 m/s	3.2 kHz	0.5 m
120 m/s	300 Hz	40 cm
108 m/s	0.9 kHz	12 cm

7 **a** Wavelength (in metres, m): The distance from one peak to the next.
  b Frequency (in hertz, Hz): The number of waves passing a point per second.
  c Amplitude (in metres, m): Maximum height of the wave, measured from the middle of the wave.

8

Upright	The image is the right way up.
Laterally inverted	The image is flipped around horizontally.
Virtual	The image cannot be projected onto a screen.

9 Red-shift (so the universe is expanding) and cosmic microwave background radiation.
10 **a** billion
   b small
   c exploded; expanding
11 Longitudinal: sound.
   Transverse: radio waves, light, infrared, water waves, X-rays, microwaves, gamma waves.
   Could be either: mechanical waves or springs.
12

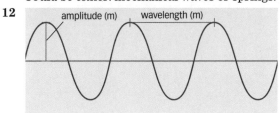

13

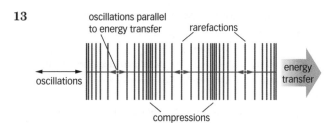

14 Light has a much smaller wavelength so does not diffract as much. Sound has a wavelength similar to the size of the gap (door frame) and so strong diffraction takes place.

15 a the wavelength decreases and the frequency increases.

b the wavelength increases and the frequency decreases.

16 When the car moves towards the observer the wavelength is compressed and so it sounds higher pitched. When it moves passed the observer the wavelength is stretched (increases) and so it sounds lower pitched.

17 First diagram – lower pitch, lower frequency, loud sound.
Second diagram – higher pitch, higher frequency, quiet sound.

18 Transverse: vibrations are perpendicular to the direction of energy transfer.
Longitudinal: vibrations are parallel to the direction of energy transfer.

19 a vibrates
b vibrations; vibrate
c longitudinal; vibrations; parallel

20

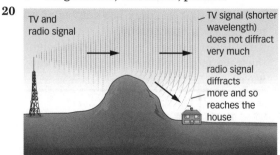

21

Wave speed (m/s)	Frequency (Hz)	Wavelength (m)
3500	75	47
340	1700	0.2
12000	200	60
3×10^8	150000000	2

P1 16–23 Examination questions: Waves and the Big Bang theory

1 a Energy (1)

b

Term	Description	
amplitude	The maximum height of the wave, from the middle to the peak.	(1)
wavelength	The minimum distance from one peak to another.	(1)
frequency	The number of waves passing a point per second.	(1)

c i Perpendicular (1) to the direction of energy transfer/wave motion (1).

ii Any two from: water waves; radio waves; microwaves; infrared; visible light; ultraviolet; X-rays; gamma rays. (2)

2 a incidence (1); reflection (1); normal (1)

b i Both diagrams showing diffraction (waves spreading out) (1).
Wavelength (distance between the lines) stays approximately the same (1).
Stronger diffraction (waves spread out more) from the smaller gap (1).

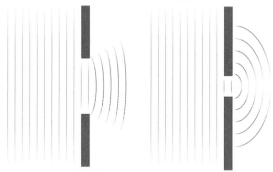

ii When the wavelength is the same size as the gap (1).

3 a wave speed = frequency × wavelength
= 1200 × 0.30
= 360 m/s (2 marks for answer; 1 mark for units)
(An answer of 36 000 or 0.36 only gains 1 mark.)

b Amplitude – no effect (1);
Wavelength – decreases (1).

4 Your answer should be well structured, with few spelling and grammatical errors. The answer might include:
Expanding universe (red shift): most galaxies are moving away from us; furthest galaxies are moving fastest; implies Universe is expanding; in the past was smaller.
Cosmic microwave background radiation: heat left over from the Big Bang; same everywhere in the universe; as the universe has expanded it has cooled; only the Big Bang theory can explain the origin of this heat (6).

How Science Works: Electrical energy and waves

1

Angle of incidence (°)	Angle of reflection (°)			
	1	2	3	Average
15	15	14	16	15
30	30	35	29	31 (or 30 if the 35 result is ignored)
45	45	45	45	45
60	62	65	62	63
75	69	75	76	73 (or 75 if the 69 result is ignored)

2   Line graph: axis labelled (including units); sensible scale and graph takes up at least 1/3 of the graph paper; points plotted in the correct place; line of best fit (curve) drawn.
The results generally support the hypothesis. However, there are some random errors which mean a few results do not show that the angle of incidence is equal to the angle of reflection.

3   a   Most results are quite close to the true value and so they are quite accurate.
   b   In general there is very little spread from the mean value, except at 30° where there is one reading of 35° and at 75° where one reading was 69°.
   c   If repeated the experiment should produce similar results.
   d   If somebody else did the experiment, they should get a very similar set of results.

4   a   Random.
   b   Human error in misreading the protractor; the mirror not being lined up perfectly.

5   A systematic error.

6   To ensure there is no bias in their findings/conclusions.

Appendices

Periodic table

Times of discovery

before 1800	1900–1949
1800–1849	1949–1999
1849–1899	

Group

	relative atomic mass
	atomic number
	name
	atomic (proton) number

1.0
H
hydrogen
1

Group	1	2											3	4	5	6	7	8
																		4 **He** helium 2
Period 2	7 **Li** lithium 3	9 **Be** beryllium 4											11 **B** boron 5	12 **C** carbon 6	14 **N** nitrogen 7	16 **O** oxygen 8	19 **F** fluorine 9	20 **Ne** neon 10
3	23 **Na** sodium 11	24 **Mg** magnesium 12											27 **Al** aluminium 13	28 **Si** silicon 14	31 **P** phosphorus 15	32 **S** sulfur 16	35.5 **Cl** chlorine 17	40 **Ar** argon 18
4	39 **K** potassium 19	40 **Ca** calcium 20	45 **Sc** scandium 21	48 **Ti** titanium 22	51 **V** vanadium 23	52 **Cr** chromium 24	55 **Mn** manganese 25	56 **Fe** iron 26	59 **Co** cobalt 27	59 **Ni** nickel 28	63.5 **Cu** copper 29	65 **Zn** zinc 30	70 **Ga** gallium 31	73 **Ge** germanium 32	75 **As** arsenic 33	79 **Se** selenium 34	80 **Br** bromine 35	84 **Kr** krypton 36
5	85 **Rb** rubidium 37	88 **Sr** strontium 38	89 **Y** yttrium 39	91 **Zr** zirconium 40	93 **Nb** niobium 41	96 **Mo** molybdenum 42	(98) **Tc** technetium 43	101 **Ru** ruthenium 44	103 **Rh** rhodium 45	106 **Pd** palladium 46	108 **Ag** silver 47	112 **Cd** cadmium 48	115 **In** indium 49	119 **Sn** tin 50	122 **Sb** antimony 51	128 **Te** tellurium 52	127 **I** iodine 53	131 **Xe** xenon 54
6	133 **Cs** caesium 55	137 **Ba** barium 56	139 * **La** lanthanum 57	178.5 **Hf** hafnium 72	181 **Ta** tantalum 73	184 **W** tungsten 74	186 **Re** rhenium 75	190 **Os** osmium 76	192 **Ir** iridium 77	195 **Pt** platinum 78	197 **Au** gold 79	201 **Hg** mercury 80	204 **Tl** thallium 81	207 **Pb** lead 82	209 **Bi** bismuth 83	(209) **Po** polonium 84	210 **At** astatine 85	222 **Rn** radon 86
7	(223) **Fr** francium 87	(226) **Ra** radium 88	(227) # **Ac** actinium 89	(261) **Rf** rutherfordium 104	(262) **Db** dubnium 105	(266) **Sg** seaborgium 106	(264) **Bh** bohrium 107	(277) **Hs** hassium 108	(268) **Mt** meitnerium 109	(271) **Ds** darmstadtium 110	(272) **Rg** roentgenium 111							

Elements with atomic numbers 112–116 have been reported but not fully authenticated

*58–71 Lanthanides

140 **Ce** cerium 58	141 **Pr** praseodymium 59	144 **Nd** neodymium 60	(145) **Pm** promethium 61	150 **Sm** samarium 62	152 **Eu** europium 63	157 **Gd** gadolinium 64	159 **Tb** terbium 65	162.5 **Dy** dysprosium 66	165 **Ho** holmium 67	167 **Er** erbium 68	169 **Tm** thulium 69	173 **Yb** ytterbium 70	175 **Lu** lutetium 71

#90–103 Actinides

232 **Th** thorium 90	231 **Pa** protactinium 91	238 **U** uranium 92	237 **Np** neptunium 93	239 **Pu** plutonium 94	243 **Am** americium 95	247 **Cm** curium 96	247 **Bk** berkelium 97	252 **Cf** californium 98	(252) **Es** einsteinium 99	(257) **Fm** fermium 100	(258) **Md** mendelevium 101	(259) **No** nobelium 102	(260) **Lr** lawrencium 103

Equations

Equation	Description
$E = m \times c \times \theta$	E is energy transferred in joules, J m is mass in kilograms, kg θ is temperature change in degrees Celsius, °C c is specific heat capacity in J/kg °C
$\text{efficiency} = \dfrac{\text{useful energy out}}{\text{total energy in}} (\times 100\%)$	
$\text{efficiency} = \dfrac{\text{useful power out}}{\text{total power in}} (\times 100\%)$	
$E = P \times t$	E is energy transferred in kilowatt-hours, kWh P is power in kilowatts, kW t is time in hours, h This equation may also be used when: E is energy transferred in joules, J P is power in watts, W t is time in seconds, s
$v = f \times \lambda$	v is speed in metres per second, m/s t is frequency in hertz, Hz λ is wavelength in metres, m

Fundamental physical quantities	
Physical quantity	**Unit(s)**
length	metre (m) kilometre (km) centimetre (cm) millimetre (mm)
mass	kilogram (kg) gram (g) milligram (mg)
time	second (s) millisecond (ms)
temperature	degree Celsius (°C) kelvin (K)
current	ampere (A) milliampere (mA)
voltage	volt (V) millivolt (mV)

Derived quantities and units	
Physical quantity	**Unit(s)**
area	cm^2; m^2
volume	cm^3; dm^3; m^3; litre (l); millilitre (ml)
density	kg/m^3; g/cm^3
force	newton (N)
speed	m/s; km/h
energy	joule (J); kilojoule (kJ); megajoule (MJ)
power	watt (W); kilowatt (kW); megawatt (MW)
frequency	hertz (Hz); kilohertz (kHz)
gravitational field strength	N/kg
radioactivity	becquerel (Bq)
acceleration	m/s^2; km/h^2
specific heat capacity	J/kg°C
specific latent heat	J/kg

Electrical symbols			
junction of conductors	ammeter (A)	diode	capacitor
switch	voltmeter (V)	electrolytic capacitor	relay
primary or secondary cell	indicator or light source	LDR	LED
battery of cells	or	thermistor	NOT gate
power supply	motor (M)	AND gate	OR gate
fuse	generator (G)	NOR gate	NAND gate
fixed resistor	variable resistor		

Index